# PROPORTIONALITY AND FACTS IN CONSTITUTIONAL ADJUDICATION

This book considers the relationship between proportionality and facts in constitutional adjudication. Analysing where facts arise within each of the three stages of the structured proportionality test – suitability, necessity and balancing – it considers the nature of these 'facts' vis-à-vis the facts that arise in the course of ordinary litigation.

The book's central focus is on how proportionality has been applied by courts in practice, and it draws on the comparative experience of four jurisdictions across a range of legal systems. The central case study of the book is Australia, where the embryonic and contested nature of proportionality means it provides an illuminating study of how facts can inform the framing of constitutional tests. The rich proportionality jurisprudence from Germany, Canada and South Africa is used to contextualise the approach of the High Court of Australia and to identify future directions for proportionality in Australia, at a time when the doctrine is in its formative stages.

The book has three broad aims:

First, it considers the role of facts within proportionality reasoning.

Second, it offers procedural insights into fact-finding in constitutional litigation.

Third, the book's analysis of the dynamic Australian case-law on proportionality means it also serves to clarify the nature and status of proportionality in Australia at a critical moment. Since the 2015 decision of *McCloy v New South Wales*, where four justices supported the introduction of a structured three-part test of proportionality, the Court has continued to disagree about the utility of such a test. These developments mean that this book, with its doctrinal and comparative approach, is particularly timely.

**Hart Studies in Constitutional Theory: Volume 1**

## Hart Studies in Constitutional Theory

**Series Editors**



The *Hart Studies in Constitutional Theory* series publishes thought-provoking works of scholarship addressing diverse aspects of constitutional theory in a concise and crystalline manner. Authors writing for this series cover a wide range of perspectives, methods, and regions, to enhance our understanding of constitutions as central institutions of modern public life. Taken together, the books in this series aim to challenge established wisdom and advance original ideas.

This series is a natural home for books interrogating the concepts and structures of constitutions on the national, the supranational and the international level. Its guiding philosophy is that the task of constitutional theory is not only to delineate the basic structures of government and to protect human rights, but also more broadly to offer methods for grappling with the social, political, and economic problems societies face today.

The series is open to theoretical, normative, analytical, empirical and comparative approaches, stemming from legal studies as well as from political philosophy and political science. In its ambition to become a global forum for debate about constitutional theory, the series editors welcome submissions for monographs as well as edited volumes from all parts of the world.

# Proportionality and Facts in Constitutional Adjudication

Anne Carter

•HART•
OXFORD • LONDON • NEW YORK • NEW DELHI • SYDNEY

HART PUBLISHING
Bloomsbury Publishing Plc
Kemp House, Chawley Park, Cumnor Hill, Oxford, OX2 9PH, UK
1385 Broadway, New York, NY 10018, USA
29 Earlsfort Terrace, Dublin 2, Ireland

HART PUBLISHING, the Hart/Stag logo, BLOOMSBURY and the Diana logo are trademarks of Bloomsbury Publishing Plc

First published in Great Britain 2021



A catalogue record for this book is available from the British Library.

Library of Congress Cataloging-in-Publication data

Names: Carter, Anne, 1980- author.

Title: Proportionality and facts in constitutional adjudication / Anne Carter.

Description: Oxford ; New York : Hart, 2021. | Series: Hart studies in constitutional theory ; volume 1 | Based on author's thesis (doctoral - Melbourne Law School, 2018) issued under title: Proportionality and the proof of facts in Australian constitutional adjudication. | Includes bibliographical references and index.

Identifiers: LCCN 2021042760 (print) | LCCN 2021042761 (ebook) | ISBN 9781509936984 (hardback) | ISBN 9781509955497 (paperback) | ISBN 9781509937004 (pdf) | ISBN 9781509936991 (Epub)

Subjects: LCSH: Constitutional law—Australia—Cases. | Proportionality in law—Australia—Cases.

Classification: LCC KU1890 .C37 2021 (print) | LCC KU1890 (ebook) | DDC 342.94—dc23/eng/20211005

LC record available at https://lccn.loc.gov/2021042760

LC ebook record available at https://lccn.loc.gov/2021042761

ISBN: HB: 978-1-50993-698-4
ePDF: 978-1-50993-700-4
ePub: 978-1-50993-699-1

Typeset by Compuscript Ltd, Shannon

*For Greta, Ned and Imogen*

# *Foreword*

DR CARTER FOCUSES on the role of facts in determining challenges to the constitutional validity of legislation. Constitutional cases involving facts have occurred in the context of the defence power, s 90 prior to *Ha v New South Wales*[1] and Australia's GST legislation, and s 92, most particularly after *Cole v Whitfield*.[2] However, it is the recent use of structured proportionality to determine whether a burden imposed by legislation on the implied freedom of political communication can be justified, which has refocused interest in constitutional adjudication involving facts.

Dr Carter charts the Australian High Court's recent shift away from the language of 'reasonably appropriate and adapted' towards a structured test of proportionality to assess burdens on the implied freedom, which she does by reference to Australia's constitutional framework and also by comparison with relevant developments in Germany, Canada and South Africa.

Accepting that proportionality is a legal test and that the conclusion as to whether a legislative measure is proportionate is best characterised as a question of law, Dr Carter argues that underlying the three sub-tests of structured proportionality – suitability, necessity and balancing – are issues of fact different in kind from adjudicative facts, which may require different modes of proof.

For some time, the Special Case procedure utilised in cases of this kind before the High Court has usually resulted in agreement between the parties as to what are the necessary, relevant facts. But it cannot be assumed that agreement will always be possible or that the facts as agreed will be sufficient to enable the determination of questions of proportionality. Not only does this book enhance an understanding of the role of facts in proportionality reasoning, it also offers insights into unresolved procedural ambiguities related to the separation of powers – the burden and standard of proof for constitutional facts, the scope of judicial notice and the role, if any, of deference to legislators.

This book deals with an important topic. Whilst it draws upon comparative experiences, it chiefly offers a scholarly, lucid and practical analysis of the issues for an Australian audience.

The Honorable Susan Crennan AC QC
*Retired Justice of the High Court of Australia*

[1] *Ha v New South Wales* (1997) 189 CLR 465.
[2] *Cole v Whitfield* (1988) 165 CLR 360.

# *Editors' Foreword*

THIS IS THE first volume in the new *Hart Studies on Constitutional Theory* series. We are delighted to see this addition to Hart's existing catalogue and hope that readers will relish the opportunity to take nourishment from the serious food for thought that this series aims to provide. The monograph before you is, in many ways, a perfect exemplar of our aspirations and the contribution that the *Studies on Constitutional Theory* seeks to make to the scholarly state of the art. Proportionality reasoning and related notions of balancing have been embraced by national and transnational courts from around the globe, with a healthy amount of academic commentary developing in its wake. Anne Carter has managed to identify an aspect of this phenomenon that is theoretically underexplored, yet of immense importance: the role and treatment of facts and fact-finding in proportionality analysis. While outwardly focused primarily on a single country, viz. Australia, the analysis offered of this case study serves as a springboard for the formulation of insights intended to be of more general use far beyond that jurisdiction. This, then, is a book that showcases the practical as well as contemporary relevance of academic scholarship that is solidly grounded in constitutional theory.

A word about the cover. The image featured is a fragment of a photograph by Czech-born artist Erika Kiffl, who is known for questioning the distinction between documentary and artistic photography. We wish to place on record our heartfelt thanks to her for so readily consenting to the use of her photographs as well as add our appreciation to art historian Anne Rodler, who first drew our attention to Erika Kiffl's work. Her series of marble figures from antiquity, like constitutions themselves, evoke a profound concern with the structures and forms that inevitably constrain and guide human life. To us, this neatly matches the series' understanding of constitutional theory as concerned with lived and desired realities for states or societies, rather than a field characterised by its abstraction and detachment from the human condition.

# *Acknowledgements*

THIS BOOK BEGAN life as my doctoral thesis, completed at the University of Melbourne under the supervision of Cheryl Saunders and Jeremy Gans. I would like to thank both Cheryl and Jeremy for their advice and encouragement throughout the PhD. In particular, I am grateful for their confidence, in me and in this project, right from the beginning. I am also indebted to my two PhD examiners, Paul Rishworth and James Stellios, and to the two anonymous Hart Publishing reviewers. Each provided thoughtful comments which have helped me to revise the manuscript for publication.

The intellectual roots of this book, however, stretch back much further. I first became interested in facts when I studied evidence with Andrew Ligertwood at the University of Adelaide, and I remain grateful for Andrew's ongoing support and enthusiasm for all things evidential. Jeff King, who supervised my MPhil in Oxford, also helped to shape my thinking on this topic and has remained a source of much encouragement. My interest in public law has been fostered by my experience as a practising lawyer, and in particular the time I spent working for the Honourable Pamela Tate SC, the then Solicitor-General for Victoria.

There are many others who have helped both during the PhD years and in the process of developing and refining my research for this book. Special mention must go to Adrienne Stone, who has provided guidance at key stages and whose work I have benefited from enormously, and to Matthew Groves, who read the entire book manuscript and provided sage advice in the lead-up to publication. Others have offered advice at critical points and commented on draft chapters, including Gabrielle Appleby, Janina Boughey, Anna Dziedzic, Penny Gleeson, Tanya Josev, Stephen McDonald, Dan Meagher, Anna Olijnyk, Oscar Roos, Joe Tomlinson and Lael ('Lulu') Weis. I am fortunate to be involved in the public law communities at both Melbourne Law School and Deakin Law School, and I am grateful to my friends and colleagues for their encouragement and support.

In preparing this book for publication, I am honoured that the Honourable Susan Crennan AC QC, retired justice of the High Court of Australia, agreed to write the Foreword and I thank her for her contribution. I would also like to thank Kate Whetter and Sinead Moloney at Hart Publishing for their enthusiasm about this project right from our initial conversations, as well as Rosie Mearns and Jon Lloyd for their assistance during the publication process. I am also grateful to Michelle Bendall in the Deakin Law Library, who helped with referencing queries, and to Rhyse Collins, who provided invaluable research assistance.

My PhD studies were supported by an Australian Government Research Training Program Scholarship (previously called an Australian Postgraduate Award). I was incredibly fortunate to spend five months of my PhD candidature at the Max Planck Institute for Comparative Public Law and International Law in Heidelberg, and I benefited enormously from the Institute's rich intellectual environment.

Finally, I would like to thank my family and friends for all their support along the way. I am ever grateful to my parents for encouraging my academic endeavours over many years. My husband, Henry, bore the emotional and financial burden of this project, and encouraged me both to commence the PhD and then to see it through to its final form. This book would not have been possible without him.

# *Table of Contents*

# *Table of Cases*

## Australia

## Canada

**Germany**

**New Zealand**



**South Africa**

## UK



## US



## Other

# *Table of Legislation*

**Australia**



**Canada**

## Germany



## South Africa



## UK



## US

# 1

# *Introduction*

THE IDEA THAT the constitutional validity and content of a law may depend on facts is controversial. In Australia the High Court has traditionally avoided fact-dependent standards, but the rise of proportionality reasoning in recent decades challenges this conventional position. Although the global popularity of proportionality as a tool of constitutional review has sparked considerable academic interest, the empirical dimensions of proportionality have been overshadowed by debates about the potential of proportionality to resolve complex moral questions, and consternation over the appropriateness of judges 'balancing' conflicting interests. Yet, in applying tests of proportionality, judges must necessarily proceed on the basis of certain factual claims or assumptions about the world, and these often concern complex and contested social, political or economic issues. A failure to address this problem systematically risks courts making factual assessments in intuitive and inconsistent ways. If judicial assessments of proportionality are to be empirically grounded and to reflect the realities of how the world works, it is imperative that greater attention is given to the problem of judicial fact-finding.

This book seeks to address this problem. It demonstrates that while facts are relevant to all three stages of proportionality reasoning, they are most prominent at the necessity stage. The Australian and comparative jurisprudence reveals that there is variation in the extent to which questions of fact have been recognised in practice; courts do not always openly acknowledge the factual underpinnings of proportionality and there has been considerable judicial disagreement about whether it is necessary or appropriate to adduce evidentiary material to establish these facts. This book argues that there is a need to distinguish more clearly between the *types* of empirical claims that arise at the different stages of proportionality reasoning. While it is possible to draw on existing categorisations of fact, such as legislative or constitutional facts, proportionality contains its own distinctive set of questions and it is instructive to consider the facts that arise at each stage separately. In developing this new framework for thinking about facts, this book also offers suggestions about the potential implications this has for court procedure.

## I. PROPORTIONALITY AND FACTS

### A. What is Proportionality?

'Proportionality' is a relational concept. It is used as a legal test to reconcile conflicting interests, and it has become particularly prominent in constitutional and human rights adjudication to assess whether a restriction or limitation on a right can be justified in relation to some other end or goal. It is sometimes referred to as either a method or standard of review, but the terminology is not always used consistently.[1] In this book I am concerned with the use of proportionality as a method of review, but take the view that it can be applied with different degrees of intensity.[2] As Thomas Poole has explained, proportionality is a 'plastic' concept 'that can be applied almost infinitely forcefully or infinitely cautiously'.[3]

This very flexibility inherent in proportionality means that between and even within jurisdictions, there are considerable differences in what is meant by proportionality.[4] When attempting to define the concept, Stephen Gardbaum points out the need not only to identify what proportionality is, but also to identify what it is not.[5] Importantly, Gardbaum highlights the need to distinguish proportionality, as a 'specific technique or tool', from both more abstract arguments made in support of a 'culture of justification' and from general notions of balancing or reasonableness review.[6] This book focuses on proportionality as a specific methodological formula or tool employed by judges to resolve competing interests.[7] When used in this sense, proportionality commonly comprises three separate stages or sub-tests: (i) 'suitability'; (ii) 'necessity'; and (iii) 'balancing' or 'proportionality *stricto sensu*'.[8] At the suitability stage,

[1] C Henckels, *Proportionality and Deference in Investor-State Arbitration: Balancing Investment Protection and Regulatory Autonomy* (Cambridge, Cambridge University Press, 2015) 31.

[2] See, eg, J Rivers, 'Proportionality and Variable Intensity of Review' (2006) 65 *Cambridge Law Journal* 174.

[3] T Poole, 'The Reformation of English Administrative Law' (2009) 68 *Cambridge Law Journal* 142, 146.

[4] See, eg, D Kenny, 'Proportionality and the Inevitability of the Local: A Comparative Localist Analysis of Canada and Ireland' (2018) 66 *American Journal of Comparative Law* 537; S Chordia, *Proportionality in Australian Constitutional Law* (Sydney, Federation Press, 2020) 4.

[5] S Gardbaum, 'Positive and Horizontal Rights: Proportionality's Next Frontier or a Bridge Too Far?' in VC Jackson and M Tushnet (eds), *Proportionality: New Frontiers, New Challenges* (Cambridge, Cambridge University Press, 2017) 222.

[6] ibid.

[7] Note that in some jurisdictions, such as Germany, proportionality is understood as a substantive and rights-optimising doctrine; see R Alexy, *A Theory of Constitutional Rights*, reprinted edn (J Rivers trans, Oxford, Oxford University Press, 2010) 47, 66–8. See also A Stone, 'Proportionality and its Alternatives' (2020) 48 *Federal Law Review* 123, 132–36.

[8] The final stage of proportionality is sometimes described as 'proportionality in the narrow sense' or 'proportionality as such', but more commonly the Latin phrase 'proportionality *stricto sensu*' is used.

the court assesses the connection between a particular measure and the aim it is stated to advance, asking whether the measure is capable of achieving the particular objective. At the second stage, necessity, the court asks whether the measure in question is necessary by inquiring into whether there are other, less restrictive alternatives that might achieve the same end. Finally, at the balancing stage, the court is required to evaluate whether the benefit (the achievement of the legitimate aim) is worth the cost of limiting the right.[9]

The history of this formula of proportionality is by now well-known and requires little elaboration. While the general concept of proportionality is an ancient one,[10] its use as a tool of constitutional adjudication is usually traced to Prussian administrative law, where, in the late nineteenth century, the administrative courts developed a notion of proportionality in the context of limiting police powers.[11] The concept was then picked up, and further refined, by the German Federal Constitutional Court in the 1950s.[12] From there, proportionality was adopted by a range of jurisdictions around the world, and it is now widely regarded as one of Germany's most successful legal 'transplants' or 'exports'.[13] This transplantation of proportionality in both the domestic and international spheres has been well-documented, and some have suggested that it now represents a 'global' model of constitutional rights.[14]

Proportionality, at least when used in the procedural sense described above, does not determine the 'correct' answer to a legal dispute, but

[9] For an overview of the three stages, see A Barak, *Proportionality: Constitutional Rights and Their Limitations* (Cambridge, Cambridge University Press, 2012) chs 10–12.

[10] Poole, for instance, has noted that aspects of the concept can be found in the works of Plato and Cicero: T Poole, 'Proportionality in Perspective' [2010] *New Zealand Law Review* 369. See also Craig, who has traced the use of similar concepts in England from the late sixteenth century onwards: P Craig, 'Proportionality and Judicial Review: A UK Historical Perspective' in S Vogenauer and S Weatherill (eds), *General Principles of Law: European and Comparative Perspectives* (Oxford, Hart Publishing, 2017).

[11] See, eg, KF Ledford, 'Formalizing the Rule of Law in Prussia: The Supreme Administrative Law Court, 1876–1914' (2004) 37 *Central European History* 203, 212; A Stone Sweet and J Mathews, 'Proportionality Balancing and Global Constitutionalism' (2008) 47 *Columbia Journal of Transnational Law* 72, 97–102; M Cohen-Eliya and I Porat, 'American Balancing and German Proportionality: The Historical Origins' (2010) 8 *International Journal of Constitutional Law* 263, 271–76.

[12] D Grimm, 'Proportionality in Canadian and German Constitutional Jurisprudence' (2007) 57 *University of Toronto Law Journal* 383, 385.

[13] It has, for instance, been described as Germany's 'export hit': N Marsch and V Tünsmeyer, 'The Principle of Proportionality in German Administrative Law' in S Ranchordás and B de Waard (eds), *The Judge and the Proportionate Use of Discretion: A Comparative Study* (London, Routledge, 2016) 13 (citing R Wahl, 'Der Grundsatz der Verhältnismäßigkeit: Ausgangslage und Gegenwartsproblematik' in D Heckmann, RP Schenke and G Sydow (eds), *Verfassungsstaatlichkeit im Wandel: Festschrift für Thomas Würtenberger zum* 70 Geburtstag (Berlin, Duncker & Humblot, 2013) 823). For a diagrammatic representation of the spread of proportionality to different legal systems, see Barak (n 9) 182.

[14] See, eg, K Möller, *The Global Model of Constitutional Rights* (Oxford, Oxford University Press, 2012). See also DM Beatty, *The Ultimate Rule of Law* (Oxford, Oxford University Press, 2004) ch 5.

merely provides a transparent and structured process for courts to follow.[15] While proportionality is often praised for promoting transparency and accountability in adjudication, it is not without its critics.[16] Some have suggested, for example, that proportionality in fact serves to conceal, rather than to illuminate, the choices made by judges.[17] Despite the proliferation of academic interest in proportionality, there has been little attention given to the role of facts. In general, the normative aspects of proportionality – such as the desirability of judges adjudicating complex moral claims and their capacity to 'balance' conflicting interests – have dominated existing accounts. Although there has been some recognition of the empirical aspects of proportionality reasoning and the problem of empirical uncertainty,[18] there has been no sustained examination of the role of facts. This book addresses this gap. It does so by examining where and how facts are relevant to judicial assessments of proportionality and the nature of those facts. Although the evaluative elements of proportionality cannot be avoided, this book demonstrates that underlying these value judgments, courts must rely on certain empirical claims about the world.

## B. Proportionality in Australia

In contrast to the widespread popularity of proportionality abroad, its reception in Australia has been more controversial. Proportionality arrived rather late in Australia,[19] only gaining a foothold in the constitutional context in the 1980s. At times the High Court has used the language of proportionality in a

[15] See, eg, ADP Brady, *Proportionality and Deference under the UK Human Rights Act: An Institutionally Sensitive Approach* (Cambridge, Cambridge University Press, 2012) 35; A Stone Sweet and J Mathews, *Proportionality Balancing & Constitutional Governance: A Comparative & Global Approach* (Oxford, Oxford University Press, 2019) 30.

[16] See, eg, J Habermas, *Between Facts and Norms: Contributions to a Discourse Theory of Law and Democracy* (William Rehg trans, Cambridge, Polity Press, 1996) 256–59; S Tsakyrakis, 'Proportionality: An Assault on Human Rights?' (2009) 7 *International Journal of Constitutional Law* 468.

[17] See, eg, GCN Webber, *The Negotiable Constitution: On the Limitation of Rights* (Cambridge, Cambridge University Press, 2009) 88ff; J von Bernstorff, 'Proportionality without Balancing: Why Judicial Ad Hoc Balancing is Unnecessary and Potentially Detrimental to the Realisation of Individual and Collective Self-determination' in L Lazarus, C McCrudden and N Bowles (eds), *Reasoning Rights: Comparative Judicial Engagement* (Oxford, Hart Publishing, 2014).

[18] See, eg, M Kumm, 'Political Liberalism and the Structure of Rights: On the Place and Limits of the Proportionality Requirement' in G Pavlakos (ed), *Law, Rights and Discourse: The Legal Philosophy of Robert Alexy* (Oxford, Hart Publishing, 2007) 137–40; M Elliott, 'Proportionality and Deference: The Importance of a Structured Approach' in C Forsyth et al (eds), *Effective Judicial Review: A Cornerstone of Good Governance* (Oxford, Oxford University Press, 2010); Alexy (n 7) 414ff; Barak (n 9) 307–08, 321, 337–38; C Chan, 'Proportionality and Invariable Baseline Intensity of Review' (2013) 33 *Legal Studies* 1.

[19] G Appleby, 'Proportionality and Federalism: Can Australia Learn from the European Community, the US and Canada?' (2007) 26 *University of Tasmania Law Review* 1, 8.

general sense, referring to the *fit* between legislative means and ends, whereas more recently it has adopted a test of 'structured proportionality' that contains the three elements of suitability, necessity and balancing.[20] This book adopts the terminology 'proportionality reasoning' to capture the various different tests applied by the High Court that contain elements of the tripartite formula of proportionality.

For much of its history, the High Court of Australia has preferred to frame its tests of constitutional validity by using the language of 'reasonably appropriate and adapted'. Both the Court and commentators have acknowledged that this language is analogous to, or contains elements of, proportionality reasoning. In the seminal decision of *Lange v Australian Broadcasting Corporation*, a unanimous High Court observed that the test of validity for the implied freedom of political communication had been expressed in various ways, but that it was not necessary to distinguish between 'proportionality' and 'appropriate and adapted'.[21]

Despite the prevalence of this view – that the two expressions are merely alternative ways to describe the same test – divisions began to emerge over the proper part of proportionality in the Australian constitutional context. As will be elaborated in Chapter 5, a critical turning point came in late 2015, when, in the decision of *McCloy v New South Wales*, a bare majority of four justices supported the introduction of a structured three-part test of proportionality in the context of the implied freedom of political communication.[22] This test incorporated the familiar three elements of 'suitability', 'necessity' and 'adequate … balance'.[23] In *Murphy v Electoral Commissioner*, decided less than a year after *McCloy*, six of the seven members of the High Court of Australia declined to apply a structured proportionality test in the context of Parliament's power to regulate elections.[24] In subsequent cases, a majority of the Court has endorsed, with only slight modification, the *McCloy* approach to structured proportionality in relation to the implied freedom of political communication.[25] Despite this growing consensus, structured proportionality testing continues to attract

[20] The adoption of proportionality in Australia is discussed further in ch 5.

[21] *Lange v Australian Broadcasting Corporation* (1997) 189 CLR 520, 562 (Brennan CJ, Dawson, Toohey, Gaudron, McHugh, Gummow and Kirby JJ).

[22] *McCloy v New South Wales* (2015) 257 CLR 178.

[23] ibid 193–95 [2] (French CJ, Kiefel, Bell and Keane JJ). For further discussion, see A Carter, 'Political Donations, Political Communication and the Place of Proportionality Analysis: Case Note on *McCloy v New South Wales*' (2015) 26 *Public Law Review* 245.

[24] *Murphy v Electoral Commissioner* (2016) 261 CLR 28, 53 [39] (French CJ and Bell J), 72 [101] (Gageler J), 94 [202] (Keane J), 107 [244] (Nettle J), 122 [297] (Gordon J). See ch 5, n 133.

[25] *Brown v Tasmania* (2017) 261 CLR 328, 363–64 [104], 368–69 [123]–[127] (Kiefel CJ, Bell and Keane JJ), 416–17 [277]–[278] (Nettle J); *Clubb v Edwards; Preston v Avery* (2019) 267 CLR 171, 200–02 [70]–[74] (Kiefel CJ, Bell and Keane JJ), 264–65 [266] (Nettle J), 330–31 [463] (Edelman J); *Comcare v Banerji* (2019) 267 CLR 373, 400 [32] (Kiefel CJ, Bell, Keane and Nettle JJ), 451 [188] (Edelman J).

vigorous dissent and debate and it remains unclear whether it will be extended to other contexts.[26]

## C. Why Facts Matter

This book is primarily concerned with how courts adjudicate questions of proportionality; that is, its focus is on *how* tests of proportionality are applied by judges. Facts are important to the application of tests of proportionality for a number of reasons. First, a rational and accurate method of fact-finding ensures that decisions will, as far as possible, reflect the real world. In this way, the work of this book broadly follows the rationalist tradition of evidence scholarship,[27] which assumes that the world is knowable and can be reconstructed by the trier of fact for the purposes of adjudication.[28] The book thus proceeds on the correspondence theory of knowledge,[29] which is based on the idea that the facts found by courts can produce an 'approximation to reality'.[30] Second, understanding the role of facts is important as it can elucidate the process of legal reasoning itself. As William Twining has observed, issues of fact, and the processes by which they are proved, are as important as legal rules in understanding law and legal reasoning.[31]

Although courts routinely engage in fact-finding in order to apply the applicable legal rule to a concrete factual scenario, there has been some recognition that facts may *also* be relevant to the content and validity of a legal rule itself. While the relevance of facts in this way might be 'seen to throw the whole positivist edifice into doubt',[32] both courts and commentators have recognised that these types of facts are different in nature from ordinary facts.

[26] In *Palmer v Western Australia* (2021) 95 ALJR 229, three justices applied a test of structured proportionality in the context of s 92 of the *Australian Constitution*.

[27] W Twining, 'The Rationalist Tradition of Evidence Scholarship', first published in E Campbell and L Waller (eds), *Well and Truly Tried: Essays on Evidence in Honour of Sir Richard Eggleston* (Sydney, Law Book Co, 1982), and republished with some additions in WL Twining, *Rethinking Evidence Exploratory Essays*, 2nd edn (Cambridge, Cambridge University Press, 2006).

[28] Note that this is also the dominant theory that underpins the practice of law: A Ligertwood and G Edmond, *Australian Evidence: A Principled Approach to the Common Law and Uniform Acts*, 6th edn (Sydney, LexisNexis Butterworths, 2017) 7–8 [1.6]. *cf* BS Jackson, *Law, Fact and Narrative Coherence* (Liverpool, Deborah Charles, 1988); IH Dennis, *The Law of Evidence*, 5th edn (London, Sweet & Maxwell, 2013) 120–26.

[29] Twining, 'The Rationalist Tradition of Evidence Scholarship' (n 27) 76–78. Note that there are competing views about whether the adjudicative system aims for truth; see D Nicolson, 'Truth, Reason and Justice: Epistemology and Politics in Evidence Disclosure' (1994) 57 *Modern Law Review* 726; Dennis (n 28) ch 4.

[30] WAN Wells, *Natural Logic, Judicial Proof and Objective Facts* (Sydney, Federation Press, 1994) 19. See also J Stone and WAN Wells, *Evidence: Its History and Policies* (Sydney, Butterworths, 1991) 59.

[31] W Twining, 'Taking Facts Seriously – Again' in P Roberts and M Redmayne (eds), *Innovations in Evidence and Proof: Integrating Theory, Research and Teaching* (Oxford, Hart Publishing, 2007) 66–69.

[32] Ligertwood and Edmond (n 28) 700 [6.71].

Most influentially, in the US, Kenneth Culp Davis developed the distinction between 'adjudicative facts' and 'legislative facts'.[33] As Chapter 3 explains, there is now a fairly broad consensus that courts are at times required to make factual findings which extend beyond the immediate parties to the dispute, and various labels have been adopted to explain these types of facts.

In Australia, the High Court has, since at least the 1940s, recognised that constitutional validity will at times depend on facts.[34] While a number of scholars have considered the problem of facts in constitutional adjudication, this work has concentrated predominantly on section 92 of the *Australian Constitution* and the defence power.[35] There has been little discussion of this issue in the context of the implied freedom of political communication or in relation to proportionality more generally, and the factual dimensions of the Court's reasoning often remain obscured.[36] The recent adoption of structured proportionality in Australia suggests it is timely to revisit the question of facts.

## II. THE AIM AND SCOPE OF THIS BOOK

This book has three broad aims. First and foremost, it seeks to understand the role of facts within proportionality reasoning. This involves identifying *where* facts are relevant within the tripartite structure of proportionality and also examining the *nature* of those facts. In this way, this book provides insights into how facts can affect the framing of constitutional tests of validity and therefore offers important doctrinal clarification. In particular, it helps to reveal some of the choices made by judges which are often hidden in applications of proportionality reasoning. The challenges of fact-finding are not unique to Australia and will arise, to varying degrees, wherever tests of proportionality are applied.

[33] KC Davis, 'An Approach to Problems of Evidence in the Administrative Process' (1942) 55 *Harvard Law Review* 364; KC Davis, 'Official Notice' (1949) 62 *Harvard Law Review* 537; KC Davis, 'Judicial Notice' (1955) 55 *Columbia Law Review* 945.

[34] See, eg, *Stenhouse v Coleman* (1944) 69 CLR 457, 469. See also the lengthy discussion by Heydon J in *Thomas v Mowbray* (2007) 233 CLR 307, 511–22 [612]–[639].

[35] *Commonwealth of Australia Constitution Act 1900* (Imp) 63 & 64 Vict, c 12, s 9 (hereinafter '*Australian Constitution*'), ss 92, 51(vi). See, eg, JD Holmes, 'Evidence in Constitutional Cases' (1949) 23 *Australian Law Journal* 235; P Brazil, 'The Ascertainment of Facts in Australian Constitutional Cases' (1970) 4 *Federal Law Review* 65; S Kenny, 'Constitutional Fact Ascertainment' (1990) 1 *Public Law Review* 134; AS Bell, 'Section 92, Factual Discrimination and the High Court' (1991) 20 *Federal Law Review* 240; J Lennan, 'How to Find Facts in Constitutional Cases' (2011) 30 *Civil Justice Quarterly* 304.

[36] Writing extra-judicially, Kiefel CJ has suggested that the second stage of proportionality, that of reasonable necessity, has been treated in Canada as a question to be determined by evidence, but that 'This possibility has not been raised in Australian cases': S Kiefel, 'Standards of Review in Constitutional Review of Legislation' in C Saunders and A Stone (eds), *The Oxford Handbook of the Australian Constitution* (Oxford, Oxford University Press, 2018) 503.

Second, the book offers procedural insights into fact-finding in constitutional litigation. As it demonstrates, in many jurisdictions the courts have failed to develop a consistent or coherent approach to the proof of facts within proportionality reasoning. Given this, the book hopes to clarify important questions about both the identification of the relevant facts and also how such facts should be ascertained. By highlighting the distinctive nature of the factual claims that arise as part of proportionality reasoning, it contributes to a developing dialogue about the proof of facts in constitutional adjudication.

Third, the book's analysis of the dynamic Australian case law on proportionality means it also serves to clarify the nature and status of proportionality in Australia at a critical moment in the doctrine's development. As explained above, for much of its history, the Australian High Court has preferred to frame its tests of constitutional validity by using the language of 'reasonably appropriate and adapted'.[37] While a majority of the High Court has now shifted towards a more structured test of proportionality, this continues to be subject to disagreement and debate.

This book focuses on proportionality in constitutional adjudication. While there are other areas of constitutional law where questions of facts might arise,[38] proportionality provides a particularly prominent example of a legal test that depends upon facts. Therefore, the book does not attempt to provide a comprehensive account of fact-finding in constitutional law. Nor does it explicitly address the question of whether proportionality ought to be adopted in Australia.[39] While it draws on some Australian cases about the validity of delegated legislation[40] (where analogous tests of proportionality have been developed), it does not examine the broader question of the role of proportionality in the judicial review of administrative decisions.[41] Finally, it does not attempt an empirical survey of the prevalence of factual findings in judicial assessments of proportionality, though such work may present a fruitful avenue of further inquiry. Instead, it is directed towards understanding how and why facts matter in proportionality reasoning.

[37] See, eg, *Lange* (n 21) 562 (Brennan CJ, Dawson, Toohey, Gaudron, McHugh, Gummow and Kirby JJ).

[38] In Australia, for instance, similar issues might arise in relation to s 90 of the *Australian Constitution*; see C Caleo, 'Section 90 and Excise Duties: A Crisis of Interpretation' (1987) 16 *Melbourne University Law Review* 296, 315ff.

[39] See Chordia (n 4), who addresses the question of whether, and if so when, structured proportionality is an appropriate method in Australian constitutional law.

[40] This is usually understood as an aspect of administrative law; see A Edgar, 'Judicial Review of Delegated Legislation: Why Favour Substantive Review over Procedural Review?' in J Bell, M Elliott, JNE Varuhas and Philip Murray (eds), *Public Law Adjudication in Common Law Systems: Process and Substance* (Oxford, Hart Publishing, 2016).

[41] For some discussion of this issue, see P Craig, 'Proportionality, Rationality and Review' [2010] *New Zealand Law Review* 265; J Boughey, 'The Reasonableness of Proportionality in the Australian Administrative Law Context' (2015) 43 *Federal Law Review* 59.

## III. METHODOLOGY AND COMPARATIVE CONTEXT

This book is directed to the work of the courts themselves; it examines how judges have applied proportionality reasoning,[42] and the extent to which they have recognised and articulated proportionality's empirical aspects. Australia forms the central case study of the book for a number of reasons. First, Australia has not, traditionally, been associated with proportionality reasoning, and proportionality is in its formative stages in Australia. Second, the High Court is still working out how the doctrine will be developed and applied, so an analysis of facts is particularly timely. Third, the High Court has already recognised the existence of 'constitutional facts' as a distinctive category of fact, so this presents an opportunity to examine how proportionality fits, or does not fit, with the Court's conventional thinking about facts.

This book concentrates on decisions of the High Court of Australia. The cases selected are those that have been significant in the development of the Court's approach to proportionality reasoning, as well as some examples where particular attention has been paid to questions of fact. Although the book is organised thematically and not by reference to discrete areas of constitutional law, as part of its analysis, it deals with constitutional characterisation (in relation to the defence power and the external affairs power), the guarantee in section 92 of the *Australian Constitution* and the implied freedom of political communication. The use of proportionality reasoning in these areas is considerably more developed than in other contexts,[43] meaning they provide the most fruitful areas of analysis.

Although Australia forms the central case study, the almost-universal reach of proportionality means that the application of the doctrine gives rise to common problems. These include empirical questions about the factual basis on which courts decide questions of proportionality, and the extent that they can (or should) be informed by evidence. For this reason, the book also draws upon the experiences of the courts in Germany, Canada and South Africa. In each of these jurisdictions, proportionality is firmly entrenched as a tool of constitutional review. These comparative experiences can offer doctrinal

[42] See R Leckey, *Bills of Rights in the Common Law* (Cambridge, Cambridge University Press, 2015) 10–11.

[43] For example, nascent elements of proportionality reasoning might be discerned in relation to other provisions in the *Australian Constitution*: s 116 (free exercise of religion), s 117 (discrimination based on State residence) and s 51 (xxxi) (acquisition of property on just terms). Note that in *Falzon v Minister for Immigration and Border Protection* (2018) 262 CLR 333, the joint judgment of Kiefel CJ, Bell, Keane and Edelman JJ rejected the use of proportionality in the context of Chapter III: 343–44 [25]–[32]; *cf Minister for Home Affairs v Benbrika* (2021) 95 ALJR 166, 223 [226] (Edelman J).

clarification about the nature and operation of proportionality,[44] and can inform how courts in Australia approach the role of facts and evidence.[45]

## A. Choice of Comparators

Germany, Canada and South Africa form useful comparators for reasons of both similarity and difference. Like Australia, each has an entrenched written constitution and in each jurisdiction the courts are empowered to invalidate legislation that is found to be in breach of the written constitution.[46] Significantly, courts in all three jurisdictions have considerable experience in applying tests of proportionality and, as part of this, grappling with the problem of facts. Therefore, this rich jurisprudence can and does offer insights for other jurisdictions, including Australia.

Against these similarities, though, there are also considerable differences between these three jurisdictions and Australia. These concern, amongst other things, different legal traditions, court structures, and constitutional traditions and cultures. This diversity, rather than hindering the possibilities of comparison, offers the potential to enrich the inquiry. As Danneman has noted, restricting one's inquiry to legal systems that are as similar as possible 'may be unduly restrictive for the purpose of finding new solutions'.[47] This selection of jurisdictions that span a range of different legal systems and traditions, then, offers the potential for developing a fuller understanding of the place of fact-finding within proportionality reasoning.

There are some notable exclusions from the scope of this inquiry. For a start, the focus on national courts means that international and supra-national courts and tribunals have been omitted.[48] While the jurisprudence from these

[44] Such an approach might be seen to contain both classificatory and normative elements; see VC Jackson, 'Comparative Constitutional Law: Methodologies' in M Rosenfeld and A Sajó (eds), *The Oxford Handbook of Comparative Constitutional Law* (Oxford, Oxford University Press, 2012) 57, 60–61.

[45] This involves elements of both 'self-reflection' and 'functionalism': VC Jackson, 'Methodological Challenges in Comparative Constitutional Law' (2009) 28 *Penn State International Law Review* 319, 320. See also M Tushnet, 'The Possibilities of Comparative Constitutional Law' (1999) 108 *Yale Law Journal* 1225, 1236; R Michaels, 'The Functional Method of Comparative Law' in M Reimann and R Zimmermann (eds), *The Oxford Handbook of Comparative Law*, 2nd edn (Oxford, Oxford University Press, 2019).

[46] The UK and New Zealand have been excluded from this study. Both are traditionally described as adopting a 'weak' form of judicial review, where a court's finding of incompatibility has no effect upon the continuing operation of the legislation.

[47] G Danneman, 'Comparative Law: Study of Similarities or Differences?' in M Reimann and R Zimmermann (eds), *The Oxford Handbook of Comparative Law*, 2nd edn (Oxford, Oxford University Press, 2019) 414.

[48] In this context, see, eg, AD Mitchell, *Legal Principles in WTO Disputes* (Cambridge, Cambridge University Press, 2008); Henckels (n 1); MA Newton and L May, *Proportionality in International Law* (New York, Oxford University Press, 2014).

bodies might also offer comparative insights, there are considerable differences when compared to national courts. For example, the European Court of Human Right's well-known 'margin of appreciation' reflects the Court's supervisory role and the differences that exist between its Member States.[49] These considerations are less relevant in a domestic context where a court is tasked with enforcing its own constitution. In terms of national courts, it is worth noting that the US has not been included in this inquiry. Unlike the courts in Germany, Canada and South Africa, the Supreme Court of the United States has resisted the turn towards proportionality and has instead developed a categorical approach to review that incorporates a tiered level of scrutiny, ranging from 'rational basis' to 'strict scrutiny'.[50] While there is a robust academic debate about the extent to which these standards in fact incorporate tests of 'proportionality or 'balancing', the status of proportionality in the US remains contested.[51]

Despite the benefits of comparative inquiry, there are also considerable challenges. These have been well-documented elsewhere, but include the risk of distorted or partial comparisons, and the problem of 'cherry-picking' cases or examples.[52] Functionalism, in particular, has been subject to much criticism, especially insofar as it attempts to carry normative force. As Ralf Michaels notes: 'Functionalist comparison can open our eyes to alternative solutions, but it cannot tell us whether those alternative solutions are better or not.'[53] Nevertheless, an inquiry into how other jurisdictions perform functionally similar tasks may be helpful as a means of identifying alternative solutions. There is also the problem that similar institutions do not necessarily perform identical roles in other constitutional settings, and even common concepts and terms can have a different complexion. This is particularly the case with proportionality, where commonalities in language can conceal considerable differences in practice. These differences, though, do not militate against comparative inquiry

[49] G van der Schyff, *Judicial Review of Legislation: A Comparative Study of the United Kingdom, the Netherlands and South Africa* (Dordrecht, Springer, 2010) 147. More generally, see A Legg, *The Margin of Appreciation in International Human Rights Law: Deference and Proportionality* (Oxford, Oxford University Press, 2012).

[50] For a brief overview, see P Yowell, 'Proportionality in United States Constitutional Law' in L Lazarus, C McCrudden and N Bowles (eds), *Reasoning Rights: Comparative Judicial Engagement* (Oxford, Hart Publishing, 2014).

[51] For some discussion, see ET Sullivan and RS Frase, *Proportionality Principles in American Law: Controlling Excessive Government Actions* (Oxford, Oxford University Press, 2009) ch 3; M Cohen-Eliya and I Porat, *Proportionality and Constitutional Culture* (Cambridge, Cambridge University Press, 2013); VC Jackson, 'Constitutional Law in an Age of Proportionality' (2015) 124 *Yale Law Journal* 3094.

[52] For some discussion of these difficulties in the context of judicial engagement with comparative sources, see C Saunders, 'The Use and Misuse of Comparative Constitutional Law' (2006) 13 *Indiana Journal of Global Legal Studies* 37; C McCrudden, 'Judicial Comparativism and Human Rights' in E Örücü and D Nelken (eds), *Comparative Law: A Handbook* (Oxford, Hart Publishing, 2007) 387–91.

[53] Michaels (n 45) 385.

altogether, but point to the need to gain a thorough and nuanced understanding of each jurisdiction.[54]

## B. The Australian Constitutional Framework

At this point it is useful to say something about the distinctive features of Australian constitutional adjudication which set it apart from the other jurisdictions considered here. This provides important context for the analysis of the High Court's approach in later chapters.

The High Court sits at the apex of the Australian judicial system and exercises both original and appellate jurisdiction.[55] Australia adheres to a 'diffuse' model of review that is generally favoured among common law jurisdictions. While matters commenced in lower courts can be 'removed' to the High Court,[56] absent such removal, State and Federal courts can entertain constitutional matters. In practice, questions involving novel or contested issues of constitutional law will generally be determined by the High Court.[57] Although the power of the courts to invalidate legislation is not specifically provided for in the *Australian Constitution*, it is widely regarded as being implied from the provisions of Chapter III which effect a separation of the judicial power of the Commonwealth from legislative and executive power.[58]

This separation of the judicial power of the Commonwealth from the legislative and executive power has been interpreted very strictly by the High Court.[59] Although the framers of the *Australian Constitution* were keen to ensure the independence and impartiality of the judiciary, it was left to the High Court to clarify the extent of the separation required by the *Constitution*.[60] Soon after federation, the Court established that the judicial power of the Commonwealth could only be exercised by a 'Chapter III court',[61] but it was not until 1956 that the reciprocal principle – namely, that a Chapter III court

[54] See, eg, Saunders (n 52) 67.

[55] The majority of constitutional matters have arisen in the Court's original jurisdiction, although some matters have come by way of appeal from State Supreme Courts or the Federal Court: P Hanks, F Gordon and G Hill, *Constitutional Law in Australia*, 3rd edn (Sydney, LexisNexis Butterworths, 2012) 17 [1.66].

[56] *Judiciary Act 1903* (Cth), s 40.

[57] M Leeming, 'The Federal and State Courts on Constitutional Law: The 2013 Term' [2014] *New South Wales Judicial Scholarship* 5.

[58] For an analysis of the historical foundations, see M Stubbs, 'A Brief History of the Judicial Review of Legislation under the Australian Constitution' (2012) 40 *Federal Law Review* 227.

[59] Note that there is no strict separation of executive and legislative power due to system of responsible government; see P Hanks, F Gordon and G Hill, *Constitutional Law in Australia*, 4th edn (Sydney, LexisNexis Butterworths, 2017) 545 [9.1].

[60] R Welsh, 'A Path to Purposive Formalism: Interpreting Chapter III for Judicial Independence and Impartiality' (2012) 39 *Monash University Law Review* 66, 68.

[61] *Waterside Workers' Federation of Australia v JW Alexander Ltd* (1918) 25 CLR 434, 442 (Griffith CJ). For some discussion, see C Saunders, *The Constitution of Australia: A Contextual Analysis* (Oxford, Hart Publishing, 2011) 196–98.

could only exercise the judicial power of the Commonwealth – was settled.[62] The effect of the twin separation rules established by the *Boilermakers* case is that there cannot be any 'mingling of judicial and non-judicial powers in the same body, except in strictly limited circumstances'.[63] This interpretation of the degree of separation that is required has led to much uncertainty about the scope and nature of judicial power.[64]

This particular understanding of judicial power has also contributed to the High Court's approach to constitutional method. The dominant method of legal reasoning adopted by the Court has been one of 'legalism'.[65] Propounded most famously by Sir Owen Dixon, 'strict and complete legalism' was considered to be the only 'safe guide' to resolving 'great conflicts'.[66] Dixon's conception of legalism was closely linked to his conception of the federation,[67] and he considered the 'sole function' of the High Court was to determine whether a measure falls within the bounds of government power.[68] While legalism is hard to define with precision, broadly speaking it encompasses an approach to interpretation that emphasises the importance of legal reasoning and excludes the personal or political preferences of judges.[69] It thus contains elements of what might be termed textualism or formalism. Although the merits of Dixonian legalism have been much debated,[70] and its influence has varied across different periods of time, its legacy still looms large.[71] In terms of facts, the influence of legalism has contributed to the Court's traditional reluctance to develop standards that depend on findings of fact.[72]

Another 'exceptional' feature of the Australian constitutional landscape is, of course, the lack of a bill of rights at the federal level.[73] Rather than

[62] *R v Kirby; Ex parte Boilermakers' Society of Australia* (1956) 94 CLR 254.

[63] Welsh (n 60) 72.

[64] For some discussion, see J Stellios, *Zines's The High Court and the Constitution*, 6th edn (Sydney, Federation Press, 2015) ch 10; J Stellios, 'The Masking of Judicial Power Values: Historical Analogies and Double Function Provisions' (2017) 28 *Public Law Review* 138.

[65] A Stone, 'Judicial Reasoning' in C Saunders and A Stone (eds), *The Oxford Handbook of the Australian Constitution* (Oxford, Oxford University Press, 2018) 475.

[66] O Dixon, 'Address upon Taking the Oath of Office as Chief Justice of the High Court' in S Crennan and W Gummow (eds), *Jesting Pilate and Other Papers and Addresses by the Rt Hon Sir Owen Dixon*, 3rd edn (Sydney, Federation Press, 2019) 289.

[67] S Gageler, 'Foundations of Australian Federalism and the Role of Judicial Review' (1987) 17 *Federal Law Review* 162, 175.

[68] Dixon (n 66) 249.

[69] C Saunders, 'Australia: Interpretation and Review' in AR Brewer-Carías (ed), *Constitutional Courts as Positive Legislators: A Comparative Law Study* (Cambridge, Cambridge University Press, 2011) 231–32.

[70] See, eg, D Dawson and M Nicholls, 'Sir Owen Dixon and Judicial Method' (1986) 15 *Melbourne University Law Review* 543; J Goldsworthy, 'Australia: Devotion to Legalism' in J Goldsworthy (ed), *Interpreting Constitutions: A Comparative Study* (Oxford, Oxford University Press, 2007).

[71] M Kirby, 'Judicial Activism? A Riposte to the Counter-Reformation' (2004) 24 *Australian Bar Journal* 219, 221.

[72] For some discussion, see Stellios, *Zines's The High Court and the Constitution* (n 64) 682ff.

[73] B Galligan and FL Morton, 'Australian Exceptionalism: Rights Protection without a Bill of Rights' in T Campbell, J Goldsworthy and A Stone (eds), *Protecting Rights without a Bill of Rights: Institutional Performance and Reform in Australia* (Aldershot, Ashgate, 2006) 18.

adopting a US-style bill of rights, the framers of the *Australian Constitution* placed their faith in parliamentary supremacy and the common law. Despite numerous attempts to introduce more explicit rights-protections over many decades, there is still no comprehensive bill of rights in either constitutional or legislative form.[74] The *Constitution* contains a small and somewhat patchy collection of explicit rights-protections, very much reflecting the history of the federation.[75] More significant in practice has been the advent of an implied rights jurisprudence, most notably the implied freedom of political communication, which has been found to be derived from the text and structure of the *Constitution*.[76] It is in this context that structured proportionality has emerged as a test of constitutional review.

## C. The Comparative Context

This brief sketch of the Australian constitutional framework reveals that while there are some similarities, there are also many differences when compared to Germany, Canada and South Africa. In order to provide some context for the analysis in later chapters, this section examines some of the key differences that exist between these jurisdictions and Australia. These differences bear upon how receptive the courts are towards proportionality reasoning, and also upon the extent to which facts have been recognised as relevant.

First, there are differences at the level of the legal system or family. Canada,[77] like Australia, has inherited the common law tradition from England,[78] including the institutions and practices of adversarial adjudication.[79] Germany, in contrast, is modelled along civilian lines and has been influenced by the Roman legal tradition. Between these two extremes sits South Africa, which contains elements of both traditions.[80] Although South Africa's jurisdiction is a 'mixed'

[74] M Groves, J Boughey and D Meagher, 'Rights, Rhetoric and Reality: An Overview of Rights Protection in Australia' in M Groves, J Boughey and D Meagher (eds), *The Legal Protection of Rights in Australia* (Oxford, Hart Publishing, 2019) 7–10.

[75] S Stephenson, 'Rights Protection in Australia' in C Saunders and A Stone (eds), *The Oxford Handbook of the Australian Constitution* (Oxford, Oxford University Press, 2018).

[76] A Stone, 'Australia's Constitutional Rights and the Problem of Interpretive Disagreement' (2005) 27 *Sydney Law Review* 29.

[77] Apart from the province of Quebec, which is a civil law jurisdiction, modelled on the French Code; see M Deturbide and EJ Hughes, 'Canada' in JM Smits (ed), *Elgar Encyclopedia of Comparative Law*, 2nd edn (Cheltenham, Edward Elgar, 2012) 132.

[78] J Stoljar, 'Invisible Cargo: The Introduction of English Law into Australia' in JT Gleeson, JA Watson and RCA Higgins (eds), *Historical Foundations of Australian Law* (Sydney, Federation Press, 2013) vol 1, 202.

[79] In the Australian context, note that some aspects, such as the jury system, were introduced only gradually: M Chesterman, 'Criminal Trial Juries in Australia: From Penal Colonies to a Federal Democracy' (1999) 62 *Law and Contemporary Problems* 69.

[80] VV Palmer, 'Mixed Jurisdictions' in JM Smits (ed), *Elgar Encyclopedia of Comparative Law*, 2nd edn (Cheltenham, Edward Elgar, 2012).

or 'hybrid' one, its evidentiary and procedural laws emanate from the common law approach, meaning its court procedures are largely adversarial.[81]

These differences, while by no means absolute,[82] continue to have implications for the procedures by which courts operate. In particular, despite some procedural modifications to the adversarial process,[83] constitutional adjudication in Australia, Canada and South Africa remains heavily influenced by the common law tradition. This includes, for instance, the traditional party-led process,[84] a more passive judicial role[85] and a binding system of precedent.[86] In contrast, constitutional adjudication in Germany has strong civilian overtones.[87] For instance, oral hearings are relatively rare and the judges play a more active role, with explicit powers to obtain further evidence or assistance from other agencies.[88]

Second, there are considerable differences in terms of court structures and the allocation of responsibility for constitutional questions. Canada, like Australia, has a diffuse system of judicial review that reflects Canada's common law heritage. The Supreme Court, at the top of the Canadian judicial hierarchy, hears appeals from provincial, territorial and federal courts.[89] This means lower courts are empowered to determine constitutional issues, although these will be subject to appeal to the Supreme Court. The Supreme Court also has a special advisory jurisdiction by which it determines 'references' on questions referred to it by the Governor in Council.[90] In contrast, in both Germany and South Africa judicial review is centralised and the creation of the new constitutional orders in the 1940s and 1990s respectively included the

[81] PJ Schwikkard and SE van der Merwe, *Principles of Evidence*, 4th edn (Cape Town, Juta, 2016) 26.

[82] See, eg, MR Damaška, *Evidence Law Adrift* (New Haven, Yale University Press, 1997) ch 1; JD Jackson and SJ Summers, *The Internationalisation of Criminal Evidence: Beyond the Common Law and Civil Law Traditions* (Cambridge, Cambridge University Press, 2012) ch 1.

[83] See further the discussion in chs 4 and 7.

[84] JA Jolowicz, 'Adversarial and Inquisitorial Models of Civil Procedure' (2003) 52 *International and Comparative Law Quarterly* 281, 289.

[85] Though note that reforms in procedural law, such as the introduction of active case management rules, have contributed to a more active judicial role.

[86] See N Duxbury, *The Nature and Authority of Precedent* (Cambridge, Cambridge University Press, 2008).

[87] For some elaboration, see RA Miller, 'Germany's German Constitution' (2017) 57 *Virginia Journal of International* Law 95.

[88] For some discussion, see PL Murray and R Stürner, *German Civil Justice* (Durham, NC, Carolina Academic Press, 2004) 262–63, 413–17; G Vanberg, *The Politics of Constitutional Review in Germany* (Cambridge, Cambridge University Press, 2005) ch 3; RA Miller and DP Kommers, 'Das Bundesverfassungsgericht: Procedure, Practice and Policy of the German Federal Constitutional Court' (2009) 3 *Journal of Comparative Law* 194.

[89] *Supreme Court Act*, RSC 1985, c S-26, s 35. For a discussion of the Court's jurisdiction, see PW Hogg, *Constitutional Law of Canada*, 2014 student edn (Toronto, Carswell, 2014) ch 8.

[90] *Supreme Court Act*, RSC 1985, c S-26, s 53. Note that similar powers exist at the provincial level and while provincial references are usually heard by appellate courts, there is some precedent for trial-level references: see *Reference re: Section 293 of the Criminal Code of Canada*, 2011 BCSC 1588. For some analysis, see M Da Silva, 'Trial Level References: In Defence of a New Presumption' (2012) 2(2) *Western Journal of Legal Studies* 2.

establishment of specialised constitutional courts, modelled along Kelsenian lines.[91] This reflected the troubled legacies of the past and the desire that the new rights-protective regimes would be backed up by powerful judicial bodies,[92] as well as a belief that certain types of questions should not be entrusted to the ordinary judiciary.[93] In Germany the Federal Constitutional Court has exclusive jurisdiction to declare legislation unconstitutional, meaning that lower courts are obliged to refer constitutional questions to the Constitutional Court.[94] Contrastingly, in South Africa the lower courts are empowered to make certain orders in relation to constitutional validity, but the Constitutional Court sits as an apex court.[95]

Third, there are significant differences between all four jurisdictions in terms of the judicial role and the conception of judicial power. These differences bear upon the types of decisions which are considered to be within the province of the courts. In contrast to Australia's rather confined approach to judicial power, in Germany, Canada and South Africa, the introduction of bills of rights prompted a considerable expansion of judicial power.[96] Judges were expected, and indeed required, to determine what might previously have

[91] H Kelsen, 'Who Ought to Be the Guardian of the Constitution? Kelsen's Reply to Schmitt' (1931) in L Vinx (ed), *The Guardian of the Constitution: Hans Kelsen and Carl Schmitt on the Limits of Constitutional Law* (Cambridge, Cambridge University Press, 2015). Note that the German Federal Constitutional Court provided a model for the South African Constitutional Court: J de Waal, 'Constitutional Law' in GC van der Merwe and JE du Plessis (eds), *Introduction to the Law of South Africa* (The Hague, Kluwer Law International, 2004) 64.

[92] See, eg, M Borowski, 'The Beginnings of Germany's Federal Constitutional Court' (2003) 16 *Ratio Juris* 155; L du Plessis and H Corder, *Understanding South Africa's Transitional Bill of Rights* (Cape Town, Juta, 1994) 194. See also M Hailbronner, 'Rethinking the Rise of the German Constitutional Court: From Anti-Nazism to Value Formalism' (2014) 12 *International Journal of Constitutional Law* 626.

[93] M Cappelletti and W Cohen, *Comparative Constitutional Law: Cases and Materials* (Indianapolis, Bobbs-Merrill, 1979) 81–83.

[94] *Basic Law for the Federal Republic of Germany* (C Tomuschat and DP Currie trans, revised by C Tomuschat and DP Kommers in cooperation with the Language Service of the German Bundestag (2014)), www.gesetze-im-internet.de/englisch_gg, art 100. Note that the Court has jurisdiction to resolve conflicts between organs of the State, abstract and concrete judicial review, and also constitutional complaints brought by individuals. For a brief overview, see Miller and Kommers (n 88) 206; J Bröhmer, 'Legislative and Executive Branch versus the Federal Constitutional Court and the Judiciary – Conflict or Cooperation?' in J Bröhmer (ed), *The German Constitution Turns 60: Basic Law and Common Constitution German and Australian Perspectives* (Frankfurt, Peter Lang, 2011) 145–48. Although the Federal Constitutional Court is separate to and does not sit above the other courts, in practice the distinction between its role and a normal appellate court is not always clear.

[95] Only certain types of disputes are exclusively reserved for the Constitutional Court under s 167(4), but any order of invalidity made by a lower court has no force until it is confirmed by the Constitutional Court: *Constitution of the Republic of South Africa 1996* (South Africa), s 172(2)(a). In addition, since 2012, the Constitutional Court's jurisdiction has been expanded to include general appellate jurisdiction, meaning it now sits as an apex court: *Constitution of the Republic of South Africa 1996* (South Africa), s 167(3)(b).

[96] Note, however, that these changes need to be understood against the backdrop of the existing constitutional systems. In Germany, for instance, the framers of the *Basic Law* remained firmly committed to the idea of Rechsstaat (a constitutional State). Similarly, in both Canada and South Africa, the received British notions of the rule of law and the separation of powers continued to be influential. See *Basic Law for the Federal Republic of Germany* (n 94), arts 20(3), 28(1), 79(iii);

been thought to be political questions.[97] In both South Africa and Germany the constitutional courts were part of a suite of deliberately transformative constitutional changes. In Canada, while the *Canadian Charter of Rights and Freedoms*[98] lacks the deliberately transformative elements of the South African and German constitutions, it too heralded a considerable expansion of the Supreme Court's existing powers of judicial review.

Finally, and relatedly, there are some broad differences between the interpretive method adopted in each jurisdiction. In Germany the dominant interpretive tradition has been that of *Begriffsjurisprudenz* – conceptual jurisprudence – which reflects a positivist understanding of the law.[99] Under this approach, law is considered to be a rational and self-contained discipline that is separate from politics, psychology and sociology.[100] This reflects the code-based nature of the German legal system, which was at its high point during the 'legal science' movement of the nineteenth century.[101] Although this understanding of the law was challenged by the 'free law movement' in Germany, which is sometimes viewed as the counterpart to legal realism in the US, this movement did not completely dislodge the dominant positivist tradition.[102] Even though the *Basic Law* has introduced a more explicit reliance on values,[103] the preference

V Götz, 'Legislative and Executive Power under the Constitutional Requirements Entailed in the Principle of the Rule of Law' in C Starck (ed), *New Challenges to the German Basic Law: The German Contributions to the Third World Congress of the International Association of Constitutional Law* (Baden-Baden, Nomos Verlagsgesellschaft, 1991) 143; T Roux, *The Politics of Principle: The First South African Constitutional Court, 1995–2005* (Cambridge, Cambridge University Press, 2013) 206; PW Hogg, 'Canada: From Privy Council to Supreme Court' in J Goldsworthy (ed), *Interpreting Constitutions: A Comparative Study* (Oxford, Oxford University Press, 2007).

[97] See, eg, H Botha, 'Democracy and Rights: Constitutional Interpretation in a Postrealist World' (2000) 63 *Journal of Contemporary Roman-Dutch Law* 561, 575.

[98] *Canada Act 1982* (UK) c 11, sch B, pt 1 (hereniafter '*Canadian Charter of Rights and Freedoms*').

[99] This doctrinal approach to adjudication has clear parallels with German approaches to constitutional scholarship, which is not surprising given the close connection in Germany between academia and legal practice; see, eg, A von Bogdandy, 'The Past and Promise of Doctrinal Constructivism: A Strategy for Responding to the Challenges Facing Constitutional Scholarship in Europe' (2009) 7 *International Journal of Constitutional Law* 364.

[100] DP Kommers and RA Miller, *The Constitutional Jurisprudence of the Federal Republic of Germany*, 3rd edn (Durham, NC, Duke University Press, 2012) 55.

[101] M Reimann, 'Nineteenth Century German Legal Science' (1989) 31 *Boston College Law Review* 837.

[102] See, eg, H Dedek and MJ Schermaier, 'German Law' in JM Smits (ed), *Elgar Encyclopedia of Comparative Law*, 2nd edn (Cheltenham, Edward Elgar, 2012) 364; KR Grechenig and M Gelter, 'The Transatlantic Divergence in Legal Thought: American Law and Economics vs German Doctrinalism' (2008) 31 *Hastings International and Comparative Law Review* 295, 307.

[103] See, eg, *Lüth*, Bundesverfassungsgericht [German Constitutional Court], 1 BvR 400/51, 15 January 1958 reported in (1958) 7 BVerfGE 198 (extracts translated in Jürgen Bröhmer, Clauspeter Hill and Marc Spitzkatz (eds), *60 Years German Basic Law: The German Constitution and its Court – Landmark Decision of the Federal Constitutional Court of Germany in the Area of Fundamental Rights*, 2nd edn (Kuala Lumpur, Malaysian Current Law Journal Sdn Bhd, 2012) 350). See also D Grimm, 'Values in German Constitutional Law' in D Davis, A Richter and C Saunders (eds), *An Inquiry into the Existence of Global Values: Through the Lens of Comparative Constitutional Law* (Oxford, Hart Publishing, 2015); E Klein, 'The Importance and Challenges of Values-Based Legal Orders' (2015) 10 *Intercultural Human Rights Law Review* 1, 9–10.

for doctrinal reasoning continues to be influential.[104] Traces of the formalist approach are particularly evident in the style and format of the Federal Constitutional Court's reasoning. As Mattias Kumm has observed, separate concurring or dissenting judgments remain rare and decisions are presented as a 'monolithic whole'.[105] The Court's judgments, including the way in which they are reported, often exclude 'all the information that would help to ground the case and its resolution in a specific political context'.[106]

In contrast, in both Canada and South Africa there has been a discernible shift away from legalist approaches to constitutional interpretation. Although in Canada legal realism did not take hold like it did in the US,[107] the proximity of the two jurisdictions and the prominence of the US *Bill of Rights* have influenced the Court's interpretation of the *Charter*. Motivated in part by the ineffectiveness of the 1960 *Bill of Rights*,[108] the Supreme Court has from its earliest *Charter* decisions emphasised that constitutional interpretation is distinct from ordinary statutory interpretation. The Court has insisted upon a 'purposive' and 'generous' method of interpretation that is cognisant of the history of the *Charter*, the values underpinning it, and the nature of Canadian society.[109] In South Africa, too, the new constitutional order[110] prompted a change in interpretive approach. Under the apartheid regime, the judiciary's role, which has since been subjected to extensive scrutiny,[111] was dominated by a formalist style of adjudication and a literal approach to statutory interpretation. The new constitutional order, which was deliberately transformative, clearly foreshadowed a value-based style of adjudication.[112] At the same time, however, the Constitutional Court of South Africa has

[104] Kommers and Miller (n 100) 56, 62–63. See also Hailbronner, who describes the approach as one of 'value formalism', which reflects the hierarchical understanding of authority and privileging of expertise which run deep in the German and continental legal tradition: Hailbronner (n 92) 646ff.

[105] M Kumm, 'On the Past and Future of European Constitutional Scholarship' (2009) 7 *International Journal of Constitutional Law* 401, 414.

[106] ibid.

[107] EM Adams, 'Canada's "Newer Constitutional Law" and the Idea of Constitutional Rights' (2006) 51 *McGill Law Journal* 435, 453.

[108] *Canadian Bill of Rights*, SC 1960, c 44.

[109] See, eg, *Law Society of Upper Canada v Skapinker* [1984] 1 SCR 357, 365–67 (Estey J); *Hunter v Southam* [1984] 2 SCR 145, 155 (Dickson J). See also Hogg (n 96) 89.

[110] This transformation of the constitutional order was accompanied by the creation of a whole new set of administrative law rights: see the *Promotion of Administrative Justice Act 2000* (South Africa).

[111] For an introduction to the extensive literature, see J Dugard, *Human Rights and the South African Legal Order* (Princeton, Princeton University Press, 1978); H Corder, *Judges at Work: The Role and Attitudes of the South African Appellate Judiciary, 1910–50* (Cape Town, Juta, 1984); I Currie, 'Judicious Avoidance' (1999) 15 *South African Journal on Human Rights* 138; H Botha, 'Metaphoric Reasoning and Transformative Constitutionalism (Part 1)' [2002] *Tydskrif vir die Suid-Afrikaanse Reg* 612.

[112] For some discussion of the changes, see M Wesson and M du Plessis, 'Fifteen Years On: Central Issues Relating to the Transformation of the South African Judiciary' (2008) 24 *South African Journal on Human Rights* 187.

emphasised the importance of not straying too far from the constitutional text.[113] Some commentators have suggested that these notes of caution perhaps reflect the Court's relatively weak institutional position,[114] and others have criticised the Court for failing to live up to its transformative ideals.[115]

## IV. THE STRUCTURE OF THE BOOK

This book is organised into six substantive chapters. Chapter 2 begins by examining the link between proportionality and facts at a conceptual level. It examines the three-part structure of proportionality and analyses the nature of the questions that arise at each of the three stages of suitability, necessity and balancing. It argues that although the ultimate conclusions at each of these stages are best characterised as questions of law, underpinning these conclusions are a series of factual propositions. These factual claims are both relevant and necessary to enable courts to make rational and reliable assessments of proportionality.

Chapter 3 then examines in more detail the types of facts that underpin the proportionality inquiry. It considers the various classifications of fact that have been developed by scholars, beginning with the influential classification between 'adjudicative facts' and 'legislative facts' pioneered by Kenneth Culp Davis.[116] The chapter argues that in the context of proportionality reasoning, it is necessary to distinguish more clearly between the facts that arise at the different stages of the analysis, and it suggests that the facts that are relevant at each stage will often exhibit different characteristics.

Against this conceptual framework, Chapter 4 investigates how courts in Germany, Canada and South Africa have approached the role of facts within proportionality. It examines the extent to which the courts have recognised the factual aspects of proportionality reasoning. In doing so, it considers whether it is possible to discern differences in the courts' treatment of facts at the different

[113] See the discussion in H Klug, 'South Africa: From Constitutional Promise to Social Transformation' in J Goldsworthy (ed), *Interpreting Constitutions: A Comparative Study* (Oxford, Oxford University Press, 2007) 285.

[114] N Petersen, *Proportionality and Judicial Activism: Fundamental Rights Adjudication in Canada, Germany and South Africa* (Cambridge, Cambridge University Press, 2017) 112.

[115] See, eg, A Cockrell, 'Rainbow Jurisprudence' (1996) 12 *South African Journal on Human Rights* 1, 2–3, 10–13, 37; KE Klare, 'Legal Culture and Transformative Constitutionalism' (1998) 14 *South African Journal on Human Rights* 146; J Dugard, 'Judging the Judges: Towards an Appropriate Role for the Judiciary in South Africa's Transformation' (2007) 20 *Leiden Journal of International Law* 965. *cf* T Roux, 'Transformative Constitutionalism and the Best Interpretation of the South African Constitution: Distinction without a Difference' (2009) 20 *Stellenbosch Law Review* 258.

[116] See, eg, KC Davis, 'Judicial Notice' (1955) 55 *Columbia Law Review* 945. The occasional Australian references to the distinction remain rare; see, eg, C Tran, 'Facts and Evidence in Litigation under the *Charter of Human Rights and Responsibilities Act 2006* (Vic) and the *Human Rights Act 2004* (ACT)' (2012) 36 *Melbourne University Law Review* 287.

stages of proportionality, drawing upon the revised framework for thinking about facts that was developed in the previous chapter. It also assesses how the courts in the three jurisdictions have sought to deal with the factual aspects of proportionality reasoning, including the processes by which such facts are established.

Chapters 5 and 6 turn to the Australian experience with proportionality. Chapter 5 assesses and explains the current status of proportionality reasoning in Australian constitutional law. It delineates the historical trajectory of the High Court towards a structured test of proportionality, and it analyses the key areas of ambiguity that linger since the 2015 decision of *McCloy*.[117] It demonstrates that the High Court has developed various tests of constitutional validity that incorporate aspects of the tripartite proportionality formula and that convey differing levels of judicial scrutiny. The adoption by a majority of the Court of a structured three-part proportionality test brings the Australian approach closer to that used in other jurisdictions, but a number of uncertainties remain. Building on this analysis, Chapter 6 seeks to investigate whether, and how, the framing of constitutional tests might affect the need for factual inquiry. In doing so, it examines whether the shift in Australia towards a more structured form of proportionality has been accompanied by an increased focus on facts.

Chapter 7 assesses the procedural implications that follow from the revised framework for thinking about facts that was developed in the earlier chapters. In particular, it considers three central, and as yet unresolved, issues: the burden and standard of proof; the scope of judicial notice; and the role of deference or restraint. The analysis in this chapter focuses on constitutional adjudication in the High Court of Australia, but also draws upon the experiences of the comparative jurisdictions. Finally, Chapter 8 brings together the main themes and findings of the book, as well as reflecting more broadly upon the various ways in which facts matter in constitutional adjudication.

[117] *McCloy* (n 22).

# 2

# *The Fact-Dependent Nature of Proportionality*

THE IDEA OF rationality – namely, that decisions will be grounded in reason and not made arbitrarily – is central both to proportionality reasoning and the adjudicative system. Proportionality reasoning provides, or at least claims to provide, a structured and principled means of resolving conflicting interests. The common law adjudicative system, within which Australian judges apply proportionality reasoning, is similarly predicated on the idea of rational decision-making.[1] This assumes that the facts that are discovered, through a rational process of proof, will reflect the realities of the external world. Despite this centrality of rationality to both adjudication and proportionality, there remains a need for closer attention to the connection between the two.

This chapter explores the link between facts and proportionality at a conceptual level, arguing that factual propositions are both relevant and necessary to enable courts to make rational and reliable assessments of proportionality. This argument is developed in two main parts. First, the chapter examines the structured nature of proportionality reasoning and the three key stages of suitability, necessity and balancing. Second, it investigates the types of decisions that courts are required to make at each of the three stages and whether these are best characterised as questions of law or questions of fact. As part of this analysis, it considers the role of value judgments within proportionality reasoning. It argues that facts are relevant at all three stages of proportionality, but are most prominent at the necessity stage. This analysis provides the foundation for Chapter 3, which examines the *nature* of the facts that arise within proportionality reasoning.

## I. PROPORTIONALITY: A STRUCTURED APPROACH

Though it takes various forms and is used in different ways, proportionality is essentially a legal tool for evaluating conflicting or competing interests.[2]

[1] Although rationality is a presumption and often a guiding principle, it is not a freestanding ground of review.

[2] J Kirk, 'Constitutional Guarantees, Characterisation and the Concept of Proportionality' (1997) 21 *Melbourne University Law Review* 1, 9–10. Note that proportionality is typically employed as part of a two-stage process of rights analysis. The first stage asks whether there is a

It is a judge-made concept that, on its own, does not determine or dictate a particular legal outcome;[3] rather, proportionality provides a method of analysis for adjudicating between competing claims.[4] The benefits of proportionality reasoning have been widely acknowledged and debated by academic commentators.[5] Chief among the benefits is the claim that it provides a structured means of choosing between conflicting interests.[6] In this way, it is said to increase the transparency, and even the objectivity, of judicial decision-making.[7] Although the three sub-tests of proportionality are well-known and often-recited, when applied in practice, courts sometimes adopt a composite approach and do not clearly distinguish between the different sub-tests.[8] This type of approach tends to conceal the process of judicial reasoning and means that the factual questions inherent in proportionality analysis often escape close attention.

To gain a better understanding of the role of facts, it is necessary to consider in further detail the various steps that are typically employed as part of proportionality analysis. The three sub-tests, derived from the German principle of proportionality, are commonly described in terms of (i) suitability, (ii) necessity and (iii) balancing. The chapter is not concerned with how each of these sub-tests is employed in different jurisdictional contexts, as that is examined in more detail later in the book in relation to the three comparative jurisdictions of Germany, Canada and South Africa (Chapter 4) and Australia (Chapters 5 and 6). Instead, this chapter examines the types of decisions the court must make at each of the three steps of proportionality reasoning.

prima facie infringement of a right and the second stage assesses whether this infringement can be justified. For some discussion, see LE Weinrib, 'The Postwar Paradigm and American Exceptionalism' in S Choudhry (ed), *The Migration of Constitutional Ideas* (Cambridge, Cambridge University Press, 2007) 93ff; LK Weis, 'On Just Terms, Revisited' (2017) 45 *Federal Law Review* 223, 230–31, 252–53.

[3] A Stone Sweet and J Mathews, 'Proportionality Balancing and Global Constitutionalism' (2008) 47 *Columbia Journal of Transnational Law* 72, 77.

[4] As explained in ch 1, while it is sometimes understood as a substantive and rights-optimising doctrine, this book focuses on its use as a methodological tool; see A Stone, 'Proportionality and its Alternatives' (2020) 48 *Federal Law Review* 123, 132–36.

[5] See, eg, VC Jackson, 'Constitutional Law in an Age of Proportionality' (2015) 124 *Yale Law Journal* 3094, 3142–53.

[6] Whether it in fact provides any real guidance for deciding between competing claims remains a matter of some dispute: D Réaume, *Limitations on Constitutional Rights: The Logic of Proportionality*, University of Oxford Legal Research Paper Series, Paper No 26/2009 (2009) 26.

[7] See, eg, S Free, 'Commentary on Chapter 6' in J Griffiths and J Stellios (eds), *Current Issues in Australian Constitutional Law: Tributes to Professor Leslie Zines* (Sydney, Federation Press, 2020) 204; DM Beatty, *The Ultimate Rule of Law* (Oxford, Oxford University Press, 2004) 166. There is considerable debate surrounding the objectivity of proportionality; see, eg, VC Jackson, 'Being Proportional about Proportionality: The Ultimate Rule of Law' (2004) 21 *Constitutional Commentary* 843; Aharon Barak, *Proportionality: Constitutional Rights and Their Limitations* (Cambridge, Cambridge University Press, 2012) 477–80.

[8] T Hickman, 'Proportionality: Comparative Law Lessons' (2007) 12 *Judicial Review* 31, 33; Jackson (n 5) 3098–99.

### A. Legitimate Aim

Proportionality reasoning is typically applied in circumstances where there is a conflict between a legitimate government end and the protection of a right.[9] The question of whether there is a legitimate aim recognises that not every purpose pursued by a government will be considered from a judicial perspective to be a valid or appropriate reason to limit a right.[10] The legitimate aim inquiry is sometimes characterised as a distinct sub-test (meaning that proportionality analysis itself is understood as a four-stage inquiry).[11] However the various stages of proportionality are defined, it is clear enough that this question needs to be examined prior to the suitability, necessity and balancing stages. Whether an aim is considered 'legitimate' in a particular constitutional context will ultimately involve a normative judgment, and so is not dependent on factual claims. However, as explained below, the identification of the legislative purpose may be viewed as an empirical question.

### B. Suitability

The first sub-test of proportionality examines the connection between a particular measure and the legitimate aim which it is said to advance. This requirement emerged from the German doctrine of proportionality and is often described as a test of 'suitability' (*geeignetheit*).[12] In other words, it asks whether the measure is a suitable way of achieving a particular purpose: does the use of such means 'rationally lead to the realization of the law's purpose'?[13] In some jurisdictions, such as Canada, the suitability test is described in terms of rational

[9] Note that Chordia argues that structured proportionality is only a useful analytical tool in situations where there is a conflict between two sets of rights or interests: S Chordia, *Proportionality in Australian Constitutional Law* (Sydney, Federation Press, 2020) 55–56, 200. Note also that Chordia argues that structured proportionality is appropriate even in jurisdictions – such as Australia – without an express bill of rights (at 5–9, 40–41, 182–84). See also Stone, who argues that the link between proportionality and rights can be severed: Stone (n 4) 135–36.

[10] Barak (n 7) 245.

[11] See, eg, G Huscroft, BW Miller and G Webber, 'Introduction' in G Huscroft, BW Miller and G Webber (eds), *Proportionality and the Rule of Law: Rights, Justification, Reasoning* (New York, Cambridge University Press, 2014) 2. This is the approach adopted by courts in the UK: see *Bank Mellat v Her Majesty's Treasury (No 2)* [2014] AC 700, 771 [20] (Lord Sumption JSC); ACL Davies and JR Williams, 'Proportionality in English Law' in S Ranchordás and B de Waard (eds), *The Judge and the Proportionate Use of Discretion: A Comparative Study* (London, Routledge, 2016).

[12] N Emiliou, *The Principle of Proportionality in European Law: A Comparative Study* (London, Kluwer Law International, 1996) 26–29. Nolte points out that the term 'suitability' can lead to misunderstandings, and that '*geeignetheit*' is more accurately translated as 'capacity of furthering an aim': G Nolte, 'General Principles of German and European Administrative Law: A Comparison in Historical Perspective' (1994) 57 *Modern Law Review* 191, 193.

[13] Barak (n 7) 303.

connection.[14] When framed in this way, the test asks whether there is a rational connection between the purpose of the law and the means employed by the legislature to achieve that objective.

The purpose of the inquiry at this stage is not to assess whether the measure is a desirable or even effective way of achieving the claimed objective, but only to assess whether it is *capable of* achieving the objective. In this way, the suitability test is often described as a test of purpose as it is designed to test whether the claimed or stated purpose is the real purpose.[15] As Aharon Barak observes:

> The question raised by the rational connection test is not whether the means are proper and correct, or whether there are other, more proper and correct means; rather, the question is: are the means chosen by the limiting law capable of advancing the underlying purpose?[16]

When assessing suitability, a court analyses the purpose of the law by probing the connection between the law and the stated purpose. It does not matter, at this stage of the analysis, whether the measure chosen is the *only* measure capable of achieving the purpose, that it only partially realises the purpose, or even that it is a harsh or excessive means of achieving the purpose.[17] It simply needs to be *capable* of achieving the purpose.

The inquiry at the suitability stage is therefore directed towards the relationship between the law and the objective that it is designed to achieve. It is not, at least directly, concerned with the corresponding limitation on a right. However, some scholars have pointed out that the suitability test serves to determine whether there is any real conflict between protecting a right and pursuing a legitimate objective. Kai Möller, for instance, suggests that if the measure does not contribute to the legitimate goal at all, there is no conflict between the protection of the right and the legitimate goal, meaning there is no need to pursue proportionality reasoning any further.[18] In this way, the suitability test serves to interrogate whether the objective is actually engaged by the law in question. As Denise Réaume explains, 'if the alleged justification for … [a] provision is a particular objective, and the provision does not actually serve that objective, the conflict is only skin deep'.[19] That is, there may be no connection with the objective: 'the value of the objective is not outweighed, but rather shown not to be operative at all, i.e. not to be a reason supporting the rights infringement'.[20]

[14] D Grimm, 'Proportionality in Canadian and German Constitutional Jurisprudence' (2007) 57 *University of Toronto Law Journal* 383, 387.

[15] Kirk (n 2) 6.

[16] Barak (n 7) 305.

[17] J Rivers, 'Proportionality and Variable Intensity of Review' (2006) 65 *Cambridge Law Journal* 174, 198.

[18] K Möller, 'Proportionality: Challenging the Critics' (2012) 10 *International Journal of Constitutional Law* 709, 713. Note that Chordia (n 9) has argued that structured proportionality is only appropriate in situations of conflicting rights or interests.

[19] Réaume (n 6) 10.

[20] ibid.

The suitability test is usually considered to provide a fairly low hurdle and one that will be relatively easy to satisfy in most cases.[21] Legislative measures will only rarely fail proportionality analysis at this stage, and the question of suitability is sometimes characterised (along with the identification of the legitimate aim) as a threshold question.[22] In the UK, where the advent of the *Human Rights Act 1998* has prompted much discussion about proportionality review, these threshold questions have been compared to 'a purified idea of *Wednesbury* reasonableness'.[23] In this way the suitability sub-test is said to provide a 'quick solution in extreme cases'.[24] It is the following two sub-tests of necessity and balancing that are, in contrast, considered to be the 'crunch' questions of proportionality analysis.[25]

### C. Necessity

The second stage of proportionality reasoning is that of necessity. Under this sub-test, the court asks whether the legitimate aim could be achieved through other measures that are less restrictive of the right in question. This test is often described as the 'least restrictive means' test and it requires that the measure be 'narrowly tailored' to the objective.[26] It involves a two-stage inquiry. First, it asks whether there are any alternative measures available to achieve the same objective. Any hypothetical alternatives must be equally effective at achieving the objective, and so measures that only partially achieve the objective will not qualify as alternatives. Second, the test focuses on the impact on the particular right, asking whether any of the potential alternatives restrict the right to a lesser extent.[27]

As with the suitability test, the necessity test is not concerned with evaluating whether the particular measure is desirable or beneficial. These are largely legislative judgments which, in many constitutional systems, are seen as outside the domain of the courts. Instead, the test of 'necessity' is equated with the concept of efficiency. As Julian Rivers explains:

> The test of necessity thus expresses the idea of efficiency or Pareto-optimality. A distribution is efficient or Pareto-optimal if no other distribution could make at least one person better off without making any one else worse off. Likewise an act is necessary if no alternative act could make the victim better off in terms of rights-enjoyment without reducing the level of realisation of some other constitutional interest.[28]

[21] J Rivers, 'The Presumption of Proportionality' (2014) 77 *Modern Law Review* 409, 422.
[22] C Chan, 'Proportionality and Invariable Baseline Intensity of Review' (2013) 33 *Legal Studies* 1, 8.
[23] Rivers (n 17) 198.
[24] Barak (n 7) 316. See *Clubb v Edwards; Preston v Avery* (2019) 267 CLR 171, 335 [472] (Edelman J).
[25] Chan (n 22) 8.
[26] Barak (n 7) 317, 333.
[27] For a more detailed discussion of the two stages, see ibid 317ff.
[28] Rivers (n 17) 198.

In short, the necessity test is concerned with minimising the impact on the right in question. It is designed to ensure that there is no equally practicable alternative that could achieve the same objective but with a smaller impact on the right.

In this way, the necessity test invites a comparison between the law in question and the hypothetical alternative. It asks whether both of these achieve the particular objective to the same extent, and then assesses which has a lesser impact on the particular right. As Barak observes, the only factor that should change with the consideration of the hypothetical alternative is that the limitation on the right is decreased.[29] The other factors, including the goal advanced, the costs incurred and the rights impacted, should remain constant. There are two different scenarios in which a law will be found to have breached the necessity sub-test.[30] First, there is the situation where the law goes beyond what is necessary; that is, it achieves the objective, but goes further and does more than is required to achieve the objective. The second scenario is where there are several policy choices available that impact upon the right to varying degrees.[31] If either of these scenarios are realised, the law cannot be said to be a necessary way of achieving the objective, and so it will be found to be disproportionate. Depending on the nature of judicial review that operates in a particular constitutional context, the law may be found to be invalid.[32]

## D. Balancing

The final and most controversial aspect of proportionality reasoning is the third stage, often labelled by the metaphor of 'balancing'[33] or proportionality *stricto sensu*. At this stage the court is required to evaluate whether the benefit (the achievement of the legitimate aim) is worth the cost of limiting the right. It is here that the impact on the right comes squarely into play. It may be that a particular law is both suitable (in that it is rationally connected to the legitimate aim) and necessary (in that there is no other equally effective measure that could secure the legitimate aim), but that a court will still not consider it a proportionate limitation. Some scholars have suggested that this inquiry essentially

[29] Barak (n 7) 325.

[30] These two situations are identified by Möller (n 18) 713.

[31] ibid.

[32] Note that in some jurisdictions, such as the UK and New Zealand, a court's finding of incompatibility has no effect upon the continuing operation of the legislation.

[33] Balancing in proportionality analysis needs to be distinguished from the doctrine of balancing that exists in US constitutional law. See M Cohen-Eliya and I Porat, 'American Balancing and German Proportionality: The Historical Origins' (2010) 8 *International Journal of Constitutional Law* 263; M Cohen-Eliya and I Porat, *Proportionality and Constitutional Culture* (Cambridge, Cambridge University Press, 2013).

involves a cost-benefit analysis,[34] although this description has been subject to criticism.[35] The inquiry at the third stage is whether the particular benefit to be achieved by the law can be justified in light of the cost to the right. As will be discussed below, the nature of the exercise undertaken by courts at this stage has been subject to extensive academic discussion and disagreement.

The balancing stage of proportionality requires a court to assess the benefits gained by the measure against the harm to the particular right. This involves considering the nature of the right or interest at stake and the degree of interference with that right. As such, this inquiry requires certain evaluative judgments to be made. When faced with a conflict, the decision-maker must ultimately prioritise which value is more important. This is sometimes described as the process of allocating weight to different values.[36] As Jeremy Kirk explains:

> That which is weighed up must be understood. On the detriment side, the extent of the restriction of a protected interest is relevant. A slight or marginal infringement can easily be justified. Account must also be taken of the nature of the protected right or interest. Not all rights, interests or guarantees are of equal importance … What is actually balanced is the *significance* of the detriment, which is a function of the level of restriction and the importance of the interest affected.[37]

One of the most influential contributors to the theory of proportionality is German scholar Robert Alexy, who has attempted to characterise this process of assigning weight in terms of a mathematical formula.[38] Essentially, Alexy's 'Law of Balancing' seeks to measure the degree or intensity of interference with one principle with the importance of satisfying another principle. Alexy adopts a 'triadic' approach that distinguishes between light, moderate and serious interferences with principles,[39] and also takes account of both abstract and concrete weights. Numbers are then assigned to the various values in the triadic model to determine which principle will prevail. Alexy's theoretical work represents

[34] Kirk (n 2) 8; Grimm (n 14) 387; M Cohn, 'Legal Transplant Chronicles: The Evolution of Unreasonableness and Proportionality Review of the Administration in the United Kingdom' (2010) 58 *American Journal of Comparative Law* 583, 609.

[35] See, eg, A Legg, *The Margin of Appreciation in International Human Rights Law: Deference and Proportionality* (Oxford, Oxford University Press, 2012) 185; Möller (n 18) 715.

[36] On the risks of resorting to 'values' in public law, see D Feldman, 'Comparison, Realism and Theory in Public Law' in J Bell, M Elliott, JNE Varuhas and P Murray (eds), *Public Law Adjudication in Common Law Systems: Process and Substance* (Oxford, Hart Publishing, 2016) 369–70.

[37] Kirk (n 2) 8. See also Cohen-Eliya and Porat, who suggest that 'normative assessments are indispensable and unavoidable in any kind of proportionality or balancing test' and that courts 'must take into account the relative importance of the conflicting rights and interests': Cohen-Eliya and Porat (n 33) 270.

[38] R Alexy, *A Theory of Constitutional Rights*, reprinted edn (J Rivers trans, Oxford, Oxford University Press, 2010) 401ff. Petersen has suggested that such a mathematical approach 'creates a false illusion of rationality and determination': N Petersen, 'Alexy and the "German" Model of Proportionality: Why the Theory of Constitutional Rights Does Not Provide a Representative Reconstruction of the Proportionality Test' (2020) 21 *German Law Journal* 163, 165. Alexy has been cited by the Australian High Court in *Murphy v Electoral Commissioner* (2016) 261 CLR 28, 74 [110] (Gageler J); *Clubb* (n 24) 307–08 [397]–[398] (Gordon J), 333 [468] (Edelman J).

[39] Note that Alexy conceives of rights as principles. See the discussion in the text accompanying n 50.

an attempt to provide a rational and mathematical structure to proportionality reasoning; it highlights, whether or not such a process is openly acknowledged, that judges will be required to evaluate the strength of various interests as part of performing the balancing exercise.[40]

## II. THE NATURE OF PROPORTIONALITY REASONING

The apparently simple, three-part structure of proportionality belies a more complex reality. Courts are not always explicit about applying the three stages, and in practice the different stages sometimes overlap. The question of the legitimacy of particular ends, for instance, may be considered as part of the other stages of analysis. In addition, the suitability test can become entwined with the necessity test as the use of excessive means to pursue a particular end may indicate that the actual purpose is different from the claimed purpose.[41] Furthermore, in practice, there are variations between jurisdictions both as to whether a structured inquiry is undertaken and as to where the 'work' of proportionality reasoning takes place.[42] For example, several scholars have noted a difference in approach between Germany and Canada in this regard.[43] In Canada, most laws that fail to meet the proportionality test in section 1 of the *Canadian Charter of Rights and Freedoms*[44] are found to contravene the necessity stage. When the necessity test is applied in this way, it essentially involves the court asking whether the more restrictive policy is 'really necessary'.[45] This inquiry involves the type of evaluative judgments that in other jurisdictions, such as Germany, are typically carried out at the third stage of proportionality analysis.[46]

In addition to these considerable variations in the application of proportionality in practice,[47] there are fundamental differences between the ways in which the theoretical underpinnings of proportionality have been conceptualised. In recent years, theoretical accounts of proportionality – both defending it as a tool of adjudication and criticising its shortcomings – have abounded. Many of

[40] B Pirker, *Proportionality Analysis and Models of Judicial Review: A Theoretical and Comparative Study* (Groningen, Europa Law Publishing, 2013) 39; N Petersen, 'How to Compare the Length of Lines to the Weight of Stones: Balancing and the Resolution of Value Conflicts in Constitutional Law' (2013) 14 *German Law Journal* 1387.

[41] Kirk (n 2) 6.

[42] For instance, in South Africa the Constitutional Court has rejected the structured approach adopted in other contexts, such as Germany and Canada, and instead considers the five factors itemised in s 36 of the *Constitution of the Republic of South Africa 1996* in a global fashion: see ch 4, n 28 and accompanying text.

[43] Grimm (n 14); Möller (n 18) 714–15.

[44] *Canada Act 1982* (UK) c 11, sch B, pt I (hereinafter '*Canadian Charter of Rights and Freedoms*').

[45] Möller (n 18) 714.

[46] Grimm suggests that the Canadian Supreme Court may avoid the third step 'out of fear that a court might make policy decisions at this stage rather than legal decisions': Grimm (n 14) 394.

[47] See further the discussion in ch 4, section I.

the theoretical discussions concentrate on the place of balancing in proportionality analysis and what this task entails. Francesco Urbina has helpfully pointed out that there are two main groupings into which most of the major theoretical accounts of proportionality can be placed.[48] First, the traditional account follows Alexy's influential work in the German context and can be described as the 'maximization account of proportionality'.[49] Alexy's theory is based on his understanding of rights as principles, which he sees as 'optimization requirements' that can be satisfied to varying degrees.[50] According to Urbina, Alexy and the other scholars in this vein conceive of proportionality as a rational tool that is 'structured through technical legal categories designed to shape the reasoning of the judge in doing so'.[51] In contrast, there is what Urbina describes as the 'unconstrained moral reasoning' view of proportionality.[52] This view, which he attributes to scholars such as Kai Möller, is characterised by Urbina as one that essentially requires judges to engage in an 'open-ended moral and factual inquiry'.[53] These different theoretical conceptions of proportionality have implications, as later chapters will show, in terms of how receptive courts are to tests of proportionality.

Within this theoretical literature, there has been some recognition of the empirical problems thrown up by proportionality reasoning. Alexy, for example, in his 'Postscript' develops an 'epistemic Law of Balancing', which requires that the level of empirical certainty be calibrated to the intensity of interference with the right.[54] In other words, 'a high intensity of interference demands a high degree of certainty about the underlying empirical premisses'.[55] Alexy's proposal for 'epistemic balancing' has been subject to criticism and modification by other scholars.[56] This book, although not attempting to resolve the

[48] FJ Urbina, 'Is it Really That Easy? A Critique of Proportionality and "Balancing as Reasoning"' (2014) 27 *Canadian Journal of Law and Jurisprudence* 167. See also Rivers (n 17) 177–82.

[49] Urbina (n 48) 174.

[50] ibid. See also Alexy (n 38) 47–48. There is some debate about the degree to which Alexy's view of rights as principles complements or contradicts Dworkin's view of rights as 'trumps'. See, eg, K Möller, 'Balancing and the Structure of Constitutional Rights' (2007) 5 *International Journal of Constitutional Law* 453; George Letsas, *A Theory of Interpretation of the European Convention on Human Rights* (Oxford, Oxford University Press, 2007) ch 5; Legg (n 35) 181–92; S Wheatle, *Principled Reasoning in Human Rights Adjudication* (Oxford, Hart Publishing, 2017) 22–26; K Möller, 'Dworkin's Theory of Rights in the Age of Proportionality' (2018) 12 *Law & Ethics of Human Rights* 281.

[51] Urbina (n 48) 174. See also Schauer, who argues there is a 'difference between the structured inquiry of proportionality review and an open-ended mandate simply to "do the right thing," or "take everything into account," or make the best decision on the "balance of reasons."': F Schauer, 'Balancing, Subsumption, and the Constraining Role of Legal Text' (2010) 4 *Law & Ethics of Human Rights* 35, 36–37 (footnote omitted).

[52] Urbina (n 48) 178.

[53] ibid.

[54] Alexy (n 38) 418ff.

[55] ibid 419.

[56] See, eg, J Rivers, 'Proportionality, Discretion and the Second Law of Balancing' in G Pavlakos (ed), *Law, Rights and Discourse: The Legal Philosophy of Robert Alexy* (Oxford, Hart Publishing, 2007) 170ff; M Klatt and J Schmidt, 'Epistemic Discretion in Constitutional Law' (2012) 10 *International Journal of Constitutional Law* 69.

theoretical debates surrounding proportionality, draws upon this literature in order to identify the extent to which proportionality reasoning is informed by questions of fact.

## A. Types of Decisions Involved in Assessing Proportionality

One of the major criticisms levelled against proportionality is that it requires judges to make policy-based judgments. This raises concerns in terms of both institutional capacity and democratic legitimacy, leading to arguments that courts are ill-equipped to make these types of decisions and that such decisions are better suited to the elected branches of government.[57] Defenders of proportionality suggest that judges make these types of evaluative decisions all the time[58] and that proportionality provides a structured and transparent process for such decisions.[59] To make sense of these criticisms, it is necessary to consider in more detail exactly *what* the court is required to do at each stage of proportionality reasoning. Although the suitability, necessity and balancing stages are well-rehearsed, there has been little attention given to the extent to which these inquiries depend upon findings of fact. In addition, there is ambiguity over whether a court's conclusions at each stage are best characterised as questions of fact or questions of law. In the context of proportionality, this distinction has relevance in terms of whether it is necessary or appropriate to adduce evidence, and whether a court's findings will constitute binding precedent.

The distinction between questions of law and questions of fact has long commanded the attention of both scholars and practitioners.[60] The distinction carries considerable practical ramifications in terms of the availability of defences in criminal law, the division of responsibility between judge and jury, the availability and scope of rights of appeal, and the application of the doctrine of precedent.[61] Yet, despite the centrality of the distinction, its application and conceptual foundations remain problematic.[62] There are some issues, such as those of procedure, jurisdiction or the content of applicable law, that are always questions of law.[63] In contrast, there are some issues, such as the interpretation of a statutory text, which will sometimes be questions of law and other times be questions of fact. For example, the interpretation of an ordinary, non-technical

[57] These concerns reflect broader concerns with the judicial review of legislation. See J Waldron, 'The Core of the Case against Judicial Review' (2006) 115 *Yale Law Journal* 1346.

[58] See, eg, P Craig, 'The Nature of Reasonableness Review' (2013) 66 *Current Legal Problems* 131.

[59] See, eg, ADP Brady, *Proportionality and Deference under the UK Human Rights Act: An Institutionally Sensitive Approach* (Cambridge, Cambridge University Press, 2012) 8, 35–36.

[60] In the context of administrative law, see M Aronson, M Groves and G Weeks, *Judicial Review of Administrative Action and Government Liability*, 6th edn (Sydney, Thomson Reuters, 2017) ch 4.

[61] T Endicott, 'Questions of Law' (1998) 114 *Law Quarterly Review* 292, 294; W Twining and D Miers, *How to Do Things with Rules* (Cambridge, Cambridge University Press, 2010) 126.

[62] Endicott (n 61).

[63] Twining and Miers (n 61) 130.

English word has been held to be a question of fact, but whether a word is to be given its ordinary meaning or a technical meaning is a question of law.[64]

Notwithstanding this lack of clarity, there are some questions that are considered quintessentially questions of fact. For example, as William Twining and David Miers suggest: 'Questions whose answers depend upon the existence of evidence showing that a fact is true or more likely than not to be true are always questions of fact.'[65] In other words, empirical questions will almost certainly be questions of fact. A fact is essentially a descriptive statement about the world.[66] To establish the facts, the court draws inferences from the available evidence,[67] which may consist of physical traces from the past, the testimony of witnesses or the opinion of experts. In this way, facts are legal constructs. They do not have an independent existence, but are selected (or 'found') on the basis of the relevant evidence. Although facts can never be established with complete certainty, they can be established to a degree of likelihood or probability.[68]

Yet, this traditional model of adjudication, under which judges 'find' facts based on the available evidence and then apply the relevant law to these facts, presents too simple a picture. The categories of law and fact are not fixed or immutable, and there are some decisions that cannot be neatly characterised.[69] In addition, the division between fact and law is complicated by the intrusion of value judgments. At times courts must make decisions that have an evaluative character and for which there may be no guidance in either empirical materials or previous cases. Proportionality reasoning is a prime example.

## B. Factual Elements in Proportionality

To understand how proportionality reasoning might fit into the law-fact dichotomy, it is necessary to revisit each of the different stages of analysis. This next part of the chapter considers how the questions at each of these stages might best be characterised, and examines when and how facts are relevant to the court's analysis.

[64] See Aronson, Groves and Weeks (n 60) 219 [4.230], who suggest that this distinction is no longer useful. See also Endicott (n 61) 299–300.

[65] Twining and Miers (n 61) 129–30.

[66] The nature of facts is explored in more detail in ch 3, sections I and II.

[67] JH Wigmore, *The Science of Judicial Proof, as Given by Logic, Psychology, and General Experience, and Illustrated in Judicial Trials*, 3rd edn (Boston, Little, Brown, 1937) ch 2; T Anderson, DA Schum and WL Twining, *Analysis of Evidence*, 2nd edn (Cambridge, Cambridge University Press, 2005) ch 5; A Ligertwood and G Edmond, *Australian Evidence: A Principled Approach to the Common Law and Uniform Acts*, 6th edn (Sydney, LexisNexis Butterworths, 2017) 8–15 [1.8]–[1.11].

[68] As explained in ch 1, in this book I am adopting the correspondence theory of knowledge, which assumes that the real world is knowable and can be discovered by the court for the purposes of adjudication.

[69] S Gageler, 'Fact and Law' (2009) 11 *Newcastle Law Review* 1, 22. See also Cane, who discusses the difficulty of distinguishing between 'law', 'fact' and 'policy': P Cane, *Controlling Administrative Power: An Historical Comparison* (Cambridge, Cambridge University Press, 2016) 238–41.

### *i. Purpose and Suitability*

The suitability sub-test of proportionality assesses the connection between the purpose of the law and the means employed, asking whether the law can rationally achieve what it is designed to do. As explained above, a preliminary step is to ascertain the purpose of the law and whether this purpose qualifies as legitimate.[70] While the question of legitimacy is ultimately a normative one, and one that will differ between jurisdictions, the identification of the relevant purpose may be seen to involve empirical issues. The ascertainment of legislative purpose is a familiar element of statutory construction, and it is well-recognised that it is not the subjective intention of the legislature that is relevant, but the objective purpose intended to be pursued by the enacted law.[71] While the task will often be straightforward and courts will often be able to rely on the statutory text alone, there may be instances where the purpose is unclear or contested. In those circumstances, it may be that extrinsic materials can assist with identifying the legislative purpose.[72] Such materials may include parliamentary materials, such as Second Reading speeches, explanatory memoranda or committee reports.[73]

Once a legitimate purpose has been identified, the suitability inquiry involves asking whether the law is capable of achieving that purpose. Amongst the scholars who have considered this question, there is some divergence in terms of whether the suitability test involves a question of fact or law. Writing in the context of the UK's *Human Rights Act 1998*, Julian Rivers has suggested that the inquiry into suitability can be characterised as a legal question:

> [T]he question of which state aims are legitimate in the context of the limitation of a specific right, and the question of whether a particular action be subsumed under such an aim, are questions of law of which the court can take judicial notice.[74]

[70] See section I.A above. For a discussion of the difference between 'purpose' and 'motive', see N van Wees, 'Judicial Review of Legislators' Motives' (2017) 45 *Federal Law Review* 681.

[71] On the difference between 'statutory purpose' and 'legislative intention', see *Lacey v Attorney-General (Qld)* (2011) 242 CLR 573, 591–92 [43]–[44] (French CJ, Gummow, Hayne, Crennan, Kiefel and Bell JJ). For further discussion, see B Selway, 'The Rise and Rise of the Reasonable Proportionality Test in Public Law' (1996) 7 *Public Law Review* 212, 217; A Simpson, 'Grounding the High Court's Modern Section 92 Jurisprudence: The Case for Improper Purpose as the Touchstone' (2005) 33 *Federal Law Review* 445, 465–70; DC Pearce, *Statutory Interpretation in Australia*, 9th edn (Sydney, LexisNexis Butterworths, 2019) 35–36 [2.3].

[72] Such materials already have a recognised role in the sphere of statutory construction: at the Australian federal level, see *Acts Interpretation Act 1901* (Cth), s 15AB. See also Pearce (n 71) 87 [3.3]ff; MT Stubbs, 'From Foreign Circumstances to First Instance Considerations: Extrinsic Material and the Law of Statutory Interpretation' (2006) 34 *Federal Law Review* 103.

[73] J Dharmanda, 'Using Parliamentary Material in Interpretation: Insights from Parliamentary Process' (2018) 41 *University of New South Wales Law Journal* 4. In terms of the role and impact of Parliamentary Committees more generally, see S Moulds, *Committees of Influence: Parliamentary Rights Scrutiny and Counter-Terrorism Lawmaking in Australia* (Singapore, Springer, 2020).

[74] Rivers does acknowledge that proportionality involves both factual and normative questions that are 'intertwined' with each other: Rivers (n 21) 415.

Although Rivers employs the term 'judicial notice', it appears that he is not referring to the traditional understanding of that concept as an evidentiary short-cut by which certain types of facts can be established without the need for formal proof;[75] rather, he appears to be using the concept to refer to the assumption that judges know the law and are relatively free in terms of their search for, and exposition of, the law.[76] This use of judicial notice of law, along with Rivers' characterisation of the suitability inquiry as a legal question, seems to omit any role for facts at this stage of the analysis.

In contrast, other scholars have characterised the suitability test as a predominantly factual test, emphasising the empirical nature of the inquiry.[77] Mattias Kumm, for instance, views the suitability and necessity tests as ones 'focus[ing] on empirical concerns'.[78] Drawing upon Alexy's work, Kumm explains that both of these stages 'express the requirement that principles be realised to the greatest possible extent relative to what is factually possible'.[79] Similarly, Barak describes the rational connection test as a factual test: 'It asks an empirical question regarding the ability of the means used by the limiting law to advance or realize the proper purpose.'[80] In recognising the empirical nature of the inquiry, Barak also acknowledges the problem of factual uncertainty, namely that whether a particular objective will be achieved can rarely be established conclusively. Barak suggests that this calls for a middle-ground framing of the test.[81] A test cannot demand complete certainty (or governments could never legislate), yet at the same time courts should not simply accept the government's statements of purpose at face value. Barak suggests that generally the test of rational connection can be fulfilled on the basis of 'logic and common sense', but that at times the text of the law will be insufficient to make this evaluation and evidence will be needed.[82]

[75] JD Heydon, *Cross on Evidence*, 12th Australian edn (Sydney, LexisNexis Butterworths, 2020) ch 2. See further the discussion in ch 7, section I.B.ii.

[76] The term 'judicial notice' is sometimes used in this way, but it has been described as a 'misnomer': Heydon (n 75) 222 [3075]. See also PB Carter, 'Judicial Notice: Related and Unrelated Matters' in E Campbell and L Waller (eds), *Well and Truly Tried: Essays on Evidence in Honour of Sir Richard Eggleston* (Sydney, Law Book Co, 1982) 90–91.

[77] See, eg, Henckels, who suggests the suitability stage (together with necessity) is factual 'in the sense that it can be objectively ascertained whether the measure is rationally connected to the objective': C Henckels, *Proportionality and Deference in Investor-State Arbitration: Balancing Investment Protection and Regulatory Autonomy* (Cambridge, Cambridge University Press, 2015) 28–29.

[78] M Kumm, 'Political Liberalism and the Structure of Rights: On the Place and Limits of the Proportionality Requirement' in G Pavlakos (ed), *Law, Rights and Discourse: The Legal Philosophy of Robert Alexy* (Oxford, Hart Publishing, 2007) 137.

[79] ibid. See also Alexy (n 38) 397.

[80] Barak (n 7) 307.

[81] ibid 309.

[82] ibid 310. Note that in the context of discussing the Canadian test of rational connection, Hickman suggests that empirical evidence 'will be of probative value but not necessary': Hickman (n 8) 39.

As will be recalled, under the suitability test, the relevant question is whether the law is *capable of* fulfilling a particular legitimate purpose. A court's overall conclusion in relation to the suitability test is likely to be construed as a legal conclusion. However, just as with ordinary tasks of statutory construction, a court does not operate in a vacuum;[83] rather, in assessing whether the law is rationally related to a particular purpose, the court must necessarily rely on background facts or assumptions. For example, a court may need further information about the policy objectives pursued by the law, the regulatory context in which it operates and the mechanics of how the law itself works. As explained above, the suitability test is generally considered to impose a low threshold and, in most cases, it is relatively easily satisfied. This has implications, which will be explored in Chapter 7, in terms of the standard of proof and whether the factual claims need to be supported by evidence.

### *ii. Necessity*

It is at the necessity stage of proportionality reasoning that empirical questions are particularly pertinent.[84] Although a court's conclusion as to whether a measure is necessary is likely to be characterised as a question of law,[85] this conclusion rests upon various propositions of fact. Unlike the suitability test, which asks only whether the measure is capable of achieving an objective, the necessity test involves the court assessing the *likelihood* that a particular objective will be achieved and the degree to which it will be achieved. As explained above, it involves considering the probability that a given measure, and also any hypothetical alternative, will achieve the interest in question. This requires making predictions about how the measure might operate in the real world. That is, the court must determine whether the measure is actually likely to advance the particular objective and also whether another measure might advance the objective without such a great restriction on the right. In this way, the necessity test is informed by questions of fact and it will often raise 'complex questions of empirical prognosis'.[86]

The necessity test is not completely free of normative judgment. In reaching a conclusion about whether there are any equally practicable alternatives that affect the right to a lesser degree, the court must evaluate the effectiveness of the real and hypothetical solutions.[87] Yet, underpinning this conclusion, there

[83] Heydon (n 75) 209.

[84] Amongst those who have considered the issue, there is general agreement on this point. See, eg, M Elliott, 'Proportionality and Deference: The Importance of a Structured Approach' in C Forsyth et al (eds), *Effective Judicial Review: A Cornerstone of Good Governance* (Oxford, Oxford University Press, 2010) 267–72; Kumm (n 78) 137; Pirker (n 40) 29; Rivers (n 21) 415.

[85] This has been recognised by Barak (n 7) 328.

[86] Rivers (n 21) 415. See also Jackson (n 5) 3145–46.

[87] As Dixon explains, assessing necessity is an 'inherently difficult evaluative exercise': R Dixon, 'Proportionality & Comparative Constitutional Law versus Studies' (2018) 12 *Law & Ethics of Human Rights* 203, 213.

will be various propositions – whether in the form of unstated assumptions or findings of fact – that the measure is *likely* to achieve the stated aim. These propositions, although they may not look like conventional facts, can be understood as factual questions.[88] They help to inform the predictive judgment the court must ultimately make at the necessity stage. Although the factual claims are unlikely, on their own, to provide a complete answer to the necessity question, it would be difficult, and probably impossible, to answer the necessity sub-test without relying on at least some facts or assumptions about how the measures will operate in practice. In this way, the necessity test relies on facts, even if these factual propositions are not always clearly or explicitly articulated by courts. The empirical nature of the questions raised by the necessity test has led to some recognition that evidence can and will be relevant to this stage of the inquiry. As Barak observes:

> In order to properly answer the question of whether the alternative means – which limit the right to a lesser extent – equally advance the purpose as the means chosen by the legislator, an understanding of both the purpose and the probability of its being achieved through the alternative means is necessary. An estimate is insufficient; the understanding should be of the concrete factual data, as well as of the probabilities and risks involved.[89]

Even in circumstances where there is no evidence or insufficient evidence, a court will still be required to reach a conclusion on the question of necessity.[90] Therefore the court's conclusion will, at least implicitly, rest upon a factual finding that the measure is or is not likely to advance the objective.

### *iii. Balancing*

The third stage of proportionality analysis – balancing or proportionality in the strict sense – is often seen as a 'bolder judicial endeavour' than the earlier two stages.[91] This is because it compels the court to make evaluative judgments about the importance of the different interests at stake.[92] As Adrienne Stone explains, balancing is 'a metaphor for a judgment about the relative importance of competing values or interests'.[93] It is this 'balancing' of interests that has led to debate about the extent to which proportionality can provide a principled, or objective, way of resolving disputes.

[88] See further the discussion in ch 3, sections III.B and IV.

[89] Barak (n 7) 321.

[90] For a discussion of how the burden of proof applies in this context, see the discussion in ch 7, section I.B.i.

[91] Elliott (n 84) 4. As Bomhoff has observed, the language of 'balancing' may carry a range of different meanings and describe different processes: J Bomhoff, 'Genealogies of Balancing as Discourse' (2010) 4 *Law and Ethics of Human Rights* 107, 113.

[92] Though even when courts avoid an overt 'balancing' of interests, similar evaluative judgments are performed during the other stages. See, eg, Petersen (n 40) 1395.

[93] Stone (n 4) 141.

Some, such as Canadian scholar David Beatty, advocate a neutral concept of proportionality.[94] Under this conception, proportionality allows conflicting interests and ideas to be compared and resolved 'on the basis of reason and rational argument'.[95] According to Beatty:

> Judgments are based on findings of fact about the parties' own evaluation of the significance of whatever government initiative or decision is before the court. Applied in this way, proportionality offers judges a clear and objective test to distinguish coercive action by the state that is legitimate from that which is not. When they stick to the facts, the personal sympathies of the judges towards the parties in the case never come into play.[96]

Beatty's conception of proportionality, which has been subject to some criticism,[97] elevates the place of factual questions. On his account, proportionality is an objective legal standard that directs attention to the facts rather than to interpretation or moral principles.[98] Beatty goes so far as to contend that proportionality 'transforms questions that in moral philosophy are questions of value into questions of fact'.[99] Although he sees facts as determinative, he offers little analysis of the contestability of facts. He seems to assume, for instance, that the facts can be objectively determined and easily separated from questions of law or policy.

In contrast, others take the view that proportionality cannot possibly offer an objective way to resolve disputes as it is, in essence, a value-laden exercise. This view emerges most strongly from the criticism of incommensurability – namely, that proportionality requires judges to bring into relation two things that cannot properly be compared.[100] There is, according to this criticism, no common metric and as a matter of logic, it is impossible to measure the cost of limiting a right against the benefit to some other interest. Timothy Endicott, for instance, argues that the balancing stage of proportionality requires judges to reconcile incommensurable interests.[101] The lack of any equivalent 'units of gravity'[102] to measure competing interests means that judges have to 'throw the scales out the window and just choose'.[103] For Endicott, however, this type of

[94] Beatty (n 7) 161.
[95] ibid 169.
[96] ibid 166.
[97] See especially Jackson (n 7). See also G Webber, 'Proportionality, Balancing, and the Cult of Constitutional Rights Scholarship' (2010) 23 *Canadian Journal of Law and Jurisprudence* 179, 187–90; G Webber, *The Negotiable Constitution: On the Limitation of Rights* (Cambridge, Cambridge University Press, 2009) 107–10.
[98] Beatty (n 7) 171.
[99] ibid 170.
[100] See, eg, TA Aleinikoff, 'Constitutional Law in the Age of Balancing' (1987) 96 *Yale Law Journal* 943, 972–76; Webber, *The Negotiable Constitution* (n 97) ch 3.
[101] T Endicott, 'Proportionality and Incommensurability' in G Huscroft, BW Miller and G Webber (eds), *Proportionality and the Rule of Law: Rights, Justification, Reasoning* (New York, Cambridge University Press, 2014) 311.
[102] ibid 316.
[103] ibid 315.

choice is not inimical to the rule of law; rather, the rule of law demands a system in which judges reconcile incommensurable interests.[104]

Yet, even accepting that at the third stage, judges are required to make a choice between two competing interests – which ultimately requires a value judgment to be made – this does not necessarily exclude any role for facts. When performing this evaluative exercise, judges must proceed on the basis of certain facts about the extent of the benefit to be achieved and the extent of the detriment to the right. That is, when considering whether the benefit is worth the cost of limiting the right, they must necessarily be informed by some empirical understanding of the real-world impacts of the law in question. These issues may already have been considered at an earlier stage of the analysis, depending on how a court structures its proportionality inquiry, but they remain relevant at the balancing stage. Even though balancing ultimately involves a normative judgment, judges cannot 'balance' competing interests in isolation; rather, they undertake this process of evaluation against the backdrop of the previous two inquiries. While recognising the relevance of facts does not, as Beatty suggests, transform proportionality into a purely objective standard,[105] it can help to reveal when and how value judgments come into play.

The criticism of incommensurability, then, does not necessarily deny that facts are relevant to the proportionality assessment; rather, it points to the distinctive nature of the facts that might arise. As Endicott observes, adjudication under the UK's *Human Rights Act 1998* involves 'circumstances of radical uncertainty'.[106] It therefore depends upon 'massively complex social facts' for which the social sciences cannot provide 'accurate and verifiable' answers.[107] These comments suggest that, unlike ordinary facts that arise between the parties in most litigation, the types of facts involved in applying proportionality reasoning will be different. They will often be general in nature and involve broader claims about society or predictive judgments about future events. The nature of such facts will be explored more fully in the next chapter, but for now it suffices to note that this has implications in terms of how proportionality tests are framed and applied.

In addition, to focus *only* on value judgments at the balancing stage, and to ignore the empirical issues, may encourage judicial assessments of proportionality that are not adequately justified. Again in the context of the UK's *Human Rights Act 1998*, Cora Chan observes that courts have upheld legislative measures that interfere with rights based on 'insufficient evidence to demonstrate the justifiability of the measures, or on the basis of untested assertions or presumptions'.[108] Chan argues that courts should be satisfied on the balance of

[104] ibid 311.
[105] See Beatty (n 7) 170–71.
[106] Endicott (n 101) 337.
[107] ibid 336.
[108] Chan (n 22) 14. See also S Greer, '"Balancing" and the European Court of Human Rights: A Contribution to the Habermas-Alexy Debate' (2004) 63 *Cambridge Law Journal* 412, 431–33.

probabilities that a rights-infringing measure is proportionate, and highlights the need for evidence in performing this task:

> I acknowledge that the kind of evidence required to prove a fact may differ from that required to prove the soundness of a judgment. Yet the idea of the court being certain of a proposition to a requisite degree is applicable to evaluative as much as it is to factual questions.[109]

Chan here recognises that proportionality will involve questions that are evaluative in nature and contends that courts need to apply more scrutiny to the evaluative exercises performed by government. She suggests that the relevant evidence may consist of first-order reasons (those that relate to the merits of the particular case) or second-order reasons (institutional reasons that relate to the government's expertise, institutional capacity or democratic legitimacy).[110] Therefore, even where the effectiveness of a measure cannot be established by direct evidence, it may still be possible to probe the government's justification by examining the second-order reasons.

## III. CONCLUSION: PROPORTIONALITY AND FACTS

When undertaking proportionality reasoning, courts are applying a legal test to evaluate conflicting rights or interests. A court's ultimate conclusion about whether a measure is proportionate is best characterised as a question of law. However, even if courts do not explicitly distinguish between the different stages, this conclusion about proportionality depends upon the application of (at least some of) the three sub-tests of suitability, necessity and balancing. A court's conclusion in relation to each of these questions is also likely to be characterised as legal rather than factual, as it represents the application of a legal test.

However, underpinning the three sub-tests are issues of fact. First, the suitability stage of proportionality involves assessing the connection between the law and its purpose. Although this will often be seen as a task of statutory interpretation, it depends on certain background facts about the purpose to be pursued by the law, the context in which the law operates and the technicalities of how the law works in practice. Second, at the necessity stage of proportionality, facts become particularly relevant as the court must, even if implicitly, be proceeding on the basis of certain views about how the law is likely to work in practice. The court must form a judgment about whether the law and any alternative

[109] Chan (n 22) 15.

[110] ibid 11–14, 18–21. See also C Chan, 'Deference, Expertise and Information-Gathering Powers' (2013) 33 *Legal Studies* 598; Legg (n 35) 194–96. For further discussion of this distinction, see J Raz, *Practical Reason and Norms* (first published by Hutchinson 1975; Oxford, Oxford University Press, 1999) ch 1; SR Perry, 'Second-Order Reasons, Uncertainty and Legal Theory' (1988) 62 *Southern California Law Review* 913.

measures are actually likely to advance a particular objective, and about the extent of the impact on the right. Finally, at the balancing stage, the court is ultimately confronted with a question of value judgment, but, as this chapter has explained, this takes place against the backdrop of the two earlier inquiries and so is premised on a certain understanding of the facts. Overall, this chapter has demonstrated that, at least at a conceptual level, facts *are* relevant to the application of proportionality reasoning. Before turning to look at the extent to which this has been recognised by courts in practice, it is first necessary to consider the *nature* of the facts that arise in proportionality reasoning.

# 3

# *Understanding Facts*

In most ordinary litigation, a judge applies a rule of law to a particular set of facts to determine whether the facts fall within the scope of the legal rule. In such scenarios the relevant facts are likely to be specific to the parties and will often concern a relatively discrete period of time. When it comes to proportionality reasoning, however, the relevant facts will concern the operation of a law in practice and its likely effects or consequences. These facts will often be general rather than specific to the parties, and will be interlaced with predictive and evaluative elements.

That there are different types of facts that arise within adjudication has long been recognised by scholars, and various different classifications of fact have been developed. There is some uncertainty, though, about how these categories might apply to proportionality reasoning. In Australia, former High Court justice Dyson Heydon, the author of the Australian edition of *Cross on Evidence*, has suggested that an additional category of fact might emerge in applying proportionality analysis.[1] In the context of the *Victorian Charter of Rights and Responsibilities Act 2006*, Heydon J had earlier suggested that the proportionality inquiry required under section 7(2) 'contemplates evidence or material of a kind going far beyond the evidence or material ordinarily considered by courts as going to "legislative facts"'.[2] Comments such as this raise the question of whether the 'facts' that underpin proportionality reasoning can be accommodated within existing understandings of facts or whether they compel a new and different type of fact-finding.

[1] JD Heydon, *Cross on Evidence*, 12th Australian edn (Sydney, LexisNexis Butterworths, 2020) 198 [3005]. Although Heydon suggests that this might be necessary in jurisdictions with bills of rights, referring to the New Zealand case of *R v Hansen* [2007] 3 NZLR 1, the development of proportionality reasoning in Australia means this inquiry is also pertinent in the Australian constitutional context. Citation of Heydon's work requires mention of his now-uncertain legacy. In 2020, the Chief Justice of the High Court of Australia commissioned an independent investigation into complaints of sexual harassment against Heydon. The investigation found that six former Court staff members were harassed by the former Justice and the Chief Justice expressed an unqualified apology. This chapter continues to cite Heydon's work as he remains one of the only Australian scholars to directly address these issues.

[2] *Momcilovic v The Queen* (2011) 245 CLR 1, 172 [431]. Note that Heydon J was in dissent in *Momcilovic* and the Court was divided over whether s 7(2) was applicable to the interpretive process required by s 32(1). For Heydon J, the very nature of the proportionality inquiry required by s 7(2) meant it was inappropriate for judges. See also G Webber, 'Judicial Power and Judicial Responsibility' (2017) 36 *University of Queensland Law Journal* 205.

This chapter considers this question, examining the nature of the facts that underpin proportionality reasoning. It explains and evaluates the various classifications of fact that have been developed by scholars, and considers how these might apply to proportionality reasoning. While it is possible, and indeed useful, to distinguish between case-specific or 'adjudicative' facts and more general 'non-adjudicative facts', in this chapter I argue that a more nuanced approach to facts is required. In particular, I suggest there is a need to distinguish more carefully between the facts that arise at the different stages of proportionality reasoning, as the facts that arise at each stage will often exhibit different characteristics. This revised framework for thinking about facts provides the basis for examining, in subsequent chapters, how courts have applied proportionality reasoning in practice.

## I. WHAT ARE FACTS?

A fact is essentially a descriptive statement about the world; it is based on, and referable to, the external world,[3] rather than deriving its primary meaning from rules of law. This understanding of facts, which assumes an empirical world exists and is capable of discovery, forms part of what is known as the 'rationalist tradition' of evidence scholarship.[4] As explained in the introduction, under this tradition, the goal of fact-finding is to obtain knowledge about the world by rational means (as opposed to 'irrational' means that were used historically, such as battle or ordeal).[5] According to William Twining, the leading exponent of this tradition, the main objective of adjudication is 'rectitude of decision'.[6] This recognises that while the goal of fact-finding is the 'pursuit of truth', in reality the 'truth' will always be an approximation based on probabilities or likelihood.[7]

[3] As Twining, O'Donovan and Paliwala have noted, 'facts' usually have 'empirically observable referents': WL Twining, K O'Donovan and A Paliwala, 'Ernie and the Centipede: Some Theoretical Aspects of Classification for the Purposes of Law Reform' in JA Jolowicz (ed), *The Division and Classification of the Law* (London, Butterworths, 1970) 24. Note that in adopting this understanding of facts, I reject the notion of 'alternative facts'. For some discussion, see S Gageler, 'Alternative Facts in the Courts' (2019) 93 *Australian Law Journal* 585; AO Larsen, 'Constitutional Law in an Age of Alternative Facts' (2018) 93 *New York University Law Review* 175.

[4] As Twining has observed, Anglo-American evidence scholarship is 'remarkably unsceptical' about the possibility of knowledge: W Twining, 'The Rationalist Tradition of Evidence Scholarship', first published in E Campbell and L Waller (eds), *Well and Truly Tried: Essays on Evidence in Honour of Sir Richard Eggleston* (Sydney, Law Book Co, 1982) and republished with some additions in WL Twining, *Rethinking Evidence Exploratory Essays*, 2nd edn (Cambridge, Cambridge University Press, 2006) 80. See also W Twining, 'Some Scepticism about Some Scepticism' (1984) 11 *Journal of Law and Society* 137.

[5] J Stone and WAN Wells, *Evidence: Its History and Policies* (Sydney, Butterworths, 1991) 2–8.

[6] Twining, 'The Rationalist Tradition' (n 4) 83.

[7] ibid 76. See also HL Ho, *A Philosophy of Evidence Law* (Oxford, Oxford University Press, 2008) 56–57.

Despite the dominance of the idea of *rationality* in most modern evidence scholarship, the meaning of this concept requires some elaboration. In particular, what does rationality require in the context of legal fact-finding? It is here that the literature on epistemology can assist, as a number of scholars have sought to connect understandings of knowledge to the legal processes of proof.[8] If facts are understood, as explained above, as descriptive statements about the world, it is apparent that the process of acquiring knowledge about the world lies at the heart of fact-finding. In other words, legal fact-finding is concerned with *how* courts acquire knowledge about the world.[9]

In the field of epistemology, knowledge has conventionally been understood as comprising three key elements: 'justified, true, belief'.[10] While belief may be described as a 'cognitive endorsement by the fact-finder', on its own it is insufficient for knowledge.[11] This is because a belief may be irrational or untrue; for example, someone may continue to believe the world is flat even though this idea has long been discredited. In addition, truth is also, on its own, insufficient for knowledge. While truth is often held up as an ideal, as Michael Pardo explains, 'we often are not in a position to judge whether fact-finders have knowledge because we often do not know whether their conclusions are true'.[12] In other words, something might be accidentally or coincidentally true, but not supported by reason.[13] This leaves the element of 'justification', which has become the focus of contemporary understandings of knowledge. While justifications may be either practical or epistemic, it is epistemic justification that is most relevant to the task of judicial fact-finding. This sort of justification is directed to the process of belief-formation rather than to the choice of courses of action.[14]

In the context of fact-finding by courts, therefore, the central concern is the extent to which a particular factual claim can be justified. Justification might involve considerations such as the nature and amount of empirical material (evidence) that is available, the extent to which this evidence actually supports the propositions in question, and the strengths and weaknesses of that evidence.[15] In this way, rationality can be understood as a requirement that propositions

[8] Note that the process of proof may also be described in terms of mathematical probabilities. For an overview, see A Ligertwood and G Edmond, *Australian Evidence: A Principled Approach to the Common Law and Uniform Acts*, 6th edn (Sydney, LexisNexis Butterworths, 2017) 16 [1.13]ff.

[9] Note that 'legal knowledge' might be distinguished from other types of knowledge, such as historical or philosophical accounts of knowledge; see Twining, 'Some Scepticism' (n 4) 147.

[10] MS Pardo, 'The Field of Evidence and the Field of Knowledge' (2005) 24 *Law and Philosophy* 321, 331–32. See also DM Dwyer, *The Judicial Assessment of Expert Evidence* (Cambridge, Cambridge University Press, 2008) 14ff.

[11] MS Pardo, 'The Gettier Problem and Legal Proof' (2010) 16 *Legal Theory* 37, 39.

[12] Pardo (n 10) 359.

[13] ibid 333.

[14] A Roberts, 'Probative Value, Reliability, and Rationality' in A Roberts and J Gans (eds), *Critical Perspectives on the Uniform Evidence Law* (Sydney, Federation Press, 2017) 70–74.

[15] See Dwyer (n 10) 51–52. See also S Haack, *Evidence Matters: Science, Proof, and Truth in the Law* (Cambridge, Cambridge University Press, 2014) 60.

of fact be supported, or *justified*, by evidence.[16] In other words, a court can rely on a proposition of fact (that is, find a fact to be proved) if that fact can be sufficiently justified by appropriate evidence. This understanding recognises, pragmatically, that a court is not engaged in an open-ended quest for truth, but is required to make findings of fact for the purposes of resolving a dispute.[17]

If we return then to the *type* and *nature* of the facts that arise within proportionality reasoning, this understanding of the legal process of proof can assist in two ways. First, it is useful in clarifying what is meant by a 'fact'. If facts are understood as descriptive statements about the world, it becomes apparent that the variety of facts relied on by courts is potentially very large. As will be explained below, this has led to some attempts to classify different types of facts. Second, if knowledge about facts is understood as primarily about justification, this provides guidance for how we can assess the degree to which the facts have been established.

With this working understanding of facts, the next section of this chapter considers the question of taxonomy.

## II. CLASSIFYING FACTS

The task of classification involves the arrangement or distribution of a given phenomenon into different classes or groups. As Twining, O'Donovan and Paliwala have explained: 'Each time we classify we are making a judgment that A and B should be treated together and C and D should be treated separately and so, perhaps, differently.'[18] The benefits of taxonomy have long been recognised in the private law sphere, with Birks arguing that a 'sound taxonomy, together with a keen sense of its importance, constant suspicion of its possible inaccuracy and vigorous debate on its improvement, is an essential condition of rationality'.[19] While in the public law arena there has been less attention given to the question of taxonomy, recently it has been recognised that taxonomy has the potential to enhance understandings of the law, to facilitate right answers to legal questions and to promote the rule of law.[20]

[16] As explained in the previous chapter, the concept of 'justification' is also central to proportionality reasoning.

[17] S Haack, *Evidence and Inquiry: A Pragmatist Reconstruction of Epistemology*, 2nd expanded edn (New York, Prometheus Books, 2009) 368.

[18] Twining, O'Donovan and Paliwala (n 3) 29.

[19] P Birks, 'Equity in the Modern Law: An Exercise in Taxonomy' (1996) 26 *University of Western Australia Law Review* 1, 4. While Birks' work was situated in opposition to legal realism, the recognition of legislative facts (discussed further in section II below) developed within the tradition of legal realism. See further n 37 below and the accompanying text.

[20] JNE Varuhas, 'Taxonomy and Public Law' in M Elliott, JNE Varuhas and SW Stark (eds), *The Unity of Public Law? Doctrinal, Theoretical and Comparative Perspectives* (Oxford, Hart Publishing, 2018) 48–57.

In the context of proportionality reasoning, as explained in the previous chapter, the types of inquiries the court must perform do not fit neatly into the categories of either 'law' or 'fact'. A consideration of taxonomy, then, might assist in clarifying the nature of facts within proportionality reasoning.[21] While a number of scholars have considered the types of facts that arise in the course of adjudication and have developed various taxonomies, this literature has not been specific to proportionality reasoning. The existing classifications of fact, developed first in the US and then modified in Australia, seek to show that the types of evidentiary material and the applicable evidentiary rules will not be the same for all types of facts. The major distinction that emerges is that between 'ordinary' or 'adjudicative' facts (that is, those that are specific to the parties) and other 'non-adjudicative' facts that contain more general propositions about the world. It is this second category that is most relevant to this book and, as will be shown below, a variety of labels have been adopted to describe and explain these sorts of facts.

Before proceeding to examine these different classifications, it is necessary to mention briefly the role of what can be called background assumptions of knowledge. Evidence scholars are in broad agreement that the process of fact-finding cannot be performed in isolation. Rather, the trier of fact, in drawing inferences from the available evidence, must necessarily rely on their general understandings and background knowledge of how the world works.[22] These assumptions are often described as 'generalisation[s] of knowledge',[23] but they have also been referred to as the 'teachings of ordinary experience',[24] 'natural logic'[25] and 'common sense and experience'.[26] While these background assumptions will usually not be substantiated by evidence or an explicit reliance on judicial notice,[27] at other times courts have received evidence to verify such assumptions.[28] Whether or not supported by evidence, these background

[21] Classification can serve a variety of purposes and be organised by a variety of different criteria: JA Jolowicz, 'Fact-Based Classification' in JA Jolowicz (ed), *The Division and Classification of the Law* (London, Butterworths, 1970).

[22] GF James, 'Relevancy, Probability and the Law' (1941) 29 *California Law Review* 689, 696.

[23] Ligertwood and Edmond (n 8) 16–17 [1.13].

[24] Heydon (n 1) 268 [3200]ff.

[25] WAN Wells, *Natural Logic, Judicial Proof and Objective Facts* (Sydney, Federation Press, 1994) 8.

[26] AJ Serpell, *The Reception and Use of Social Policy Information in the High Court of Australia* (Sydney, Lawbook Co, 2006) 11. Note that this category overlaps somewhat with what is sometimes described as 'judicial values'. See, eg, J Malbon, 'Judicial Values' in I Freckelton and H Selby (eds), *Appealing to the Future: Michael Kirby and His Legacy* (Sydney, Lawbook Co, 2009) 579; K Mason, 'Ethics and the Environment' (2011) 10 *The Judicial Review* 187.

[27] Heydon (n 1) 268 [3200].

[28] In the US, for example, courts have received evidence relating to eyewitness identification, risk assessment of violence, battered woman syndrome and rape trauma syndrome: J Monahan, L Walker and G Mitchell, 'Contextual Evidence of Gender Discrimination: The Ascendance of "Social Frameworks"' (2008) 94 *Virginia Law Review* 1715. Note that Monahan and Walker use the term 'social frameworks', but the concept is similar to what I describe as 'background generalisations of knowledge': L Walker and J Monahan, 'Social Frameworks: A New Use of Social Science in Law' (1987) 73 *Virginia Law Review* 559. In the Australian context, see also H Douglas, 'Social Framework Evidence: Its Interpretation and Application in Victoria and Beyond'

generalisations can assist the trier of fact either in determining questions of relevance or in drawing inferences from the available evidence.[29] The important thing to note is that these background generalisations of knowledge, as they are commonly understood, are used to understand and interpret the specific *adjudicative facts* in issue between the parties. They can therefore be distinguished from the more general facts that concern the operation of a law (and which are the primary focus of this book).

### A. Kenneth Culp Davis and the Distinction between Adjudicative Facts and Legislative Facts

The most influential classification of facts remains the distinction between 'adjudicative facts' and 'legislative facts' that was developed in the context of administrative law by Kenneth Culp Davis in the 1940s and 1950s. Writing in the US, Davis sought to explain the ways in which courts and administrative agencies used 'extra-legal' materials in the course of their decision-making.[30] Fundamentally, he recognised that not all of the materials referred to by courts and agencies were being used in the same way, and this prompted him to distinguish between two sorts of facts. First, he defined 'adjudicative facts' as the facts that concern the immediate parties to the dispute and relate to the litigants, their properties and their businesses: 'who did what, where, when, how, and with what motive or intent'.[31] These are the facts that, in the context of a jury trial, are determined by the jury. In contrast, Davis defined 'legislative facts' as those facts that concern the content of a law or policy:

> Legislative facts are those which help the tribunal to determine the content of law and policy and to exercise its judgment or discretion in determining what course of action to take. Legislative facts are ordinarily general and do not concern the immediate parties.[32]

As Davis explained, the '[c]reation of law and determination of policy usually do not rest upon uninformed a priori judgments having only an ethical or a logical basis'.[33] Rather, when determining the content of a law or policy, a court or agency was often required to find facts. By way of an example, Davis referred to the case of *Jay Burns Baking Co v Bryan*,[34] which concerned the regulation

in K Fitz-Gibbon and A Freiberg (eds), *Homicide Law Reform in Victoria: Retrospect and Prospects* (Sydney, Federation Press, 2015).

[29] Heydon (n 1) 268 [3200].

[30] KC Davis, 'An Approach to Problems of Evidence in the Administrative Process' (1942) 55 *Harvard Law Review* 364; KC Davis, 'Official Notice' (1949) 62 *Harvard Law Review* 537; KC Davis, 'Judicial Notice' (1955) 55 *Columbia Law Review* 945.

[31] Davis, 'Judicial Notice' (n 30) 952.

[32] ibid.

[33] Davis, 'An Approach to Problems of Evidence' (n 30) 402.

[34] *Jay Burns Baking Co v Bryan* 264 US 504 (1924).

of loaves of bread, where the Court referred to a wide variety of non-legal materials concerning the nature of the baking industry to determine the validity of the regulations.[35]

In defining legislative facts in this way, Davis recognised that both agencies and judges were involved in the 'creation of law or of policy';[36] that is, their role extended beyond the mere application of existing legal rules. In this way, as Monahan and Walker have observed, Davis' work was 'a clear indication that the realists had succeeded in undercutting the classical perspective on the nature of law'.[37] This emphasis on the creation of law needs to be understood in the context in which Davis was writing. Davis was a leading administrative lawyer in the US and his work on legislative facts initially focused on administrative agencies. As Heydon has observed, Davis' work was 'part of a campaign to urge *administrative agencies*, which in America have considerable capacity to make delegated legislation, to do so with sounder empirical support'.[38] As Heydon recognises, in the US, administrative agencies have considerable law-making powers. In addition, the distinction between 'law' and 'policy' is less sharply drawn in the US than in the Australian tradition.[39]

Yet Davis' distinction also applied to the work of the courts. The courts were, in Davis' account, not concerned solely with applying existing laws, but were also engaged in the development of the law.[40] The common law, for instance, was described by Davis as being created through 'judicial legislation'.[41] In addition, in constitutional cases he observed that the Supreme Court was *already* being presented with social and economic data to assist the Court with 'forming a judgment on a question of constitutional law'.[42] Davis noted this practice had originated with the 1908 case of *Muller v Oregon*, where Mr Louis Brandeis (later a justice of the Supreme Court) had compiled a brief of reports and statistics relevant to factory conditions.[43] This practice, which has become known as

[35] Davis, 'An Approach to Problems of Evidence' (n 30) 403–04.

[36] Davis, 'Judicial Notice' (n 30) 952.

[37] J Monahan and L Walker, 'Social Authority: Obtaining, Evaluating, and Establishing Social Science in Law' (1986) 134 *University of Pennsylvania Law Review* 477, 483. See also S Gageler, 'Whitmore and the Americans: Some American Influences on the Development of Australian Administrative Law' (2015) 38 *University of New South Wales Law Journal* 1316, 1319.

[38] JD Heydon, 'Developing the Common Law' in JT Gleeson and RCA Higgins (eds), *Constituting Law: Legal Arguments and Social Values* (Sydney, Federation Press, 2011) 125.

[39] For some discussion, see P Cane, *Controlling Administrative Power: An Historical Comparison* (Cambridge, Cambridge University Press, 2016) 222–30, 240.

[40] Commentators agree that Davis' distinction had application 'well beyond the boundaries of administrative law'; see, eg, Monahan and Walker (n 37) 483.

[41] Davis, 'Judicial Notice' (n 30) 952. Although this expression is not used in Australia, it is now well-settled that judges do make law: JJ Doyle, 'Judicial Law Making – Is Honesty the Best Policy?' (1995) 17 *Adelaide Law Review* 161.

[42] Davis, 'An Approach to Problems of Evidence' (n 30) 403.

[43] *Muller v Oregon* 208 US 412 (1908). Note, however, that others have pointed out this was not in fact the first use of the Brandeis brief: Heydon (n 38) 125; P Yowell, 'Proportionality in United States Constitutional Law' in L Lazarus, C McCrudden and N Bowles (eds), *Reasoning Rights: Comparative Judicial Engagement* (Oxford, Hart Publishing, 2014) 110.

the 'Brandeis brief procedure', was used not only in constitutional litigation[44] but also in other types of cases:

> [C]onstitutional facts are only one manifestation of a larger category of facts which are utilized for informing a court's legislative judgment on questions of law and policy. In non-constitutional cases courts often use a similar type of legislative facts not developed through the evidence.[45]

As an example of this broader practice, Davis referred to a case in which extrinsic materials had been referred to in order to determine whether the refusal to sign a written contract amounted to an unfair labour practice.[46]

At the heart of Davis' distinction is a focus on the *type of function* the court or agency undertakes. When applying an existing law or policy to a particular set of facts, the court is performing an 'adjudicative function'.[47] In contrast, when acting 'legislatively', the court or agency is required to create or develop the law.[48] This might arise, for instance, where administrative agencies exercise their rule-making functions or where courts develop the common law or interpret the Constitution or other statutory provisions. When acting in this way, according to Davis, the court was likely to need to rely on extra facts about the policy behind a law, its operation in practice and its likely effects or consequences.

Davis' distinction between adjudicative and legislative facts has important ramifications for the procedures by which facts should be established.[49] Adjudicative facts, according to Davis, were typically required to be supported by evidence,[50] and the rules of evidence were developed specifically for these types of facts. In contrast, legislative facts were often not, and sometimes could not be, supported by evidence.[51] These facts were likely to require 'generalized information' about a broad array of different topics,[52] and the parties themselves may have 'little or nothing to contribute to the development of legislative facts'.[53] Unlike adjudicative facts – which concern particular circumstances or events that occurred in the past – the general nature of legislative facts means

[44] For some discussion, see P Yowell, 'Empirical Research in Rights-Based Judicial Review of Legislation' in KS Ziegler and P Huber (eds), *Current Problems in the Protection of Human Rights: Perspectives from Germany and the UK* (Oxford, Hart Publishing, 2013) 157–60.

[45] Davis, 'An Approach to Problems of Evidence' (n 30) 404.

[46] ibid 404–05, referring to *HJ Heinz Co v NLRB* 11 US 514 (1941).

[47] KC Davis, *Administrative Law Treatise* (St Paul, West Publishing Co, 1958) vol 2, 353.

[48] ibid.

[49] Scholars have noted that Davis' labels contain an element of circularity, in that they 'presuppose the distinctive treatment Davis argues each type of fact should receive': CE Borgmann, 'Appellate Review of Social Facts in Constitutional Rights Cases' (2013) 101 *California Law Review* 1185, 1193. See also DL Faigman, *Constitutional Fictions: A Unified Theory of Constitutional Facts* (New York, Oxford University Press, 2008) 146.

[50] Note there are some exceptions, such as the doctrine of judicial notice. This is discussed further in ch 7.

[51] Davis, 'Judicial Notice' (n 30) 952–53.

[52] Davis, 'An Approach to Problems of Evidence' (n 30) 407–09.

[53] KC Davis, *Administrative Law Treatise*, 2nd edn (San Diego, KC Davis Publishing Co, 1979) vol 2, 413.

they may not be referable to external events and may not be able to be verified to the same degree of certainty.[54]

These differences meant there was a fundamental mismatch between the rules of evidence in the US (as they were stated at the time) and the practice of adjudication. In the 1950s, for instance, Davis critiqued the *Model Code of Evidence* and the proposed *Uniform Rules of Evidence*, highlighting the inappropriateness of trying to fit the traditional rules of evidence to legislative facts. He suggested that confining judicial notice to indisputable facts[55] failed to recognise that 'judicial notice practices of courts vary with the different functions that courts perform'.[56]

Davis' distinction has had a considerable impact in practice, both in and beyond the US. In the US, the distinction has been part of the 'legal mainstream'[57] for decades, and both courts and commentators have recognised and applied this distinction. Davis' categorisation has also informed the *Federal Rules of Evidence*, which are now expressed to apply only to adjudicative facts.[58] Despite differences in context, the import of Davis' work also extends to other common law jurisdictions, and courts in Canada, South Africa and New Zealand have recognised Davis' distinction and adopted his terminology.[59]

When it comes to translating Davis' distinction to the Australian context, there is a need for some elaboration. As Stephen Gageler, now a justice of the High Court, has explained:

> It may well be that the terminology of 'legislative facts' and 'adjudicative facts' sits uncomfortably within the Australian judicial landscape. Our conception of the separation of judicial power and our traditionally close adherence to formal judicial technique make a definition of 'legislative fact' that involves a description of a court acting as a legislator sound somewhat jarring to an Australian lawyer. It may also be that, for some purposes, a more precise division of what is encompassed within the category of 'legislative facts' is warranted.[60]

[54] In a similar vein, Ligertwood and Edmond suggest that generalisations of knowledge 'lack independent existence' and are less susceptible to a binary answer: Ligertwood and Edmond (n 8) 705 [6.77].

[55] The formal judicial notice rules at the time confined judicial notice to 'facts and propositions of generalized knowledge as are so universally known that they cannot reasonably be the subject of dispute': Davis, 'Judicial Notice' (n 30) 946.

[56] ibid. For some critique of Davis' argument that legislative and adjudicative facts require different treatment, see Borgmann (n 49).

[57] S Gageler, 'Fact and Law' (2009) 11 *Newcastle Law Review* 1, 18.

[58] See *Federal Rules of Evidence* (US) Pub L 93–595, §1, 88 Stat 1930 (1975, as amended 2011), r 201(a). See also Advisory Committee, *Notes of Advisory Committee on Proposed Rules of Evidence*, www.law.cornell.edu/rules/fre/rule_201; KC Davis, 'Judicial Notice' [1969] *Law and the Social Order* 513; R Slovenko, 'The Superfluous Rule of Evidence on Judicial Notice' (1998) 2 *International Journal of Evidence and Proof* 51; KS Broun (ed), *McCormick on Evidence*, 6th edn (St Paul, Thomson West, 2006) vol 2, ch 35.

[59] See, eg, *Danson v Ontario (Attorney-General)* [1990] 2 SCR 1086, 1099 (Sopinka J); *R v Hansen* [2007] 3 NZLR 1, 10 [9] (Elias CJ), 75 [230] (McGrath J); *S v Lawrence; S v Negal; S v Solberg* [1997] 4 SA 1176 [52] (Constitutional Court).

[60] Gageler (n 57) 22.

Although the idea that judges do not make law has long been discarded, the considerations identified by Gageler continue to underpin the approach of the High Court.[61] Despite this, and quite apart from the influence of Davis,[62] in constitutional adjudication the High Court has long recognised the existence of different categories of fact. First, the Court has identified 'ordinary questions of fact', which are those facts that concern the immediate parties to a dispute.[63] As Dixon CJ explained in *Breen v Sneddon*, these facts 'arise between the parties because one asserts and the other denies that events have occurred bringing one of them within some criterion of liability or excuse set up by the law'.[64] Second, since at least the 1940s, the High Court has acknowledged that constitutional validity will sometimes depend on facts.[65] These facts, according to the Court, 'somehow must be ascertained by the court responsible for deciding the validity of the law'.[66] Susan Kenny, now a judge of the Federal Court of Australia, has described constitutional facts as 'the facts which either the Court has, or might reasonably have, regarded as relevant to the determination of a constitutional issue'.[67] As Chapter 6 will show, such facts have been recognised most often in the context of section 92 of the *Australian Constitution* and in relation to the characterisation of laws with respect to particular heads of Commonwealth legislative power.

More recently, there has been some recognition by the High Court of the broader category of 'legislative facts'. Consistently with Davis' approach,[68] 'constitutional facts' have been viewed as a sub-category of legislative facts.[69] In *Woods v Multi-Sport Holdings*, McHugh J adopted Heydon's definition from *Cross on Evidence*, describing a legislative fact as a fact 'which helps the

[61] In addition, in Australia there has been less adherence to legal realism in comparison with the US. See, eg, T Blackshield, 'Realism' in T Blackshield, M Coper and G Williams (eds), *The Oxford Companion to the High Court of Australia* (Melbourne, Oxford University Press, 2001) 583; T Josev, *The Campaign against the Courts: A History of the Judicial Activism Debate* (Sydney, Federation Press, 2017) 102–04.

[62] The High Court has, more recently, referred expressly to Davis' distinction between legislative and adjudicative facts (*Maloney v The Queen* (2013) 252 CLR 168, 299 [352] (Gageler J)), but did not do so in its earlier recognition of 'constitutional facts'.

[63] *Breen v Sneddon* (1961) 106 CLR 406, 411.

[64] ibid.

[65] See, eg, *Stenhouse v Coleman* (1944) 69 CLR 457, 469.

[66] *Commonwealth Freighters Pty Ltd v Sneddon* (1959) 102 CLR 280, 292 (Dixon CJ).

[67] S Kenny, 'Constitutional Fact Ascertainment' (1990) 1 *Public Law Review* 134, 135. Other scholars have adopted similar definitions: B Selway, 'The Use of History and Other Facts in the Reasoning of the High Court of Australia' (2001) 20 *University of Tasmania Law Review* 129, 140; J Lennan, 'How to Find Facts in Constitutional Cases' (2011) 30 *Civil Justice Quarterly* 304, 306; Heydon (n 1) 237 [3156].

[68] Davis, 'An Approach to Problems of Evidence' (n 30) 404. This is also the understanding that has been adopted by Australian scholars. See E Campbell, 'Fact Finding in Constitutional Cases' in Constitutional Commission, *Final Report of the Constitutional Commission* (Canberra, Australian Government Publishing Service, 1988) vol 2, 1099, 1100; PH Lane, *The Australian Federal System*, 2nd edn (Sydney, Law Book Co, 1979) 1084.

[69] *Re Day* (2017) 91 ALJR 262, 269 [21] (Gordon J). Note that this was a trial held before a single justice.

court determine the content of law and policy and to exercise its discretion or judgment in determining what course or action to take'.[70] Justice McHugh explained that, in contrast to adjudicative facts, such facts 'generally relate to the law-making function of the judicial process'.[71] This understanding of legislative facts, which is strongly reminiscent of Davis' original definition, was particularly apt in the context of *Woods*, which concerned the scope of the standard of care for negligence.[72] Yet it is also clear that legislative facts have a role *beyond* the sphere of developing the common law, and the High Court has since clarified that legislative facts might be relevant to the interpretation and application of particular statutory provisions.[73] In the case of *Aytugrul v The Queen*, which concerned the admissibility of evidence in a criminal trial, Heydon J observed that legislative facts 'reveal how existing rules work and how legal rules which do not exist might work if they were adopted'.[74] In this way, Davis' conception of legislative facts, which emphasised the creation of law or policy, has some application in the Australian setting.

### B. 'Legislative Facts' and their Alternatives

Although there is now a fairly broad consensus that courts are at times required to make factual findings that extend beyond the immediate parties to the dispute, there has been less agreement on how these 'non-adjudicative' facts should be labelled and understood. A number of scholars have developed alternative labels which they suggest better reflect the nature of the facts and, in some cases, the methods by which such facts should be established. In addition, some scholars writing in the Australian context have suggested that a twofold classification is too narrow and fails to capture the variety of ways in which courts use facts.[75]

This part of the chapter considers some of the alternative categorisations that have been developed. It examines how these categories can be seen as similar to, and different from, Davis' conception of legislative facts and points out

[70] *Woods v Multi-Sport Holdings* (2002) 208 CLR 460, 478 [65]; see also 510–11 [163] (Callinan J).

[71] ibid 479 [65].

[72] The question in issue in *Woods*, namely the scope of standard of care for negligence, clearly required the Court to develop the common law.

[73] See *Maloney* (n 62) 299 [354], where Gageler J, referring to Brennan J in *Gerhardy v Brown* (1985) 159 CLR 70, observed that the facts relevant to the characterisation of an impugned law as a 'special measure' under the *Racial Discrimination Act 1975* (Cth) were properly understood as legislative facts. See also 185 [21], 193 [45] (French CJ).

[74] *Aytugrul v The Queen* (2012) 247 CLR 170, 201 [71] (footnote omitted). Note that in *Aytugrul*, the majority held that psychological literature could not be used to take judicial notice of a general proposition about the reliability of DNA evidence, but the majority did not refer to 'legislative facts' or Heydon J's classification of facts: 183 [20]–[21].

[75] Note that in the US context, Faigman has suggested that 'constitutional facts' can be further taxonomised into the categories of 'constitutional doctrinal facts', 'constitutional reviewable facts' and 'constitutional case-specific facts': Faigman (n 49) 46–49.

some potential difficulties with these alternative classifications. As I will explain, in this book I have adopted the terminology of 'legislative facts' and 'constitutional facts' as a basis for exploring the facts that arise in proportionality reasoning.

The major alternative labels that have been developed to capture non-adjudicative facts are 'social facts', 'social authority' and 'social policy information'.[76] The reference to 'social' in all three of these categories seeks to describe statements or representations about society as well as patterns of human behaviour, though not all agree that such statements should be classified as 'facts'. Writing in the US, Donald L Horowitz defined social facts as the 'recurrent patterns of behavior on which policy must be based':[77]

> Social facts are nothing new in litigation. Courts have always had to make assumptions or inferences about general conditions that would guide their decisions. The broader the issue, the more such imponderables there are. The breadth of the issues in constitutional law has always made it a fertile field for empirical speculation.[78]

Horowitz preferred to avoid the terminology of 'adjudicative' and 'legislative' facts[79] because of what he described as the 'preconceptions they carry and the division of labor they imply'.[80] In the Australian context, the concept of 'social facts' has gained some traction amongst scholars working in the field of negligence. Kylie Burns, for instance, has defined social facts very widely as 'general statements about the nature and behaviour of people and institutions and the nature of the world and society'.[81] According to Burns, social facts might include assumptions about the social or policy consequences of particular findings, as well as background assumptions that can help the Court to interpret the adjudicative facts.[82]

Other scholars have shifted away from the concept of 'facts' and have focused more on the nature of the empirical materials used by courts. For instance, again in the US, John Monahan and Laurens Walker have adopted the

[76] Note that this survey is not exhaustive. In the US context, Keeton has proposed the terminology of 'premise facts', which encompasses what he describes as 'legislative facts' and 'lawmaking facts': RE Keeton, 'Legislative Facts and Similar Things: Deciding Disputed Premise Facts' (1988) 73 *Minnesota Law Review* 1.

[77] DL Horowitz, *The Courts and Social Policy* (Washington DC, Brookings Institution, 1977) 45.

[78] ibid 46.

[79] ibid 45.

[80] ibid.

[81] K Burns, 'The Australian High Court and Social Facts: A Content Analysis Study' (2012) 40 *Federal Law Review* 317, 317 (footnote omitted). See also K Burns, 'The Way the World is: Social Facts in High Court Negligence Cases' (2004) 12 *Torts Law Journal* 216; K Burns, 'It's Just Not Cricket: The High Court, Sport and Legislative Facts' (2002) 10 *Torts Law Journal* 234. A narrower concept of 'social facts' has been adopted in the context of family law: GR Mullane, 'Evidence of Social Science Research: Law, Practice, and Options in the Family Court of Australia' 72 *Australian Law Journal* 434.

[82] K Burns, 'The High Court and Social Facts: A Negligence Case Study' in M Bryan (ed), *Private Law in Theory and Practice* (London, Routledge-Cavendish, 2007) 90.

terminology of 'social authority' to describe the use of social science evidence by courts.[83] Similarly, in the Australian context, Andrew Serpell has adopted the label 'social policy information' to explain the High Court's use of 'information that may assist a judge in determining the social or economic consequences of a law'.[84] Serpell's definition of 'social policy information' is very broad as it includes empirical data, opinions, assumptions and what Serpell calls 'judicial knowledge'.[85]

A key point of divergence is whether such material is best classified as fact or law. For Serpell, 'social policy information' is conceived of as essentially a 'type of fact'[86] and he notes that such information is often referred to as a type of legislative fact.[87] In this way, his concept of 'social policy information' can be seen as broadly congruous with Davis' category of legislative facts. In contrast, Monahan and Davis suggest that such material is best treated as 'law' rather than 'fact'.[88] Davis' original distinction, they suggest, 'perpetuated the old pre-Realist boundaries of the distinction between "fact" and "law"'[89] and failed to provide 'clear direction' for courts in terms of how to obtain or evaluate social science material.[90] Although noting that there was some conceptual similarity between social science and fact, in that both are positive and concern the way the world is, they argued there was an 'equally clear conceptual bond' between social science and law.[91] Both were general, rather than relating specifically to individuals, and both were typically directed to 'future, as-yet-unknown contingencies'.[92] As a result of these shared characteristics, they suggested social science research should be treated as law rather than fact.

In developing these different categorisations, all of these scholars were – like Davis – concerned with the procedures by which courts could be informed.

[83] See, eg, J Monahan and L Walker, *An Introduction to Social Science in Law* (New York, Foundation Press, 2006). Note that Monahan and Walker's concept of 'social authority' forms part of their tripartite classification scheme. 'Social frameworks' are broadly analogous to the 'background generalisations of knowledge that are discussed in section II above, whereas 'social facts' are limited to those facts that are specific to the parties (and so are more akin to 'adjudicative facts'). Since their tripartite classification scheme was first published, the Supreme Court's approach to social science evidence has changed significantly, as discussed in J Monahan and L Walker, 'Twenty-Five Years of Social Science in Law' (2011) 35 *Law and Human Behavior* 72.

[84] Serpell (n 26) 7.

[85] Serpell does not include 'statements that are merely statements of policy or law', but he acknowledges that the distinction between 'social policy' and 'policy' is not always clear: ibid 8–9.

[86] ibid 4.

[87] ibid 7.

[88] As Burns notes, Monahan and Walker did not propose that social science research *is* legal authority or precedent, but that it should be *treated as* a source of authority rather than a source of facts: K Burns, 'Judicial Use and Construction of Social Facts in Negligence Cases in the Australian High Court' (PhD thesis, Griffith University 2011) 82. See also MJ Saks, 'Judicial Attention to the Way the World Works' (1990) 75 *Iowa Law Review* 1011, 1018ff.

[89] Monahan and Walker (n 37) 485.

[90] ibid.

[91] ibid 488.

[92] ibid 491.

Horowitz, for instance, argued that while the adversarial system and the rules of evidence were designed to enable courts to make findings of adjudicative or historical fact, they were ill-suited to address the kinds of behavioural questions to which social facts give rise. According to Horowitz, some questions of social fact were beyond the ability of the courts 'to answer on the basis of common experience or the usual modicum of expert testimony'.[93] Like Davis, therefore, he suggested that different procedures were required for the two different types of facts. While the parties may be expected to 'elicit all of the relevant historical facts' through testimony and documentary evidence, the same could not be said of social facts.[94] Horowitz made some suggestions for how the courts' existing processes could be modified to better accommodate social facts, but at the same time warned that too much '[r]etooling of the judicial process' may 'erode the distinctive contribution courts make'.[95]

Such changes to procedure also formed a key part of the categories of 'social authority' and 'social policy information', with these scholars suggesting an even more relaxed approach to the admission of such material. For Monahan and Walker, treating social science as 'law' meant that it should be treated by courts much like prior judicial decisions. It should be presented to the court 'in the same manner' as legal precedents – in written briefs rather than oral testimony.[96] This approach would give the courts considerable (and perhaps unrestricted) freedom: 'as courts are free to find legal precedent parties have not presented, they should also have the power to locate social science research through independent investigation'.[97] Similarly, for Serpell, the judge's role in obtaining and using social policy information seems virtually unrestrained. For instance, there should be no burden of proof or presumptions, and the judge should not be limited by submissions made by the parties.[98] Ultimately, for Serpell, social policy information 'is characterised as an integral part of the judicial reasoning process in determining the content of the law'.[99]

In contrast to these alternative conceptions of legislative facts, others have suggested that a twofold classification is too narrow and does not capture how courts actually use facts in practice. In the Australian context, for instance, Bradley Selway[100] proposed a threefold classification which distinguished between: (i) facts in issue between the parties; (ii) constitutional facts in issue; and (iii) facts used as an aspect of legal reasoning.[101] The main departure from

[93] Horowitz (n 77) 46–47.

[94] ibid 47.

[95] ibid 298.

[96] Monahan and Walker (n 37) 496.

[97] ibid 497. *cf Aytugrul* (n 74) 184 [22] (French CJ, Hayne, Crennan and Bell JJ).

[98] Serpell (n 26) 30. Note that under Serpell's proposal social policy information could be presented by the parties through submissions rather than pleadings. See also Heydon (n 38) 127.

[99] Serpell (n 26) 29.

[100] Selway was the Solicitor-General for South Australia and later a judge of the Federal Court of Australia.

[101] Selway (n 67) 131–58.

Davis' classification is the introduction of the third category. This was developed by reference to the negligence case of *Woods*, where McHugh J had referred to statistics and reports relating to sporting injuries in order to demonstrate that the relevant standard of care should have been higher.[102] Although McHugh J considered these materials were evidence of legislative facts,[103] Selway disagreed and suggested that this was better characterised as a 'step in [McHugh J's] legal reasoning' because the purpose was to indicate the way in which the common law should be developed.[104] When facts were used in this way, in contrast to constitutional facts, they were not to be considered 'evidence' and the Court was free to inform itself as it thought fit.[105]

Building upon Selway's work, Heydon has sought to distinguish five different types of facts: (i) facts in issue or facts relevant to facts in issue; (ii) constitutional facts (those facts going to the validity of statutes, other enactments or executive acts); (iii) facts going to the construction of non-constitutional statutes; (iv) facts going to the construction of constitutional statutes; and (v) facts going to the content and development of the common law.[106] While some of Heydon's five categories mirror those adopted by other scholars, his classification differs by adding in further purposes for which facts may be used.[107] Heydon also acknowledges the categories may overlap and that the same evidence might be used to establish different sorts of facts.[108]

Both of these multi-fold classifications seek to identify additional *purposes* or *uses* to which empirical material might be put. While this identification of purposes is useful in identifying the variety of ways in which facts can inform legal decision-making, it is not clear whether the nature of the facts in each category will always be different. Moreover, these distinctions do not consider the differences that might exist *within* a particular category.

## C. Evaluating the Categories

The existing taxonomies of fact that have been developed are valuable in drawing attention to the reality that not all of the facts that arise in the course of

[102] *Woods* (n 70) 477–81 [62]–[71].

[103] ibid 478 [63].

[104] ibid 140.

[105] ibid 146–47, 158. Note that in Australia, there is a sharp distinction between courts and tribunals, with tribunals generally free to inform themselves as they see fit, subject to the requirements of procedural fairness.

[106] Heydon (n 1) 197 [3005]. See also *Thomas v Mowbray* (2007) 233 CLR 307, 512 [613]ff. Note that when discussing legislative facts, Heydon distinguishes between seven different sources from which such facts can be derived: Heydon (n 38) 99.

[107] These are facts going to the construction of non-constitutional statutes and facts going to the construction of constitutional statutes.

[108] He illustrates this by reference to *Brown v Board of Education* 347 US 483 (1954): Heydon (n 1) 198 [3005].

litigation are the same. In particular, there are facts that extend beyond the immediate parties to the dispute and that concern the content or validity of the legal rule or standard to be applied. They are also helpful in questioning whether such 'facts' are really facts at all. As indicated above, in this book I have adopted the terminology of 'legislative facts' and 'constitutional facts'. Davis' distinction remains the most influential of the classifications that has been developed, and it has been widely applied by both courts and commentators in the US and beyond. More importantly, however, the description 'legislative' attempts to capture something about the nature of the judgment that the court must exercise, which is absent from the other categories.

The terminology of social facts is so broad that it is difficult to reconcile with traditional understandings of fact-finding.[109] While the language seems to suggest patterns of human behaviour, it is apparent the term is often intended to capture a wide array of statements about the empirical world, not necessarily limited to social or human behaviour. For Horowitz, for instance, the definition included 'general conditions',[110] and Burns' expansive approach expressly includes institutional behaviour and general assumptions about how the world operates.[111] The breadth of the concept may serve to conceal, rather than reveal, the different roles facts can play within legal decision-making. For instance, as I have explained above, background generalisations of knowledge or assumptions can be used to interpret the adjudicative facts and are, conceptually, distinct from legislative facts.[112]

The other categories of 'social authority' and 'social policy information' are also not without difficulties. Serpell's classification of 'social policy information', for instance, seems to blur the distinction between the *material* being relied on by the Court and the *use* the Court makes of such material. While he seems to focus on the data or raw material that is relied on by judges,[113] he also expressly refers to social policy information as a 'type of fact' and he acknowledges that it is analogous to the existing category of legislative facts.[114] This conflation of 'information' and 'fact' seems to overlook that facts are not self-evident, but are subject to a process of evaluation.[115] In this way, it runs counter to traditional understandings of the inferential process of proof.

[109] Note that for some scholars, this is intentional. See, eg, Burns, who adopts a 'social constructionist approach', which expressly departs from what she describes as a 'positivist' approach to fact-finding: Burns (n 88) 24.

[110] Horowitz (n 77) 46.

[111] Burns (n 88) 97.

[112] For example, Burns expressly includes 'social frameworks' (as that concept is described by Monahan and Walker) within the ambit of her study: ibid 85–86.

[113] Serpell (n 26) 7.

[114] ibid 4, 7.

[115] See the discussion of facts in section I above. See also McClellan and Doyle, who suggest that while legislative facts are sometimes referred to as 'social policy information', this 'tends to diminish their real character': P McClellan and A Doyle, 'Legislative Facts and Section 144: A Contemporary Problem?' (2016) 12 *The Judicial Review* 421, 436.

Likewise, Monahan and Walker's invocation to treat social science material as 'law' presents a number of challenges.[116] By emphasising the similarities between social science and law, Monahan and Walker seem to downplay the quite considerable differences that exist between the two categories. Previous judicial decisions carry normative force precisely because they were decided by a court. In contrast, social science material can come from a variety of different sources and may well be subject to disagreement or dispute. The reliability of such material cannot be assumed and, on its own, it lacks any inherent authority to guide legal decision-making.[117] In addition, Monahan and Walker's proposal seems to give judges almost free rein in terms of conducting their own research. This sits uncomfortably with traditional notions of the judicial role and raises questions in terms of the court's resources and expertise. At least in the Australian context, judges are not completely unrestrained in referring to legal materials that have not been referred to by the parties.[118] Although the facts relevant to proportionality appear quite different from conventional facts, they remain, in essence, descriptive statements about the world. For this reason, it makes sense to continue to treat them as a species of fact.

The terminology of legislative facts draws attention to the 'function the court is performing' to determine the type of fact that arises.[119] Indeed, some have suggested that the only way to distinguish between different types of facts is to look at the function being performed by the court: 'whether the fact is being utilized to create law on a disputed legal issue, making it "legislative", as contrasted to its use in the fact-to-law syllogistic process, making it "adjudicative"'.[120] This emphasis on function, however, tends to overshadow significant differences between the *nature* of the two sorts of facts. Returning to Davis' classification, it is clear he also recognised adjudicative and legislative facts would very often exhibit different characteristics. For instance, his very terminology of 'legislative facts' suggests that the types of judgments these facts require are judgments that are more typically exercised by the legislative branch.[121] Davis also acknowledged that while legislative facts could come in many different varieties, they were often predictive and evaluative.[122]

[116] See, eg, R Mounsey, 'Social Science Evidence as Proof of Legislative Fact in Constitutional Litigation: A Proposed Framework for a Reliability Analysis' (2014) 32 *National Journal of Constitutional Law* 127, 140 n 56.

[117] On the different types of authority of law and science, see Faigman (n 49) 178.

[118] Heydon (n 38) 127. *cf* AO Larsen, 'Confronting Supreme Court Fact Finding' (2013) 98 *Virginia Law Review* 1255.

[119] Davis, 'Judicial Notice' (n 30) 960.

[120] RB Cappalli, 'Bringing Internet Information to Court: Of Legislative Facts' (2002) 75 *Temple Law Review* 99, 108. In a similar vein, Keeton has suggested that the 'nature of the fact in dispute does not determine' the type of fact: Keeton (n 76) 16.

[121] This criticism is particularly apt in the Australian context, where the idea of courts acting 'legislatively' sits uncomfortably with the strict separation of powers and the High Court's approach to the judicial method: see n 60.

[122] KC Davis, 'Facts in Lawmaking' (1980) 80 *Columbia Law Review* 931. See also Monahan and Walker (n 37) 488.

In addition, he acknowledged that the requirements of proof would be different for adjudicative facts and legislative facts. In the famous Brandeis brief case of *Muller v Oregon*, for instance, the brief was introduced to establish there was a reasonable ground for the legislative action and not to establish the truth of the matters contained in the brief.[123]

While Davis' distinction remains a useful starting point, his work was not directed to the specific context of proportionality reasoning. There remains a need to consider in more detail the types of facts that arise at each of the three stages of suitability, necessity and balancing.

## III. FACTS AND PROPORTIONALITY

While a court's conclusion about proportionality will most likely be characterised as a question of law, underpinning this conclusion are various questions of fact. But what is the nature of these facts? As foreshadowed earlier, this book is concerned with the broad category of 'non-adjudicative' facts. These types of facts are not specific to the parties and are likely to concern how legislation works, or might work, in practice. Under Davis' classification, then, these facts are likely to be described as 'legislative facts'. They will also, at least for the purposes of this book, fall within the narrower sub-set of constitutional facts, as they are facts that are relevant to determining a question of constitutional validity.[124] However, if that is the end of the inquiry – namely that the facts relevant to proportionality are constitutional facts – all that can be concluded is that these facts are *different in kind* to adjudicative facts and may require different modes of proof. For instance, different types of information will be relevant to establishing the facts, there may be no relevant empirical data available, or the available material might be outside the knowledge or experience of the parties.

Instead of treating all constitutional facts as alike, it is helpful to consider the differences that might exist *within* this category. The facts relevant to the various stages of proportionality reasoning will often exhibit different characteristics. Distinguishing more precisely between these facts potentially has implications in terms of the evidentiary material available, the level of satisfaction required and the limits of the court's capacity.[125]

[123] *Muller v Oregon* (n 43) 416; Heydon (n 38) 125. Note that the brief included medical opinions, academic studies, reports of factory inspectors and bureaus of labour statistics; see Yowell (n 44) 157.

[124] As explained in the introduction, this book concerns the use of proportionality reasoning in constitutional adjudication. I do not address other uses of proportionality, such as in administrative law, or in applying statutory charters of rights.

[125] These issues are explored in ch 7.

### A. The Suitability Stage: Purpose and Rational Connection

As will be recalled from the previous chapter, at the suitability stage of proportionality, a court needs to ascertain: (i) the purpose of the challenged law; and (ii) whether the law is capable of fulfilling this purpose. While the purpose of a law may often be evident from the text and structure of the legislation itself, at times additional material may be required.[126] Further, in order to assess the connection between the law and the purpose, the court will need some knowledge of the background context in which the law operates, as well as the practicalities of how the law actually works. For instance, if a law is enacted in response to a pressing environmental problem, it will be relevant to know something about the nature of the problem, its scope and whether other measures have already been adopted. As will be recalled, at this stage the court only needs to be satisfied that the law is *capable of* achieving the purpose, not whether it will actually achieve the purpose. This is generally understood to constitute quite a low threshold.

When assessing the issues of both *purpose* and *connection*, the relevant facts will not always be matters that are within the general knowledge or experience of the courts. It may be necessary, at times, for the courts to have access to relevant evidentiary material, including parliamentary documents, reports prepared by other bodies such as law reform commissions, or expert reports or testimony that demonstrate the nature and scope of the problem to be addressed. Such material may be relevant to show that Parliament, in enacting the law, was acting in response to a genuine problem. The types of extrinsic materials relevant to the suitability inquiry are likely to be relatively familiar to courts as they are already used in the context of statutory construction.[127] In addition, the nature of the facts themselves will also be familiar, in that they tend to describe existing circumstances or events. While the question of suitability involves some element of prediction, the facts that underpin this judgment will often be backward-looking and referable to phenomena that exist in the real world.[128] In other words, they will be concerned with the existence of a current problem and the prevailing circumstances in which the legislation operates.

Of course, the facts relevant to the suitability stage may well encompass a variety of different *subject matters* or *types of expertise*; for example, depending on the issues at play, the relevant facts may be historical facts (facts about historical events), economic facts, scientific or technical facts, environmental facts or facts concerning social phenomena. What unites them as a category is that they are all descriptive of the empirical world. They do not, unlike rules

[126] See ch 2, nn 72 and 73 and accompanying text.
[127] ibid.
[128] See n 3 above and accompanying text.

of law, carry normative force. In addition, the sources from which they derive are also very different from traditional legal sources. It therefore makes sense to describe them as a species of 'fact' rather than of 'law'. Moreover, it will often be the case that the law has already engaged with the very same subject matters in the traditional sphere of expert evidence (in the context of proving adjudicative facts). To treat such facts as law, as proposed by Monahan and Walker,[129] would add unnecessary conceptual confusion.

## B. The Necessity Stage: Predictions and Counterfactuals

At the necessity stage of proportionality reasoning, it is immediately apparent that the conclusion a court must reach is quite different in nature. In contrast to the suitability stage, which requires only that a law be capable of advancing an objective, the necessity stage requires a finding about the extent to which the objective is *actually* likely to be advanced. In addition, as explained in Chapter 2, the requirement of 'least restrictive means' requires a comparison between the law in question and any hypothetical alternatives. It asks whether both the law and the alternative achieve the particular objective to the same extent, and also assesses which has the lesser impact on the right. This requires a predictive judgment about how the law, and also any alternatives, are likely to operate in practice.[130]

The facts that inform this predictive judgment will often be quite different compared to the facts that arise at the suitability stage. Whereas at the suitability stage, the relevant facts are likely to concern existing or past circumstances, at the necessity stage, the facts will tend to be future-oriented or hypothetical. As I have explained, a court's assessment of likelihood is essentially an 'empirical prognosis':[131] will the law actually achieve the legitimate objective? This requires a conclusion about the likely consequences or effects of the law at a future point in time. In addition, in considering the efficacy of alternatives, the court must consider whether any real or hypothetical alternatives may also further the legitimate objective (but with a lesser impact on the right). While sometimes the court may be able to draw upon examples of alternatives that have been used in other jurisdictions, at other times the comparison the court is invited to make will be largely hypothetical. When this occurs, the court will be required to engage in a form of counterfactual analysis. This type of inquiry looks very different compared to the conventional fact-finding process with which judges are familiar.

[129] See nn 96ff and 116ff above and accompanying text.

[130] While the 'suitability' stage also involves an element of prediction, this will be much more pronounced at the 'necessity' stage.

[131] J Rivers, 'The Presumption of Proportionality' (2014) 77 *Modern Law Review* 409, 415. See also ch 2, section II.B.ii.

The different types of inquiries at each stage of proportionality analysis mean that the relevant facts will often exhibit different characteristics. At the necessity stage, rather than involving the acquisition of knowledge about an existing state of affairs, the court will have to make a predictive assessment about the potential operation of the law (and any alternatives) in the future. The relevant facts will thus tend to be forward-looking and hypothetical.[132] This type of fact-finding sits uncomfortably with the Australian conception of judicial power. As Heydon has commented extra-judicially, in the context of legislative fact-finding by courts, the more a court engages with this type of fact-finding (as opposed to adjudicative fact-finding), the 'more it will resemble a legislature' and the 'less will it correspond with a court'.[133] Such comments reflect a broader concern with proportionality reasoning, in Australia at least, that judgments about necessity require the courts to trespass beyond the appropriate limits of the judicial role.[134]

### C. Balancing and Facts

These concerns about the nature of the facts at the necessity stage are likely to be even more acute at the balancing stage of proportionality, again reflecting a broader unease with the nature of the task required at this stage. As the previous chapter has explained, at the balancing stage, the court needs to evaluate the importance of the different interests at stake and make a determination about whether the benefit (the achievement of the legitimate aim) is worth the cost of limiting the right. While the ultimate conclusion at this stage will be a normative one, the process of evaluation takes place against the backdrop of the previous two inquiries. In particular, in 'balancing' the different interests, judges must proceed on certain understandings about the extent of the benefit to be achieved and the degree to which the right will be impacted. Depending on how a court structures and explains its proportionality inquiry, it may be that the facts relevant to the balancing stage have already been canvassed at the earlier stages of analysis.

Unlike the facts that arise at the suitability and necessity stages, the facts that arise at the balancing stage will contain a greater element of evaluation; that is, they will involve not only representations about the external world, but will also be interlaced with value judgments about the extent of the benefit or detriment. In this way, they may be seen to be even further away from the conventional understanding of facts.

[132] Note that such predictive judgments are not unique to proportionality reasoning, and similar judgments are required in other contexts such as control and preventive detention orders, which involve an assessment of future dangerousness; see, eg, I Coyle and R Halon, 'Humpty Dumpty and Risk Assessment: A Reply to Slobogin' in P Keyzer (ed), *Preventive Detention: Asking the Fundamental Questions* (Cambridge, Intersentia, 2013) 197ff.

[133] Heydon (n 38) 124.

[134] This is discussed further in chs 5 and 6.

## IV. CONCLUSION

Given the distinctive nature of the facts that underpin proportionality reasoning, a question may arise in this context about whether these facts are really facts at all. The predictive, counterfactual and evaluative nature of the inquiry involved, particularly at the necessity and balancing stages, sets such facts apart from the traditional understanding of facts. As Ann Woolhandler has observed in relation to legislative facts in the US: 'There is less a sense that legislative facts are true or knowable because such facts are predictions, and, moreover, typically predictions about the relative importance of one factor in causing a complex phenomenon.'[135]

While it is true that legislative facts, particularly those that involve predictions, will be less 'knowable' than other types of facts, they can still be understood as facts. While our capacity to acquire knowledge about these sorts of propositions of fact may well be different, this does not mean they cannot be regarded as facts at all. Rather, as the discussion of epistemological understandings of knowledge in section II shows, this directs attention to the degree of justification it is reasonable to expect when establishing such facts. Such propositions are still, like other facts, essentially descriptive statements about the world, even if that 'world' is a future state of affairs. Even though hypothetical or counterfactual reasoning may be even more tenuously connected to traditional notions of fact, such reasoning also involves propositions about the world in the sense of evaluating how something *might work* in practice. It is also clear that legislative facts concerning either the operation or likely operation of a law are different from straight rules of law in that they do not guide or compel particular behaviour. They are descriptive rather than normative. It makes sense, therefore, to continue to treat them as types of facts, notwithstanding the considerable differences that exist vis-a-vis conventional facts.

To return to Heydon's query about whether proportionality analysis might require an additional category of facts,[136] I have argued in this chapter that it is useful to distinguish more clearly between the facts that arise at the three stages of proportionality analysis. While Davis' distinction between adjudicative and non-adjudicative facts remains a useful starting point, Davis and the scholars who followed him were not specifically concerned with proportionality reasoning. When proportionality is used to determine questions of constitutional validity, the facts that inform a court's assessment of proportionality can, as this chapter has shown, be understood as constitutional facts.[137] However, as has been suggested here, not all facts within this category will be the same, and the fact relevant to the various stages of proportionality reasoning will often exhibit different characteristics.

[135] A Woolhandler, 'Rethinking the Judicial Reception of Legislative Facts' (1988) 41 *Vanderbilt Law Review* 111, 114.
[136] Heydon (n 1) 198 [3005].
[137] These are best viewed as a sub-set of the broader category of legislative facts.

As with all efforts of categorisation, there will in practice be some overlap between the facts that arise at the suitability, necessity and balancing stages. For a start, the same material might at times be relevant to several of the factual inquiries or the relevant factual elements might be intertwined. In the context of the trade and commerce limb of section 92 of the *Australian Constitution*, for instance, the court must often make a factual assessment of whether the law in question is discriminatory and protectionist.[138] This requires an examination of how the law operates in practice as well as some prediction about its future effect. In addition, proportionality is applied differently in each jurisdiction and courts do not always distinguish clearly between the different stages of the inquiry. The Canadian Supreme Court, for instance, has tended to rely mostly on the 'necessity' stage of analysis, whereas in Germany the Federal Constitutional Court has been more willing to engage explicitly in 'balancing'.[139]

Despite this potential for overlap, and the lack of distinction in some judicial reasoning, it remains helpful to distinguish between the facts that arise at the different stages of proportionality reasoning. First, identifying more precisely the use that is being made of evidentiary material will help to illuminate the degree to which particular propositions are supported, or justified, by relevant empirical material. It will, in this way, help to increase the transparency of judicial reasoning. Second, there may be practical differences in terms of the type or availability of relevant evidentiary material at the different stages. Third, distinguishing between the different stages may bear upon the level of satisfaction required for various propositions of fact. Finally, and most importantly, recognising different types of constitutional facts may provide some guidance as to the types of inquiries that it is institutionally appropriate for courts to perform.

This revised framework for thinking about facts, which draws attention to differences that arise at the three stages of proportionality reasoning, provides the basis for examining, in subsequent chapters, how courts have applied proportionality reasoning in practice.

[138] See the discussion in ch 5, section II.A.iii and ch 6, section II.C.

[139] See ch 2, nn 42ff and accompanying text.

# 4

# *Proportionality and Facts in Comparative Perspective*

GERMANY, CANADA AND South Africa all have extensive experience in applying tests of proportionality. Unlike in Australia, where the place of proportionality in constitutional adjudication remains somewhat underdeveloped, in these jurisdictions proportionality is firmly entrenched and the courts have built up a considerable body of jurisprudence. In the course of applying proportionality, the courts in Germany, Canada and South Africa have, to varying degrees, grappled with the question of facts. This chapter examines the degree to which the courts in each jurisdiction have recognised facts as *relevant* to proportionality reasoning. As part of this analysis, it considers whether it is possible to discern any differences in the treatment of facts at the suitability, necessity and balancing stages, drawing on the revised framework for thinking about facts that was developed in the previous chapter. In addition, and to the extent that facts have been recognised as relevant, the chapter assesses *how* the courts in each jurisdiction have sought to establish these facts, and identifies a number of different approaches that have been adopted. This comparative approach is instructive in terms of illustrating how the conceptual understanding of proportionality, developed in the previous chapters, has been translated as a matter of practice. Further, a consideration of how the problem of facts has been resolved in other jurisdictions potentially offers insights for Australia as it grapples with the factual elements of its emerging conception of proportionality.

## I. PROPORTIONALITY COMPARED

Although proportionality has become almost ubiquitous in its reach, it does not always take precisely the same form. Despite some differences of emphasis between Germany, Canada and South Africa, each jurisdiction applies a form of proportionality reasoning. Germany is commonly considered to be the home of modern proportionality reasoning, as proportionality was initially developed in the administrative law context in the nineteenth century.[1] In the 1950s

[1] N Marsch and V Tünsmeyer, 'The Principle of Proportionality in German Administrative Law' in S Ranchordás and B de Waard (eds), *The Judge and the Proportionate Use of Discretion: A Comparative Study* (London, Routledge, 2016) 25–28.

it was adapted and refined for use in the constitutional context. While Germany lacks a single defining case,[2] the *Pharmacies Case* of 1958 represents a significant step in the Federal Constitutional Court's development of proportionality.[3] In this case the *Bavarian Pharmacy Act*, which required pharmacists to obtain permits,[4] was challenged on the grounds of the right to occupational freedom.[5] In invalidating the legislation, the Court began to develop a framework for testing whether a limitation on a right was permissible. In doing so, the Court noted that it must determine whether the specific encroachment was 'compellingly required' and that the conflict between the fundamental right and the regulatory power could only be resolved through 'carefully balancing the importance of the respective opposing and possibly even conflicting interests'.[6] On the facts of the case, it assumed that the purpose of the legislation was to protect the pharmacy profession and also to advance the health needs of the population.[7] Ultimately, it concluded that the legislation was not necessary, as the legislature had not chosen the least restrictive means. From these beginnings, proportionality developed into a more structured test[8] containing the now-familiar stages of 'suitability' (*geeignetheit*), 'necessity' (*erforderlichkeit*) and 'balancing' (*angemessenheit*).[9] It has now crystallised into a general constitutional principle in German law.[10]

[2] N Petersen, 'Balancing and Judicial Self-Empowerment: A Case Study on the Rise of Balancing in the Jurisprudence of the Federal Constitutional Court' (2015) 4 *Global Constitutionalism* 49, 59. According to Grimm, proportionality first appeared in the Court's jurisprudence in 1954, but was more fully developed in 1958 in the *Pharmacies Case*: D Grimm, 'Values in German Constitutional Law' in D Davis, A Richter and C Saunders (eds), *An Inquiry into the Existence of Global Values: Through the Lens of Comparative Constitutional Law* (Oxford, Hart Publishing, 2015) 207.

[3] *Pharmacies Case*, Bundesverfassungsgericht [German Constitutional Court], 1 BvR 596/56, 11 June 1958 reported in (1958) 7 BVerfGE 377 (extracts translated in J Bröhmer, C Hill and M Spitzkatz (eds), *60 Years German Basic Law: The German Constitution and its Court – Landmark Decision of the Federal Constitutional Court of Germany in the Area of Fundamental Rights*, 2nd edn (Kuala Lumpur, Malaysian Current Law Journal Sdn Bhd, 2012) 599).

[4] The legislation provided that a permit would only be granted if the pharmacy was considered to be in the public interest, had a secure economic base and would not compromise the economic base of neighbouring pharmacies.

[5] *Basic Law for the Federal Republic of Germany* (C Tomuschat and DP Currie trans, revised by C Tomuschat and DP Kommers in cooperation with the Language Service of the German Bundestag (2014), www.gesetze-im-internet.de/englisch_gg) art 12.

[6] *Pharmacies Case* (n 3) 608. According to Grimm, 'balancing' was introduced by the Federal Constitutional Court and had not been part of the earlier notion of proportionality employed by the administrative courts: Grimm (n 2) 207.

[7] *Pharmacies Case* (n 3) 612.

[8] E Bjørge, *Domestic Application of the ECHR: Courts as Faithful Trustees* (Oxford, Oxford University Press, 2015) 164.

[9] For a brief overview of the German approach, see N Emiliou, *The Principle of Proportionality in European Law: A Comparative Study* (London, Kluwer Law International, 1996) ch 2; A Jasiak, *Constitutional Constraints on Ad Hoc Legislation: A Comparative Study of the United States, Germany and the Netherlands* (Cambridge, Intersentia, 2011) ch 5; G Lübbe-Wolff, 'The Principle of Proportionality in the Case-Law of the German Federal Constitutional Court' (2014) 34 *Human Rights Law Journal* 12.

[10] Emiliou (n 9) 65–66.

In Canada, the Supreme Court has adopted a similar tripartite structure in applying the limitations clause in section 1 of the *Canadian Charter of Rights and Freedoms* (hereinafter 'the *Charter*').[11] Chief Justice Dickson's interpretation of section 1 in *R v Oakes*[12] remains influential and has assumed the character of a 'holy writ'.[13] Although the extent to which Dickson CJ was influenced by comparative jurisprudence is not clear,[14] his approach followed the two-stage model of rights-protection that emerged in constitutional and international instruments following the Second World War.[15] Under the first stage of the *Oakes* test, the objective pursued by the legislation must be 'of sufficient importance to warrant overriding a constitutionally protected right or freedom'.[16] Second, the means chosen must be shown by the party invoking section 1 to be 'reasonable and demonstrably justified'.[17] This, in turn, involves a three-step proportionality inquiry:

> First, the measures adopted must be carefully designed to achieve the objective in question. They must not be arbitrary, unfair or based on irrational considerations. In short, they must be rationally connected to the objective. Second, the means, even if rationally connected to the objective in this first sense, should impair 'as little as possible' the right or freedom in question ... Third, there must be a proportionality between the effects of the measures which are responsible for limiting the *Charter* right or freedom, and the objective which has been identified as of 'sufficient importance'.[18]

The issue in *Oakes* was whether a reverse onus provision in the *Narcotic Control Act* violated the presumption of innocence in section 11(d) of the *Charter*.[19] The Court held that the provision failed the first stage of the three-part proportionality test, as there was no rational connection between the basic fact of possession and the presumed fact of possession for the purposes of trafficking. Given this conclusion, there was no need for the Court to consider the subsequent stages of the proportionality test.[20]

[11] *Canada Act 1982* (UK) c 11, sch B pt 1 (hereinafter '*Canadian Charter of Rights and Freedoms*').

[12] *R v Oakes* [1986] 1 SCR 103.

[13] PW Hogg, 'Section 1 Revisited' (1991) 1 *National Journal of Constitutional Law* 1, 3. *cf* CD Bredt and HK Pessione, 'The Death of *Oakes*: Time for a Rights-Specific Approach' (2013) 62 *Supreme Court Law Review* 486.

[14] D Grimm, 'Proportionality in Canadian and German Constitutional Jurisprudence' (2007) 57 *University of Toronto Law Journal* 383, 383–84.

[15] LE Weinrib, 'Canada's *Charter of Rights*: Paradigm Lost?' (2001) 6 *Review of Constitutional Studies* 119, 125–32; LE Weinrib, 'The Postwar Paradigm and American Exceptionalism' in S Choudhry (ed), *The Migration of Constitutional Ideas* (Cambridge, Cambridge University Press, 2007) 89ff.

[16] *Oakes* (n 12) 138, quoting *R v Big M Drug Mart Ltd* [1985] 1 SCR 295, 352.

[17] ibid 139.

[18] ibid (citations omitted).

[19] Section 8 of the *Narcotic Control Act*, RSC 1970, c N-1 provided that if a person was found to possess a particular quantity of narcotics, they were presumed to possess the narcotics for the purposes of trafficking.

[20] *Oakes* (n 12) 142. Note that in the Court's later jurisprudence, the 'rational connection' stage has rarely been decisive. In addition, it has been suggested that the decision in *Oakes* would have been better justified by the 'minimal impairment' stage; see, eg, RJ Sharpe and K Roach, *The Charter of Rights and Freedoms*, 5th edn (Toronto, Irwin Law, 2013) 72.

Both the Canadian and German approaches to proportionality served as useful models for the South African Constitutional Court when it came to interpret its own limitations clause.[21] The Constitutional Court's approach to proportionality was developed in *S v Makwanyane*, which concerned the constitutionality of the death penalty.[22] President Chaskalson observed that the provisions of section 33 required 'the weighing up of competing values, and ultimately an assessment of proportionality'.[23] This assessment was to be applied flexibly on a case-by-case basis, but was to be informed by a number of factors.[24] The Court held that life imprisonment was a severe alternative form of punishment and that 'the clear and convincing case that is required to justify the death sentence as a penalty for murder' had not been established.[25] While the *Interim Constitution* of 1993 included two different standards for assessing limitations on rights,[26] the *Constitution of the Republic of South Africa 1996* contains a single standard that was modelled on Chaskalson P's list of considerations in *Makwanyane*.[27] Unlike the general language of section 1 of the Canadian *Charter*, section 36 of the 1996 *Constitution* contains a non-exhaustive list of factors to be considered by the Court when assessing limitations.[28] The Court has emphasised that these factors are indicative only and that judges should not 'adhere mechanically to a sequential check-list'.[29]

As this brief snapshot shows, there are some important commonalities between the three jurisdictions. All adopt a flexible rather than a rule-based approach, and proportionality provides some structure for how the competing interests are to be considered. There are, however, also differences in terms of how proportionality is applied. In particular, the 'global' approach adopted

[21] Despite the clear parallels between s 33 of South Africa's interim constitution and s 1 of the Canadian *Charter*, the Constitutional Court emphasised that its approach would not simply mirror the Canadian approach: *S v Zuma* [1995] 2 SA 642 [35] (Kentridge AJ) (Constitutional Court).

[22] *S v Makwanyane* [1995] 3 SA 391 (Constitutional Court).

[23] ibid [104].

[24] ibid.

[25] ibid [146] (Chaskalson P). See also [184] (Ackermann J), [202] (Kentridge AJ), [212] (Kriegler J), [295]–[297] (Mahomed J).

[26] Relevantly, s 33(1)(a) of the *Constitution of the Republic of South Africa 1993* (South Africa) (hereinafter '*Interim Constitution*') provided that the rights could be limited by a law of general application provided that the limitation was '(i) reasonable; and (ii) justifiable in an open and democratic society based on freedom and equality'. Section 33(1)(b) then provided that for certain itemised rights any limitation *also* had to be 'necessary'. Note that the langue of 'necessary' was considered to impose a stricter standard of scrutiny: L du Plessis and H Corder, *Understanding South Africa's Transitional Bill of Rights* (Cape Town, Juta, 1994) 124–27.

[27] *Makwanyane* (n 22) [104]; I Currie and J de Waal, *The Bill of Rights Handbook*, 6th edn (Cape Town, Juta, 2013) 163 [7.2].

[28] *Constitution of the Republic of South Africa 1996* (South Africa), s 36.

[29] *S v Manamela* [2000] 3 SA 1, [32] (Madala, Sachs and Yacoob JJ) (Constitutional Court) ('*Manamela*').

in South Africa differs from the more structured approach of the other two jurisdictions, although the same types of factors are considered in all three jurisdictions.[30] In addition, the Supreme Court of Canada has traditionally placed most emphasis on the 'minimal impairment' stage, and the majority of *Charter* cases succeed or fail at this stage.[31] In contrast, the Federal Constitutional Court in Germany relies much more overtly on the 'balancing' stage than its Canadian or South African counterparts.[32] Finally, there are also differences in terms of the level of scrutiny that is applied. In Germany the courts have developed three distinct levels of scrutiny – the 'control of evidence' standard, the 'control of reasonableness' standard and the 'strict control' standard – and the level of scrutiny is dictated by the right in question.[33] In Canada, by contrast, while the Court has insisted that section 1 provides a single standard of review, in practice it has been applied variably and a number of factors appear to influence the application of section 1.[34] In South Africa, similarly, there is also a single standard of review and the Constitutional Court has indicated that it is to be applied flexibly.[35]

## II. RECOGNISING FACTS?

### A. The Relevance of Facts

In all three jurisdictions there has been some recognition that facts are relevant to proportionality analysis. The most explicit and developed discussion of the

[30] N Petersen, 'Proportionality and the Incommensurability Challenge in the Jurisprudence of the South African Constitutional Court' (2014) 30 *South African Journal on Human Rights* 405, 407; *cf* S Woolman and H Botha, 'Limitations: Shared Constitutional Interpretation, An Appropriate Normative Framework and Hard Choices' in S Woolman and M Bishop (eds), *Constitutional Conversations* (Pretoria, Pretoria University Law Press, 2008) 149, 155–56.

[31] See the discussion at n 130 below.

[32] N Petersen, *Proportionality and Judicial Activism: Fundamental Rights Adjudication in Canada, Germany and South Africa* (Cambridge, Cambridge University Press, 2017) ch 4.

[33] *Codetermination Case* (1979) 50 BVerfGE 290, 332 (referred to in *Second Abortion Case*, Bundesverfassungsgericht [German Constitutional Court], 2 BvF 2/90; 2 BvF 4/92; 2 BvF 5/92, 28 May 1993 reported in (1993) 88 BVerfGE 203 (Federal Constitutional Court, trans, www.bverfg.de/e/fs19930528_2bvf000290en.html)). For an explanation of the three levels of scrutiny, see E Benda, 'The Position and Function of the *Bundesverfassungsgericht* (Federal Constitutional Court) in a Reunited Germany' in E McWhinney, J Zaslove and W Wolf (eds), *Federalism-in-the-Making: Contemporary Canadian and German Constitutionalism, National and Transnational* (Dordrecht, Kluwer Academic Publishers, 1992) 30–31; C Koch, 'The Sky is Falling if Judges Decide Religious Controversies! – Or is it? The German Experience of Religious Freedom under a Bill of Rights' in P Babie and N Rochow (eds), *Freedom of Religion under Bills of Rights* (Adelaide, University of Adelaide Press, 2013) 194.

[34] *Thomson Newspapers Co v Canada (Attorney-General)* [1998] 1 SCR 877, 942 [90] (Bastarache J); Sharpe and Roach (n 20) 79.

[35] See, eg, *Manamela* (n 29) [33] (Madala, Sachs and Yacoob JJ).

role of facts can be seen in Canada.[36] In *Oakes* itself, Dickson CJ articulated the section 1 inquiry in a way that prioritised the importance of evidence:

> Where evidence is required in order to prove the constituent elements of a s 1 inquiry, *and this will generally be the case*, it should be cogent and persuasive and make clear to the Court the consequences of imposing or not imposing the limit.[37]

Such evidence, according to Dickson CJ, would include information about the availability of alternative measures to achieve the same purpose.[38] Despite this call for evidence, in *Oakes* itself the evidence appeared to play little role in the Court's ultimate conclusion that the reverse onus provisions lacked a rational connection to the legitimate goal of reducing drug trafficking. While Dickson CJ referred to a number of reports to demonstrate the increasing problem of drug trafficking, and also the national and international measures that had been adopted, he considered that the 'degree of seriousness' of drug trafficking meant that it was 'to a large extent, self-evident' that it constituted a sufficiently important objective for the purposes of section 1.[39] The empirical materials to which Dickson CJ referred served to bolster this conclusion, but do not appear to have been determinative. In addition, when it came to applying the rational connection test, Dickson CJ did not rely on any evidence, but instead held that the legislation was not 'internally rational'.[40]

In the decades since *Oakes*, the Canadian courts have grappled with the extent to which evidence is required for the section 1 limitations analysis. As Sujit Choudhry has observed, Dickson CJ's approach produced 'a conflict between the demand for definitive proof … and the reality of policy making under conditions of factual uncertainty'.[41] This led to an 'enormous institutional dilemma for the Court',[42] and how to reconcile this dilemma continues to trouble the Court. While social science evidence is increasingly common in *Charter* litigation,[43] there has been considerable

[36] From the early days of *Charter* litigation, the Supreme Court acknowledged the relevance of evidence in determining whether limitations can be justified under s 1: *Law Society of Upper Canada v Skapinker* [1984] 1 SCR 357, 383–84; *Singh v Minister of Employment and Immigration* [1985] 1 SCR 177, 217.

[37] *Oakes* (n 12) 138 (emphasis added). As Pepall notes, this was not the only interpretation of s 1 that could have been adopted: JT Pepall, 'What's the Evidence? The Use the Supreme Court of Canada Makes of Evidence in *Charter* Cases' in AA Peacock (ed), *Rethinking the Constitution: Perspectives on Canadian Constitutional Reform, Interpretation, and Theory* (Toronto, Oxford University Press, 1996) 163–64. See also Grimm, who notes that the German Federal Constitutional Court has never insisted upon such a high burden of proof: Grimm (n 14) 390.

[38] *Oakes* (n 12) 138.

[39] ibid 141.

[40] ibid. See the text accompanying n 20 above.

[41] S Choudhry, 'So What is the Real Legacy of *Oakes*? Two Decades of Proportionality Analysis under the Canadian *Charter*'s Section 1' (2006) 34 *Supreme Court Law Review* 501, 503.

[42] ibid.

[43] B Perryman, 'Adducing Social Science Evidence in Constitutional Cases' (2018) 44 *Queens's Law Journal* 121.

disagreement over when and how much evidence is necessary to support the section 1 inquiry.[44]

Although not as developed as the Canadian jurisprudence, in South Africa there has also been some recognition that evidence may be relevant to assessing limitations under section 36. In *Makwanyane*, for instance, Chaskalson P noted that it is for the 'legislature, or the party relying on the legislation, to establish this justification'.[45] In later cases the Court has confirmed that justification requires both 'factual material and policy considerations'[46] and that the 'facts and policy are often intertwined'.[47] The Constitutional Court has even, on occasion, directed the parties to file further evidentiary material. In *Prince v President of the Law Society of the Cape of Good Hope*, the Court had to consider whether the failure to provide an exemption for cannabis use for religious purposes was compatible with the 1996 *Constitution*.[48] The Court indicated that it could not accept 'bare allegation'[49] or 'speculation',[50] and that the evidence before it was 'neither comprehensive enough nor specific enough as to the South African context' to enable it to resolve the dispute.[51] In what has been described as a 'rare' procedural move,[52] the Court issued an interim judgment in which it directed the parties to file further affidavit evidence addressing how cannabis is used and obtained by Rastafari, internal regulations or restrictions on the use of cannabis, and the practicalities of policing an exemption.[53] Drawing upon this evidence, a majority of the Constitutional Court held that the restriction on cannabis use was justifiable.[54]

[44] For some discussion, see M Jamal, 'Legislative Facts in *Charter* Litigation: Where are We Now?' (2005) 17 *National Journal of Constitutional Law* 1; Choudhry (n 41) 503; RE Charney and SZ Green, 'Prophets of Doom, Seers of Fortune: 20 Years of Expert Evidence under the *Oakes* Test' (2006) 34 *Supreme Court Law Review* 479; D Wiseman, 'Managing the Burden of Doubt: Social Science Evidence, the Institutional Competence of Courts and the Prospects for Anti-Poverty *Charter* Claims' (2014) 33 *National Journal of Constitutional Law* 1, 17.

[45] *Makwanyane* (n 22) [102]. Although the State sought to rely upon statistical evidence to demonstrate the deterrent effect of the death penalty, the Court was not persuaded by this evidence and held that the State had failed to justify the death penalty under s 33 of the *Interim Constitution*.

[46] *Moise v Transitional Local Council of Greater Germiston* [2001] 4 SA 491, [18] (Constitutional Court). See also *Manamela* (n 29) [33].

[47] *Minister for Home Affairs v National Institute for Crime Prevention and the Re-integration of Offenders (NICRO)* [2005] 3 SA 280, [35] (Constitutional Court) (hereinafter '*NICRO*').

[48] *Prince v President of the Law Society of the Cape of Good Hope* [2001] 2 SA 388 (Constitutional Court) (hereinafter '*Prince 2001*').

[49] ibid [5].

[50] ibid [17].

[51] ibid [15]. Note that there was some evidence before the Constitutional Court, including an affidavit from an expert on the Rastafari religion.

[52] L du Plessis, 'Religious Freedom and Equality as Celebration of Difference: A Significant Development in Recent South African Constitutional Case-Law' (2009) 12 *Potchefstroom Electronic Law Journal* 10, 19.

[53] *Prince 2001* (n 48) [12]–[17], [41].

[54] *Prince v President of the Law Society of the Cape of Good Hope* [2002] 2 SA 794, [139]–[144] (Chaskalson CJ, Ackermann and Kriegler JJ, with whom Goldstone and Yacoob JJ concurred) (Constitutional Court) (hereinafter '*Prince 2002*').

In Germany the Federal Constitutional Court has been less explicit, though it has also recognised that facts may be relevant to the proportionality inquiry. The Court's dominant interpretive approach is doctrinal, and while the *Begriffsjurisprudenz* school of conceptual jurisprudence has been challenged by competing approaches to interpretation and by the enactment of the Basic Law itself,[55] aspects of the 'scientific' approach to legal reasoning and scholarship remain.[56] The Court, as a result, has attracted criticism for failing to explain the political circumstances of its decisions.[57]

Yet, at the same time, the Court has not altogether avoided the empirical dimensions of constitutional claims. Indeed, the Court can and does receive evidence,[58] and amongst German scholars, there are indications of an emerging interest in the role of empirical research in legal decision-making.[59] An early example of the Court's use of evidence can be seen in the *Pharmacies Case*, where it noted that 'the necessity of such a restriction of freedom [to choose an occupation] must meet especially stringent standards of proof'.[60] The Court was not simply prepared to assume the existence of a threat to public health, but heard expert testimony from a variety of witnesses, including public health officials in Germany and Switzerland, an economist, and pharmacists' associations in Bavaria and Switzerland.[61] The Swiss evidence was used to demonstrate that the lack of similar restrictions in Switzerland

[55] DP Kommers and RA Miller, *The Constitutional Jurisprudence of the Federal Republic of Germany*, 3rd edn (Durham, NC, Duke University Press, 2012) 55–56.

[56] For some discussion, see KR Grechenig and M Gelter, 'The Transatlantic Divergence in Legal Thought: American Law and Economics vs German Doctrinalism' (2008) 31 *Hastings International and Comparative Law Review* 295; A von Bogdandy, 'The Past and Promise of Doctrinal Constructivism: A Strategy for Responding to the Challenges Facing Constitutional Scholarship in Europe' (2009) 7 *International Journal of Constitutional Law* 364; C Möllers and H Birkenkotter, 'Towards a New Conceptualism in Comparative Constitutional Law, or Reviving the German Tradition of the *Lehrbuch*' (2014) 12 *International Journal of Constitutional Law* 603; EV Towfigh, 'Empirical Arguments in Public Law Doctrine: Should Empirical Legal Studies Make a "Doctrinal Turn"?' (2014) 12 *International Journal of Constitutional Law* 670, 670–71, 674.

[57] M Hailbronner, 'Rethinking the Rise of the German Constitutional Court: From Anti-Nazism to Value Formalism' (2014) 12 *International Journal of Constitutional Law* 626, 637. See also Alexander Somek, 'The Indelible Science of Law' (2009) 7 *International Journal of Constitutional Law* 424.

[58] *Federal Constitutional Court Act (BVerfGG)* (Germany) (Federal Constitutional Court trans (2017), www.bundesverfassungsgericht.de/EN/Verfahren/Rechtsquellen/rechtsquellen_node.html_) § 26. See also HW Baade, 'Social Science Evidence and the Federal Constitutional Court of West Germany' (1961) 23 *Journal of Politics* 421; R Alexy and R Dreier, 'Statutory Interpretation in the Federal Republic of Germany' in N MacCormick and RS Summers (eds), *Interpreting Statutes: A Comparative Study* (Aldershot, Dartmouth, 1991) 91; Grimm (n 14) 391.

[59] See, eg, N Petersen, 'Avoiding the Common-Wisdom Fallacy: The Role of Social Sciences in Constitutional Adjudication' (2013) 11 *International Journal of Constitutional Law* 294; Towfigh (n 56). Note that Möllers has observed that little research has been done on the Court's use of facts: C Möllers, 'Scope and Legitimacy of Judicial Review in German Constitutional Law – The Court versus the Political Process' in H Pünder and C Waldhoff (eds), *Debates in German Public Law* (Oxford, Hart Publishing, 2014) 15.

[60] *Pharmacies Case* (n 3) 610.

[61] Baade (n 58) 452.

had not had the detrimental effects argued for by the Bavarian government.[62] This contributed to the Court's overall finding that the restrictions on pharmacists were not necessary to achieve the stated goal.[63]

## B. Differentiating Facts: The Various Stages of Proportionality Analysis

In all three jurisdictions, then, there has been *some* recognition of the factual elements of proportionality reasoning. As the examples discussed above illustrate, the courts do receive empirical material and at times have even required the parties to file further evidence. Moreover, in some cases the lack of evidentiary material has been critical to a court's ultimate finding that a limitation on a right is not justified. Yet, as discussed in the previous chapter, rather than treating all constitutional facts as alike, it is helpful to consider differences that might exist *within* this category. This section of this chapter considers whether the comparative jurisprudence reveals any differences emerging at the suitability, necessity and balancing stages of proportionality.

### *i. The Suitability Stage: Purpose and Rational Connection*

As the previous two chapters have established, at the suitability stage the court must determine the purpose of the challenged law and whether the law is capable of fulfilling this purpose. Both of these questions involve empirical elements.

In practice there has been some recognition that facts are relevant to both of these inquiries, and at times the courts have relied on empirical material to support their conclusions. As explained above, in *Oakes* itself, the Supreme Court of Canada had before it a number of reports and other material that documented the problem of drug trafficking in Canada and the efforts that had been taken both nationally and internationally to address the problem.[64] This material was referred to by Dickson CJ primarily to support his conclusion that the *purpose* of the challenged provision was to curb drug trafficking by facilitating the conviction of drug traffickers. Another example of the Court's recognition of facts at the suitability stage is *Sauvé v Canada (Chief Electoral Officer)*.[65] The case concerned prisoners' voting rights and a majority of the Court was critical of the lack of evidence. Chief Justice McLachlin, for

[62] Petersen (n 2) 61.

[63] Note that von Brünneck has suggested that constitutional courts only rely on social science data to the extent that appears necessary to give their decisions a 'plausible foundation, making them more acceptable in the society': A von Brünneck, 'Constitutional Review and Legislation in Western Democracies' in C Landfried (ed), *Constitutional Review and Legislation: An International Comparison* (Baden-Baden, Nomos Verlagsgesellschaft, 1988) 230–31.

[64] *Oakes* (n 12) 140–41.

[65] *Sauvé v Canada (Chief Electoral Officer)* [2002] 3 SCR 519.

instance, observed that the government had failed to identify any 'particular problems' that justified denying the right,[66] commenting that 'people should not be left guessing about why their *Charter* rights have been infringed'.[67] The record before the Court, including the parliamentary debates, offered little 'illumination' of the government's objectives.[68] Although the majority went on to consider the rest of the proportionality inquiry, these doubts about the government's purpose contributed to a failure to satisfy all three aspects of the proportionality test.[69]

In other cases, however, the Supreme Court has indicated that logic and reason will play a role in determining legislative purpose. The section 1 inquiry is not, as some judges have explained, to be understood primarily as an 'evidentiary contest'.[70] This does not deny that the inquiry contains factual elements, but suggests instead that the relevant facts will not always need to be supported by evidence.[71] In *Harper v Canada (Attorney-General)*, which concerned restrictions on third-party election advertising, Bastarache J, writing for the majority, observed that the harm of electoral unfairness was difficult, if not impossible to measure.[72] In this circumstance, he was satisfied that 'logic and reason assisted by some social science evidence is sufficient proof of the harm that Parliament seeks to remedy'.[73] Justice Bastarache relied on the Lortie Commission report on third-party spending[74] and also the Court's previous decisions,[75] to conclude that the objectives pursued by the legislation were pressing and substantial.[76] Further, he held that the lower courts had erred by requiring 'scientific proof' that the absence of third-party spending limits had led to unfair elections in Canada.[77]

In South Africa, similarly, the Constitutional Court has at times required evidence of purpose. In the *NICRO* case, the Court had to determine whether a restriction on convicted prisoners voting was justified.[78] Chief Justice Chaskalson, writing for the majority, emphasised the importance of context

[66] ibid 542 [26].
[67] ibid 541 [23].
[68] ibid 540 [21].
[69] ibid 542 [26].
[70] *R v Bryan* [2007] 1 SCR 527, 547 [32] (Bastarache J). See also *R v Keegstra* [1990] 3 SCR 697, 768; *R v Butler* [1992] 1 SCR 452, 502–03.
[71] It appears that when the Court refers to 'reason' or 'logic' in this way, it is not relying explicitly on the doctrine of 'judicial notice'. See further the discussion in section III.A below.
[72] *Harper v Canada (Attorney-General)* [2004] 1 SCR 827, 875 [79].
[73] ibid.
[74] The 'Lortie Commission' refers to the Royal Commission on Electoral Reform and Party Financing that was appointed by the federal government in 1989 and that produced the report *Reforming Electoral Democracy* in 1991: see *Harper* (n 72) 834. In *Harper* this report had been before the trial judge.
[75] *Harper* (n 72) 884 [100].
[76] ibid 884–85 [101]–[103].
[77] ibid 881 [93].
[78] *NICRO* (n 47). As a majority of the Court (at [67]) found that the limitation on the right to vote could not be justified, there was no need to consider the argument based on the right to equality.

when assessing limitations under section 36. He acknowledged that legislative choice may be 'based on reasonable inferences unsupported by empirical data'[79] and that the demonstration of justification may not depend on 'disputed facts but on policies directed to legitimate governmental concerns'.[80] However, this did not relieve the party seeking justification from the burden of adducing evidence:

> If that be the case, the party relying on justification should place sufficient information before the court as to the policy that is being furthered, the reasons for that policy, and why it is considered reasonable in pursuit of that policy to limit a constitutional right. That is important, for if this is not done the court may be unable to discern what the policy is, and the party making the constitutional challenge does not have the opportunity of rebutting the contention through countervailing factual material or expert opinion.[81]

In that case the policy justifications had been introduced 'almost tangentially',[82] and the only material before the Court consisted of a statement from the Director-General of Home Affairs that it would be unfair to others who could not vote, and assertions from counsel that the government did not want to be 'soft on crime'.[83] This was considered insufficient to establish the government's purpose in restricting the prisoner franchise.

Once the purpose of the legislation has been ascertained, facts are also relevant when the court considers the connection between the law and its purpose. In Canada, the Supreme Court has indicated that while evidence may be of assistance at this stage, it will not always be essential.[84] As with the establishment of the legislative objective, reason and logic also play a role in determining whether there is a rational connection.[85] For instance, in *RJR-MacDonald v Canada (Attorney-General)*, which concerned legislation regulating the advertising, promotion and sale of tobacco products, McLachlin J reiterated that the government 'must demonstrate' the relevant causal connection.[86] She acknowledged, however, that where legislation was directed at changing human behaviour, as it was in this case, 'the causal relationship may not be

[79] ibid [35].
[80] ibid [36].
[81] ibid.
[82] ibid [66]. Due to a procedural irregularity, the Constitutional Court in this case sat as both a court of first and final instance.
[83] ibid [55]. See also [49].
[84] An early empirical survey in Canada suggests that while it is common for government parties to adduce factums of empirical material, the majority of this material is directed to whether the legislation pursues a 'pressing and substantial purpose', despite the fact that this stage is rarely determinative; see FL Morton and I Brodie, 'The Use of Extrinsic Evidence in *Charter* Litigation before the Supreme Court of Canada' (1993) 3 *National Journal of Constitutional Law* 1.
[85] See the discussion above at text accompanying n 71.
[86] *RJR-MacDonald v Canada (Attorney-General)* [1995] 3 SCR 199, 339 [153]. Note that McLachlin J formed part of the majority, which held that the impugned sections could not be justified under s 1.

scientifically measurable', and reason or logic could assist in establishing the relationship.[87] This reliance on reason or logic is consistent with the understanding, as explained in Chapter 2, that the rational connection test imposes a fairly low threshold.[88]

While a similar approach has been adopted in a number of other cases,[89] there have occasionally been signs of a more demanding approach to establishing rational connection. In *Chaoulli v Quebec (Attorney-General)*, for instance, which concerned the validity of a prohibition on private health insurance, the three judges who considered the section 1 issue found that there was no rational connection between the law and the objective of protecting the public health system.[90] In particular, they found that there was an absence of evidence that the prohibition on private health insurance would serve to protect the healthcare system.[91]

In South Africa, as explained in section I above, the Constitutional Court considers a range of factors in assessing proportionality, but these include the 'relation between the limitation and its purpose'.[92] While this aspect of the section 36 analysis has only rarely been determinative, where it has been, it appears that both evidence *and* reason will play a role.[93] For instance, in the case of *S v Bhulwana*, the Court held that a reverse onus provision in relation to the possession of dagga[94] was not justified.[95] While the objective of suppressing illicit drug trafficking was acknowledged to be 'an urgent and pressing one', O'Regan J, writing for the Court, held that it was not clear 'how, if at all' the reverse onus provision furthered that objective.[96] This conclusion was based partly on the lack of a 'logical connection' between the fact of possession and the presumption of dealing,[97] but also on the evidence placed before the Court about how many cigarettes could be made from the prescribed quantity of dagga.[98] Similarly, in *South African National Defence Union v Minister*

[87] ibid 339 [154]. See also 354 [184] (Iacobucci J).

[88] See chapter two, part IB. See also C Mathen, 'Rational Connections: *Oakes*, Section 1 and the *Charter*'s Legal Rights' (2012) 43 *Ottawa Law Review* 491, 498; Sharpe and Roach (n 20) 73.

[89] See, eg, *R v Keegstra* [1990] 3 SCR 697, 768, 777; *R v Butler* [1992] 1 SCR 452, 502; *Sauvé* (n 65) 538 [18].

[90] *Chaoulli v Quebec (Attorney-General)* [2005] 1 SCR 791, 859 [155] (McLachlin CJ and Major J, with whom Bastarache J agreed).

[91] ibid.

[92] *Constitution of the Republic of South Africa 1996* (South Africa), s 36(1)(d). See also J Brown, 'The Doctrine of Proportionality: A Comparative Analysis of the Proportionality Principle Applied to Free Speech Cases in Canada, South Africa and the European Convention on Human Right and Freedoms' (Master of Laws thesis, Central European University, 2012) 61.

[93] This is similar to the approach in Canada.

[94] Note that 'dagga' is the term used for cannabis in South Africa.

[95] *S v Bhulwana; S v Gwadiso* [1996] 1 SA 388 (Constitutional Court).

[96] ibid [24].

[97] ibid.

[98] ibid [23]. O'Regan J noted that counsel for the Attorney-General had conceded that it would 'not be unreasonable' for a regular user of dagga to possess that quantity of dagga.

*of Defence*, the Court found that a prohibition on members of the defence force participating in public protests and joining trade unions was not rationally connected to the objective of maintaining a disciplined and effective defence force.[99] In reaching this conclusion, the Court relied in part on a research memorandum submitted by one of the parties that considered the position adopted in various other countries.[100]

These cases demonstrate that the courts have, at times, recognised facts as relevant to the suitability stage of proportionality. Although the courts do not always consider it necessary for this stage of the analysis to be supported by empirical material,[101] when such material is referred to, it will often include parliamentary documents or reports, as well as reports prepared by other bodies, including Law Reform Commissions.[102] This material is used to clarify or substantiate the purposes of the legislation and to establish that the government is acting in response to a genuine problem. The courts appear to be relatively comfortable with referring to this sort of material, and have on occasion been critical of the lack of evidentiary material presented by the parties.[103] As the previous two chapters have established, at this stage the court is not concerned with whether the legislation will actually serve the objectives or whether the policy is likely to be effective. The only question is whether the law is *capable* of advancing the objective. In this context, it makes little sense to describe the court's task in conventional evidentiary terms as being concerned with the 'truth' of the asserted facts. Rather, as explained in Chapter 3, the real question is whether the empirical claims can be justified.

### *ii. The Necessity Stage: Effectiveness and Alternatives*

It is at the next stage of proportionality – necessity – that empirical questions arise most sharply. As explained in the previous chapters, the necessity stage requires an empirical assessment of how effective the law is in achieving its purpose. It might be expected, therefore, that at this stage the courts will rely more heavily upon empirical material. A review of the three jurisdictions shows that while courts *do* rely upon empirical material at this stage, they do not always insist upon evidence and there are often divisions about the extent to which evidence is required.

In Germany, as indicated above, the balancing stage of proportionality often assumes a pivotal place in the Court's reasoning, meaning that the relevant

[99] *South African National Defence Union v Minister of Defence* [1999] 4 SA 469 (Constitutional Court).

[100] ibid [34].

[101] See, eg, nn 70–71 above.

[102] In the Canadian context, such materials have been described by Charney as 'admissible evidence' of legislative purpose: RE Charney, 'Evidence in *Charter* Cases: Expert Evidence and Proving Purpose' (2004) 16 *National Journal of Constitutional Law* 1, 14.

[103] See, eg, *NICRO* (n 47); *Sauvé* (n 65).

factual analysis tends to take place at this stage. There are, however, some examples of where the necessity stage has proved decisive, such as the 1958 *Pharmacies Case*.[104] In this case, as explained above, the Federal Constitutional Court had before it varied empirical material, including evidence of the situation in Switzerland, which was used to show that the lack of similar restrictions would not have a detrimental effect upon the pharmacy profession. This evidence was relied on to support the Court's conclusion that the restrictions on pharmacists imposed by the Bavarian legislation were not necessary.[105]

Similarly, in both Canada and South Africa, evidence has also been relied upon at the necessity stage, but there have been divisions in terms of the extent to which such evidence is required. In Canada, for instance, in *Irwin Toy Ltd v Quebec (Attorney-General)*, the majority took the view that when mediating between claims of competing groups, the Court would be required to strike a balance 'without the benefit of absolute certainty'.[106] In these circumstances, it was not appropriate to take a 'restrictive approach' to the social science evidence, but there 'must nevertheless be a sound evidentiary basis' for the government's conclusions.[107] The minority justices, in contrast, were not satisfied that the risk to children from advertising had been demonstrated on the evidence.[108] Similarly, in *Little Sisters Book and Art Emporium v Canada (Minister of Justice)*, the Court divided over whether the minimal impairment limb had been established.[109] A majority of the Court was satisfied that the 'skeletal scheme' laid out by the customs legislation was capable of being administered in a way that minimally impaired the freedom of expression of importers.[110] The majority's discussion of this stage of the proportionality analysis was brief, with no discussion of possible alternatives. In contrast, the minority held that a less intrusive scheme was 'clearly possible' and Iacobucci J identified nine possible alternative measures that could have been taken.[111]

These divisions amongst the Court reveal a broader disagreement about how rigorously the 'minimal impairment' test should be applied,[112] but also suggest

[104] *Pharmacies Case* (n 3).

[105] See the discussion at text accompanying n 60 above. See also Petersen (n 2) 61ff.

[106] *Irwin Toy Ltd v Quebec (Attorney-General)* [1989] 1 SCR 927, 993 (Dickson CJ, Lamer and Wilson JJ).

[107] ibid 999.

[108] ibid 1007–08 (McIntyre J, with whom Beetz J agreed).

[109] *Little Sisters Book and Art Emporium v Canada (Minister of Justice)* [2000] 2 SCR 1120.

[110] Apart from the reverse onus provision: ibid 1199–1200 [150] (Binnie J, with whom McLachlin CJ, L'Heureux-Dubé, Gonthier, Major and Bastarache JJ joined).

[111] ibid 1245 [241]. Some of these alternatives, Iacobucci J acknowledged, had been suggested in an academic critique of the lower court's decision.

[112] See, eg, Sharpe and Roach (n 20) 75ff. For some discussion of the Court's inconsistent approach to *Charter* litigation, see LE Trakman, W Cole-Hamilton and S Gatien, '*R v Oakes* 1986–1997: Back to the Drawing Board' (1998) 36 *Osgoode Hall Law Journal* 83; CD Bredt and AM Dodek, 'The Increasing Irrelevance of Section 1 of the *Charter*' (2001) 14 *Supreme Court Law Review* 175; EP Mendes, 'Section 1 of the *Charter* after 30 Years: The Soul or the Dagger at its Heart?' in E Mendes and S Beaulac (eds), *The Canadian Charter of Rights and Freedoms*, 5th edn (Markham, LexisNexis, 2013).

diverging views about the types of inquiries that are institutionally appropriate for courts. Such differences were also apparent in *RJR-MacDonald*, discussed above, where the Court divided over whether the prohibitions on advertising in the *Tobacco Control Act* satisfied the minimal impairment inquiry.[113] The majority's finding of a lack of minimal impairment depended, in large part, on the failure of the government to establish an appropriate factual justification. As McLachlin J observed: 'The s 1 inquiry is by its very nature a fact-specific inquiry.'[114] Despite the fact that at the original trial in the Quebec Superior Court, which had lasted for over a year, a 'massive' amount of evidence was adduced, consisting both of oral testimony and documentary expert evidence, the majority held that the government had adduced no evidence to support a total ban or to demonstrate why less invasive measures would not be as effective.[115] As McLachlin J noted, the government had before it 'a variety of less intrusive measures' and had failed to demonstrate why such a broad ban was required.[116] The majority judges also attached significance to the fact that the Attorney-General had refused to disclose a government study that investigated alternatives to a total ban.[117]

In contrast, the minority judges disagreed that such evidentiary support was needed. For La Forest J, to demand 'definitive social science evidence' could 'have the effect of virtually paralyzing the operation of government in the socio-economic sphere'.[118] Instead, taking into account the legislative context, he was satisfied that the provisions in question minimally impaired the right to freedom of expression.[119] For him, it was significant that the Parliament had introduced this legislation after an intensive 20-year public policy process, which incrementally introduced various measures before determining that a full prohibition was necessary.[120] He was satisfied that the government had produced sufficient documentation to justify the legislation,[121] but also expressed concerns about the types of inquiries that it was appropriate for the Court to undertake:

> [I]t would be highly artificial for this Court to decide, on a purely abstract basis, that a partial prohibition on advertising would be as effective as a full prohibition. In my view, this is precisely the type of 'line drawing' that this Court has identified as being within the institutional competence of legislatures and not courts.[122]

[113] *RJR-MacDonald* (n 86).
[114] ibid 331 [133].
[115] ibid 338–39 [151]–[152].
[116] ibid 344 [164]. These measures included a partial ban, a ban on lifestyle advertising only, labelling requirements or prohibiting advertising aimed at children. There was testimony about these alternatives as well as examples from other jurisdictions, such as Quebec.
[117] ibid 354 [166] (McLachlin J), 352 [186] (Iacobuccui J); *cf* 311 [102] (La Forest J).
[118] ibid 275 [67].
[119] ibid 306 [97].
[120] ibid 306–07 [98].
[121] ibid 319 [111].
[122] ibid 312 [104], referring to *Irwin Toy* (n 106) and *R v Edwards Books and Art Ltd* [1986] 2 SCR 713.

Similarly, in South Africa, the Constitutional Court has at times expressed concerns about the limits of the Court's proper role in undertaking the necessity inquiry. In *Manamela*, for instance, the Court divided on the issue of whether a reverse onus provision in relation to stolen goods was compatible with the right to a fair trial.[123] The majority held that an evidential burden was a less restrictive means of achieving the same legislative object.[124] In reaching this conclusion, the majority took into account the practical impacts of the law, including the types of people likely to be adversely affected, presumably relying on its own knowledge of society.[125] In contrast, the minority disagreed that an evidential burden would fully achieve the purpose of reducing trafficking in stolen goods. The minority noted that while it was often 'possible for a court to conceive of less-restrictive means', such decisions were better made by the legislative branch.[126] This reflected the difficult policy choices involved, as well as the need to assess costs and practical implementation, and to reconcile competing interests.[127] This division amongst the Court suggests differences not only in terms of how strictly the necessity test should be applied, but also in terms of the Court's willingness to engage with the question of alternatives.

At the necessity stage, then, the courts have at times referred to evidence to demonstrate the effectiveness of a given law and any proposed alternatives. However, there has been some disagreement in terms of whether evidence is required to support the necessity inquiry.[128] In both Canada and South Africa, for example, there have been concerns about the extent to which it is appropriate for the courts to engage with the question of alternatives. As explained in the previous chapter, the facts that underpin the necessity inquiry will often involve predictive and even hypothetical judgments, and there are signs that the courts (or, at least, various judges) are wary about this type of judicial fact-finding.

### *iii. Balancing and Facts*

The final step of the proportionality inquiry is that of balancing. It is here that the court must assess whether the achievement of the legitimate aim is worth the cost of limiting the right. While this ultimately involves a value judgment as to the importance of the different interests at stake, as the previous chapter

[123] *Manamela* (n 29).

[124] ibid [49] (Madala, Sachs and Yacoob JJ).

[125] ibid [44], [49].

[126] ibid [94] (O'Regan and Cameron AJ).

[127] ibid [94]–[95], quoting Blackmun J in *Illinois State Board of Elections v Socialist Workers Party* 440 US 173, 188–89 (1979): 'And, for me, "least drastic means" is a slippery slope ... A judge would be unimaginative indeed if he could not come up with something a little less "drastic" or a little less "restrictive" in almost any situation, and thereby enable himself to vote to strike legislation down.'

[128] For example, in *Prince 2002* (n 54), the minority and majority disagreed about whether there was sufficient evidence of the harm caused by the religious use of cannabis.

explained, this assessment takes place against the backdrop of the previous two inquiries and requires the court to evaluate the extent of both the benefit and the detriment.

The extent to which facts are explicitly acknowledged at this stage will depend partly on how a court structures its proportionality inquiry. In Canada, as foreshadowed earlier, the Supreme Court has tended to concentrate on the second stage of 'minimal impairment'.[129] More recently, however, it has placed a renewed emphasis on the final balancing stage of proportionality.[130] In *R v KRJ*, for example, the balancing stage was described as the 'essence of the proportionality enquiry' as it 'allows courts to stand back to determine on a normative basis whether a rights infringement is justified in a free and democratic society'.[131] In *KRJ* the balancing stage proved decisive, and the majority invalidated legislation that retrospectively expanded sentencing judges' discretion in relation to sex offenders. The Crown had adduced fresh evidence before the Supreme Court that consisted of statistics and social science articles relating to the recidivism of sexual offenders.[132] Justice Karakatsanis, writing for the majority, reviewed this material in the context of considering the deleterious and salutary effects of the legislation. Ultimately, she concluded that the Crown had failed to establish the '*degree of enhanced* protection' offered by the amendments (in comparison to the previous version of the legislation).[133] This, combined with the finding that the benefits to society were marginal and speculative, led to a conclusion that the balancing test was not met.[134]

In Germany, where balancing has assumed a prominent part in the proportionality inquiry, there is also more emphasis on facts at this stage. Again, the Federal Constitutional Court has at times been divided over how much harm needs to be established by way of evidence. In the *Second Headscarf Case* in 2015, for instance, a majority of the Federal Constitutional Court held that a general prohibition on teachers wearing headscarves was not compatible with their freedom of faith and freedom to profess a belief.[135] The majority held

[129] See the text accompanying n 31.

[130] It had earlier been suggested that the third stage was redundant; see Hogg (n 13) 23. However, this view was rejected by the Supreme Court: *Alberta v Hutterian Brethren of Wilson Colony* [2009] 2 SCR 567, 605–07 [75]–[77] (McLachlin CJ). See also S Weinrib, 'The Emergence of the Third Step of the *Oakes* Test in *Alberta v Hutterian Brethren of Wilson Colony*' (2010) 68 *University of Toronto Faculty of Law Review* 77.

[131] *R v KRJ* [2016] 1 SCR 906, 945–46 [79] (Karakatsanis J).

[132] ibid 939 [60]. This evidence was attached to affidavits.

[133] ibid 950 [89].

[134] The minority, in contrast, held that the majority had placed an 'evidentiary burden on the state that was impossible to satisfy'; see ibid 971 [141] (Brown J).

[135] *Second Headscarf Case*, Bundesverfassungsgericht [German Constitutional Court], 1 BvR 471/10, 1 BvR 1181/10, 27 January 2015 (Federal Constitutional Court trans, www.bverfg.de/e/rs20150127_1bvr047110en.html). See also *First Headscarf Case*, Bundesverfassungsgericht [German Constitutional Court], 2 BvR 1436/02, 24 September 2003 reported in (2003) 108 BVerfGE 282 (Federal Constitutional Court trans, www.bverfg.de/e/rs20030924_2bvr143602en.html). For some discussion, see G Taylor, 'Teachers' Religious Headscarves in German Constitutional Law' (2017) 6 *Oxford Journal of Law and Religion* 93.

that there needed to be a 'specific danger' and that this must be 'proven and substantiated'.[136] The wearing of a headscarf did not, in general, have the effect of promoting or proselytising a belief.[137] The minority, in contrast, considered that an 'abstract danger to the peace at school and the neutrality of the state' was sufficient to justify the prohibition.[138] The minority referred to statements given at parliamentary hearings and considered that these illustrated the importance of a uniform Land-wide prohibition even in the case of abstract danger.[139] Although some empirical material was relied upon, ultimately it seems that the decision rested on a different balancing of the interests at stake.[140]

The above analysis shows that in each jurisdiction, facts have been considered relevant to the three stages of proportionality reasoning and at times the courts have relied on empirical material to support their conclusions. There are some differences in terms of the degree to which the relevance of facts has been acknowledged, reflecting broader differences between the constitutional and procedural traditions of each system, including different approaches to constitutional interpretation.[141] In addition, there are signs of some variation at the three stages of proportionality analysis. While the courts appear relatively comfortable with referring to extrinsic materials at the suitability stage, there is more caution – and greater judicial disagreement – at the necessity and balancing stages. These differences tend to reflect different views about how much evidence is necessary to justify a restriction, how much weight should be afforded to the views of the other branches of government, and the appropriate limits of the judicial role.

## III. FINDING FACTS?

Given that all three jurisdictions have recognised, at least to some extent, that facts are relevant to assessments of proportionality, this section of the chapter considers *how* the courts have sought to establish these facts. This raises questions about how the courts will be informed of the relevant facts and also what degree of weight, or deference, should be accorded to the legislative branch.

### A. Informing the Court

The first possibility is that the court may seek to ascertain the relevant facts itself. In other words, the court will not simply accept the asserted justification

136 *Second Headscarf Case* (n 135) [116].
137 ibid.
138 ibid [9] (Separate Opinion of Justices Schluckebier and Hermanns).
139 ibid [16].
140 ibid [11].
141 For a brief overview of some of the relevant differences, see the discussion in ch 1, section III.C.

for the legislation or its effectiveness, but will review the evidence itself to reach a conclusion about the facts. This prompts consideration of how the court is to obtain the relevant empirical material, and how it can evaluate and test this material.

In terms of the processes by which empirical material is placed before the court, there is a clear division between the adversarial and inquisitorial systems. In Germany, as foreshadowed in the introduction, the Federal Constitutional Court is not limited to the material presented by the parties. The Court's governing legislation and rules of procedure equip it with considerable investigatory powers that enable it to expand the evidentiary record.[142] For instance, the Court is empowered to call for expert opinions to inform its resolution of constitutional questions.[143] The Court also benefits from Germany's strong tradition of research institutions, including the Max Planck Institutes, and there are several examples of the Court relying on the work of these institutions.[144]

In South Africa and Canada, by contrast, the courts largely follow the common law adversarial tradition. While this tradition is premised on the idea of party presentation of evidence, in both jurisdictions there have been some modifications that enable courts to receive a wider array of evidentiary material. In South Africa, for instance, the rules of the Constitutional Court permit a non-party with an 'interest in any matter before the Court' to apply to be admitted as an amicus curiae,[145] and both parties and amici curiae may adduce relevant factual material directly to the Court.[146] In Canada, similarly, interveners and amici curiae may seek leave to appear in constitutional matters and to adduce evidentiary material directly to the Supreme Court.[147] While factums (which consist of unsworn evidence) are primarily used in the Court's reference jurisdiction, at times a similar approach has been used in appellate cases.[148]

[142] See *Federal Constitutional Court Act* (n 58) §§26, 27. For some discussion, see PL Murray and R Stürner, *German Civil Justice* (Durham, NC, Carolina Academic Press, 2004) 415.

[143] *Federal Constitutional Court Act* (n 58) § 27a. See also *Rules of Procedure of the Federal Constitutional Court of 19 November 2014* (Federal Constitutional Court trans (2015), www.bundesverfassungsgericht.de/EN/Verfahren/Rechtsquellen/rechtsquellen_node.html) § 22(5). Note that such experts are not considered witnesses in the formal sense.

[144] J Hughes and V MacDonnell, 'Social Science Evidence in Constitutional Rights Cases in Germany and Canada: Some Comparative Observations' (2013) 32 *National Journal of Constitutional Law* 23, 39. See in particular Hughes and MacDonnell's discussion of the *Second Abortion Decision* (see n 186 below) at 48–49.

[145] *Rules of the Constitutional Court 2003* (South Africa), r 10. See also G Budlender, 'Amicus Curiae' in S Woolman, T Roux and M Bishop (eds), *Constitutional Law of South Africa*, 2nd edn (Cape Town, Juta) vol 1 (at 07-06) [8.3].

[146] *Rules of the Constitutional Court 2003* (South Africa), r 31.

[147] I Brodie, *Friends of the Court: The Privileging of Interest Group Litigants in Canada* (Albany, State University of New York Press, 2002) ch 2; BRD Alarie and AJ Green, 'Interventions at the Supreme Court of Canada: Accuracy, Affiliation, and Acceptance' (2010) 48 *Osgoode Hall Law Journal* 381; GD Callaghan, 'Intervenors at the Supreme Court of Canada' (2020) 44 *Dalhousie Law Journal* 33.

[148] PW Hogg, *Constitutional Law of Canada*, 5th edn (Toronto, Thomson Carswell, 2007) vol 2, 810–13 [60.2(b)]. Note also that the Supreme Court also has the power to enable affidavit evidence to be cross-examined: *Rules of the Supreme Court of Canada*, SOR/2002-156, r 90. But see Perryman (n 43) 173, who notes there is a 'strong continuing preference' for social science to be adduced at the trial level.

In the context of appellate matters, the Canadian Supreme Court has also considered the question of how to evaluate a trial judge's findings of legislative fact. While in some earlier cases the Court had suggested that findings of legislative fact made by trial judges may be entitled to a lesser degree of deference vis-a-vis findings of adjudicative fact,[149] more recently the Court has clarified that there is no different standard for different types of facts. The Court has confirmed that: 'Absent reviewable error in the trial judge's appreciation of the evidence, a court of appeal should not interfere with the trial judge's conclusions on social and legislative facts.'[150] It has also addressed the extent to which prior Supreme Court precedents can be distinguished or overruled on the basis of changing factual circumstances.[151]

In all three jurisdictions, therefore, there are specific procedural mechanisms that operate to expand the evidentiary material before the court. This is most explicit in Germany, where, as outlined above, the Federal Constitutional Court has express powers to supplement the evidentiary record.[152] In both South Africa and Canada, the use of interventions recognises that the issues adjudicated by the courts may extend beyond the knowledge or expertise of the immediate parties. Further, in both jurisdictions, the capacity to present additional evidentiary material directly to the Constitutional or Supreme Court recognises that there may have been no lower court decision or that the factual issues may not have been fully ventilated below. This practice, of presenting evidence directly to the appellate court, raises the difficulty of how courts are to test and evaluate such material.[153]

Canada and South Africa offer the most pertinent guidance for how empirical material can be scrutinised by the court.[154] In Canada, the Supreme Court has indicated that where the social science evidence is contested, it should be presented through an expert witness who can be cross-examined as to the value and weight of the expert reports.[155] Importantly, the Supreme Court has also sought to clarify the appropriate scope of judicial notice. In *R v Spence*, which concerned the right to a fair trial, the Court had to consider whether it was appropriate to take judicial notice of the fact that

[149] See, eg, *RJR-MacDonald* (n 86) 334 [141] (McLachlin J), 287 [80] (La Forest J); *Harper* (n 72) 883 [99] (Bastarache J).

[150] *Canada (Attorney-General) v Bedford* [2013] 3 SCR 1101, 1130 [49] (McLachlin CJ for the Court). See also *Carter v Canada (Attorney-General)* [2015] 1 SCR 331, 384 [109] (McLachlin CJ, LeBel, Abella, Rothstein, Cromwell, Moldaver, Karakatsanis, Wagner and Gascon JJ). See also Perryman (n 43) 127.

[151] See ch 7, nn 156 and 157 and accompanying text.

[152] See the text accompanying n 142 above.

[153] This problem is particularly acute at the appellate level, as in common law adversarial systems it is rare for appellate courts to hear witnesses.

[154] In Germany, the different institutional features and the inquisitorial nature of the proceedings make comparison in this regard more difficult.

[155] See, eg, *R v Malmo-Levine* [2003] 3 SCR 572, 599–600 [27]–[28] (Gonthier and Binnie JJ). See also Perryman (n 43) 152ff, who discusses the approach taken in Canada to evaluating the reliability of social science evidence.

jurors have a 'natural sympathy' for victims of the same race.[156] A majority of the Court confirmed that the scope of judicial notice should vary according to the nature of the issue under consideration. For adjudicative facts, a strict formulation of judicial notice was appropriate,[157] whereas for legislative facts – which were acknowledged to be 'laced with supposition, prediction, presumption, perception and wishful thinking' – the limits of judicial notice would be 'inevitably somewhat elastic'.[158] The scope of judicial notice would thus vary depending on the degree to which the legislative fact approached the 'dispositive issue' in the case.[159] When the fact was critical to the outcome, a strict approach should be taken and judicial notice should be kept 'on a relatively short leash'.[160] In contrast, for background facts the approach could be more relaxed. In between these two extremes, Binnie J proposed that:

> [A] court ought to ask itself whether such 'fact' would be accepted by reasonable people who have taken the trouble to inform themselves on the topic as not being the subject of reasonable dispute *for the particular purpose for which it is to be used*, keeping in mind that the need for reliability and trustworthiness increased directly with the centrality of the 'fact' to the disposition of the controversy.[161]

While the application of these principles does not always yield consistent results, the Court has at least attempted to provide guidance as to the appropriate dividing line between judicial notice and expert evidence.

Similarly, in South Africa, there has been some attempt to delineate the appropriate boundaries of judicial notice. Rule 31 of the Constitutional Court's rules provides that 'factual material' that is relevant to the determination of issues before the court may be judicially noticed if the facts are either (a) common cause or otherwise incontrovertible, or (b) of an official, scientific, technical or statistical nature capable of easy verification.[162] This rule is understood to apply to legislative facts; while it represents an expansion of the approach to the judicial notice of adjudicative facts,[163] it is not unlimited.[164]

[156] *R v Spence* [2005] 3 SCR 458.

[157] ibid 486–87 [53] (Binnie J), citing McLachlin CJ in *R v Find* [2001] 1 SCR 863. Under this strict formulation, the facts need to be either: (1) so notorious or generally accepted as not to be the subject of debate among reasonable persons; or (2) capable of immediate and accurate demonstration by resort to readily accessible sources of indisputable accuracy.

[158] *Spence* (n 156) 490–91 [63].

[159] ibid 490 [61].

[160] ibid 491 [64]. The Court endorsed the 'strict' Morgan criteria, based on the approach of EM Morgan, 'Judicial Notice' (1944) 57 *Harvard Law Review* 269.

[161] *Spence* (n 156) 491–92 [65]. For criticism of the Court's restrictive approach, see R Agarwal and F Lalani, 'Noting the Obvious: A Reflection on the Supreme Court of Canada's Application of Judicial Notice under Sections 7 and 15 of the *Charter*' (2016) 35 *National Journal of Constitutional Law* 131.

[162] *Rules of the Constitutional Court 2003* (South Africa), r 31.

[163] *S v Lawrence; S v Negal; S v Solberg* [1997] 4 SA 1176, [25] (Constitutional Court); *Hoffman v South African Airways* [2001] 1 SA 1, [3] (Constitutional Court); PJ Schwikkard and SE van der Merwe, *Principles of Evidence*, 4th edn (Cape Town, Juta, 2016) 531.

[164] See, eg, *In re Certain Amicus Curiae Applications: Minister of Health v Treatment Action Campaign* [2002] 5 SA 713, [10]–[11] (Constitutional Court); *Prince 2002* (n 54) [11]; *Mabaso v Law Society of the Northern Provinces* [2005] 2 SA 117, [45] (Constitutional Court).

## B. Deference to the Legislature

A related question is that of deference or restraint. In other words, when it comes to questions of fact underpinning proportionality reasoning, how much weight should a court give to the empirical assessments made by other branches of government?[165] Proportionality, as explained in the previous chapters, is a variable standard of review, and for this reason it is said to go 'hand in hand' with the question of deference.[166] According weight, or respect, to the decisions of other branches of government is generally justified on two grounds: normative and empirical. Normative deference recognises the legislature's superior democratic legitimacy, whereas empirical deference recognises that the decision-maker's superior institutional competence or expertise.[167] It is the second of these forms of deference that is likely to be most relevant when it comes to the factual elements of proportionality reasoning.

In Germany, the Federal Constitutional Court has developed a doctrine of *Einschätzungsprärogative* or 'prerogative of judgment' which applies to questions of future prognosis.[168] Under this doctrine, the Court grants the legislature a margin of appreciation for making the relevant factual prognosis.[169] Although this latitude is not typically described in terms of judicial deference, it operates to increase or decrease the amount of political discretion.[170] Under this approach, the Court will defer to the legislature's assessment where this is based on a 'prognosis of societal or technical development, or the effectiveness of new and untested measures'.[171] For example, in the *Cannabis Case*, the Court noted that the uncertain state of the scientific knowledge meant that the legislature had a 'prerogative of forming a view and making a decision' when choosing between alternatives.[172] The level of scrutiny that the Court applies as part of its proportionality test[173] can be diluted by according a wide margin for

[165] This is discussed further in ch 7, section I.B.iii.

[166] *Handyside v UK* (1979–80) 1 EHRR 737, 754 [49]. See also A Kavanagh, *Constitutional Review under the UK Human Rights Act* (Cambridge, Cambridge University Press, 2009) 237.

[167] See, eg, M Elliott, 'Proportionality and Deference: The Importance of a Structured Approach' in C Forsyth et al (eds), *Effective Judicial Review: A Cornerstone of Good Governance* (Oxford, Oxford University Press, 2010) 269; R Alexy, *A Theory of Constitutional Rights*, reprinted edn (J Rivers trans, Oxford, Oxford University Press, 2010) 393, 414–15.

[168] M Martin and A Horne, 'Proportionality: Principles and Pitfalls – Some Lessons from Germany' [2008] *Judicial Review* 169, 175; D Lovric, *Deference to the Legislature in WTO Challenges to Legislation* (Alphen aan den Rijn, Kluwer Law International, 2010) 70 fn 44; K Meßerschmidt, 'The Race to Rationality Review and the Score of the German Federal Constitutional Court' (2012) 6 *Legisprudence* 347, 366.

[169] Grimm (n 14) 390–91.

[170] Möllers (n 59) 14; O Lepsius, 'Constitutional Review of Tax Laws and the Unconstitutionality of the German Inheritance Tax' (2015) 16 *German Law Journal* 1191, 1209.

[171] Martin and Horne (n 168) 175.

[172] *Cannabis Case*, Bundesverfassungsgericht [German Constitutional Court], 2 BvL 43/92, 9 March 1994, reported in (1994) 90 BVerfGE 145 (Michael Jewell trans, http://germanlawarchive.iuscomp.org/?p=85) [183].

[173] See discussion at the text accompanying n 33 above.

factual prognosis.[174] Although the Court has sought to articulate factors that affect the extent of the legislature's prognostic freedom, such as the subject matter, the level of uncertainty, and the interests at stake,[175] it has been suggested that in practice these 'vague' factors provide little real guidance.[176]

In Canada, too, as foreshadowed above, there has also disagreement about the appropriate weight to be accorded to the other branches of government. In *Harper*, for instance, the Court divided over the validity of the provision imposing limits on third-party spending on election advertising.[177] While all members of the Court agreed that the lower courts had erroneously required proof that the stated objective (promoting fair elections) was pressing and substantial,[178] the Court disagreed over the appropriate level of deference. For the minority, the lack of evidence was critical, as the dangers suggested were 'wholly hypothetical'[179] and the Attorney-General had failed to demonstrate that the 'draconian' limits imposed were justified.[180] In contrast, the majority judgment considered that the context of the case, and the impossibility of scientifically measuring the harm, favoured a 'deferential approach'.[181] Under this approach, 'a reasoned apprehension that the absence of third party election advertising limits will lead to election unfairness' was sufficient.[182]

As this brief discussion illustrates, deference is rarely an all-or-nothing-affair. In other words, the courts will rarely, if at all, defer entirely to the legislative branch, nor will they simply substitute their own findings of fact with total disregard of the legislature's position. The critical question will be *how much* scrutiny of the legislature is warranted. In the context of assessing questions of proportionality, this may extend to scrutinising the *processes* by which the legislature arrived at its factual findings. It might involve, for instance, inquiring into the nature of the evidence before the legislature, and whether the legislature relied on consultations, investigations or studies.[183] This form of review is sometimes described as 'process review' or 'semi-procedural' review, as it 'requires the legislature to convince the court that the law was indeed enacted on the basis of its superior expertise or democratic credentials'.[184]

[174] For some discussion, see Lepsius (n 170) 1211. See also D Bilchitz, 'Necessity and Proportionality: Towards a Balanced Approach?' in L Lazarus, C McCrudden and N Bowles (eds), *Reasoning Rights: Comparative Judicial Engagement* (Oxford, Hart Publishing, 2014) 46–48.

[175] See *Cannabis Case* (n 172) 173.

[176] Bilchitz (n 174) 48; Petersen (n 32) 126.

[177] *Harper* (n 72).

[178] ibid 844–45 [25] (McLachlin CJ and Major J), 881 [93] (Bastarache J).

[179] ibid 847 [34] (McLachlin CJ and Major J).

[180] ibid 849 [39].

[181] ibid 879 [88] (Bastarache J).

[182] ibid.

[183] I Bar-Siman-Tov, 'Semiprocedural Judicial Review' (2012) 6 *Legisprudence* 271, 274. In the UK context, see A Kavanagh, 'Proportionality and Parliamentary Debates: Exploring Some Forbidden Territory' (2014) 34 *Oxford Journal of Legal Studies* 443.

[184] P Popelier, 'Preliminary Comments on the Role of Courts as Regulatory Watchdogs' (2012) 6 *Legisprudence* 257, 267 (citation omitted).

Examples of this approach can be seen in Germany, where the Federal Constitutional Court has required the Parliament not only to develop but also to maintain a proper factual foundation for its legislative action.[185] For instance, in the *Second Abortion Case* of 1993, the Court emphasised the need for the government to have an empirical record and held that failing to keep statistics on pregnancy terminations could not be reconciled with the 'duty of protection'.[186] As a consequence, a change to the Penal Law that dispensed with the need to maintain statistics was held to be invalid.[187] A similar approach can be seen in the Court's successive decisions on the parental custody of unmarried parents. While in 2003 the Court was prepared to act upon the basis of certain assumptions about custody arrangements,[188] when the issue came before the Court again in 2010, the Court held that there was sufficient data available to indicate that the legislature's assumptions in 2003 had been incorrect.[189]

In the case of *Hartz IV*, the Court's review of the factual basis for the legislation extended to interrogating the procedures followed by the legislature.[190] In that case, the Court had to assess the constitutionality of certain reforms to the German welfare system.[191] Although the right to human dignity is in theory an absolute right, which allows no limitation, in practice the Court scrutinised the reasonableness of the legislation.[192] The Court defined its task as

[185] Meßerschmidt (n 168) 356; Hughes and MacDonnell (n 144) 55; Möllers (n 59) 14.

[186] *Second Abortion Case*, Bundesverfassungsgericht [German Constitutional Court], 2 BvF 2/90; 2 BvF 4/92; 2 BvF 5/92, 28 May 1993, reported in (1993) 88 BVerfGE 203 (Federal Constitutional Court trans, www.bverfg.de/e/fs19930528_2bvf000290en.html) [299].

[187] ibid [302].

[188] *Parental Custody Decision*, Bundesverfassungsgericht [German Constitutional Court], 1 BvL 20/99, 1 BvR 933/01, 29 January 2003, reported in (2003) 107 BVerfGE 150 (Federal Constitutional Court trans, *Decisions of the Bundesverfassungsgericht – Federal Constitutional Court – Federal Republic of Germany* (Nomos Verlagsgesellchaft, 2013) vol 5, 611).

[189] *Parental Custody Decision II*, Bundesverfassungsgericht [German Constitutional Court], 1 BvR 420/09, 21 July 2010, reported in (2010) 127 BVerfGE 132 (Federal Constitutional Court trans, bverfg.de/e/rs20100721_1bvr042009en.html) [61].

[190] *Hartz IV*, Bundesverfassungsgericht [German Constitutional Court], 1 BvL 1/09, 1 BvL 3/09, 1 BvL 4/09, 9 February 2010, reported in (2010) 125 BVerfGE 175 (Federal Constitutional Court trans, www.bverfg.de/e/ls20100209_1bvl000109en.html).

[191] These were challenged on the basis that they violated the fundamental right to guarantee a subsistence minimum that accorded with human dignity (art 1(1)) and also the principle of the social state (art 20(1)).

[192] *Hartz IV* (n 190) [141]–[144]. See the discussion by Williams, who analyses how the Court repeatedly resorted to a 'standard of reasonableness or justification': LA Williams, 'The Role of Courts in the Quantitative-Implementation of Social and Economic Rights: A Comparative Study' [2010] *Constitutional Court Review* 141, 159 fn 61. In this way, as Williams notes (at 185), the Court imported considerations of proportionality. *cf* K Meßerschmidt, 'The Good Shepherd of Karlsruhe: The "*Hartz IV*" Decision on Unemployment Benefits and Social Allowances – A Good Example of Regulatory Review by the German Federal Constitutional Court?' in P Popelier, A Mazmanyan and W Vandenbruwaene (eds), *The Role of Constitutional Courts in Multilevel Governance* (Cambridge, Intersentia, 2013) 244; S Gardbaum, 'Positive and Horizontal Rights: Proportionality's Next Frontier or a Bridge Too Far?' in VC Jackson and M Tushnet (eds), *Proportionality: New Frontiers, New Challenges* (Cambridge, Cambridge University Press, 2017) 235.

determining whether the benefits were 'evidently insufficient'[193] and considered that this required a 'review of the basis and of the method of assessment of benefits in terms of whether they do justice to the goal of the fundamental right'.[194] Accordingly, it required the legislature to disclose the facts on which it had acted and the methods it had used for its calculations.[195] The Court found several major defects in the legislature's processes in determining the reductions in expenditure, the projection of cost-of-living increases and the amount of benefits payable to children.[196] While the Court refrained from quantifying the minimum level of support that had to be provided by the State, it held that the legislation in question was unconstitutional.[197]

## IV. CONCLUSION

This chapter has demonstrated that in Germany, Canada and South Africa, the courts have recognised that the application of proportionality reasoning may depend on facts. This confirms the conceptual understanding of proportionality that was developed in Chapter 2. While this recognition of facts has been most explicit in Canada, where the Supreme Court in *Oakes* adopted a fact-sensitive approach to section 1 of the *Charter*, in all three jurisdictions there are examples of the courts relying on empirical material in their assessments of proportionality. Such extrinsic material is potentially relevant to all three aspects of the proportionality inquiry, but there are signs of some differences emerging at the various stages. Where courts are required to make future-oriented or hypothetical judgments, for instance, there have been some concerns that these types of judgment exceed the proper limits of the court's role. This chapter has also explored the question of how the courts in each jurisdiction have sought to ascertain the relevant facts and, in doing so, has considered the question of deference. This comparative experience is useful in identifying some of the key issues that need to be resolved in Australia, including institutional questions about the scope of the judicial role and procedural questions about how facts can be ascertained. Against this background, the next two chapters turn to examine proportionality and facts in Australian constitutional adjudication.

[193] *Hartz IV* (n 190) [141].
[194] ibid [142].
[195] ibid [144]. Note that the *Hartz IV* case came to the Federal Constitutional Court by way of a referral from several lower courts. The Court received submissions from a number of bodies such as the Federal Statistical Office, the German Confederation of Trade Unions, the German Association for Public and Private Welfare, and the German Caritas Association, and also held an oral hearing, which is relatively rare.
[196] *Hartz IV* (n 190) [171], [186], [191]. For a detailed explanation, see Williams (n 192).
[197] The legislature was given time to amend its legislation.

# 5

# *Proportionality in Australian Constitutional Law*

IN CONTRAST TO the position elsewhere, in Australia proportionality arrived rather late and remains contested. Although for the last few decades judges have flirted with the notion of proportionality, the High Court has traditionally preferred to frame its tests of constitutional validity in terms of the language of 'appropriate and adapted'. In late 2015, however, a majority of the Court in *McCloy v New South Wales*[1] adopted a structured three-part test of proportionality in the context of the implied freedom of political communication. This new test has been subject to considerable criticism and some revision, and the extent of its application remains uncertain. In light of this, this chapter assesses and explains the current status of proportionality in Australian constitutional law, examining the various different tests that have been adopted by the High Court.

The chapter proceeds in three main steps. Section I traces the genealogy of proportionality in Australian constitutional law. It shows that while the development of proportionality forms of reasoning has been informed by its use in other jurisdictions, until recently the High Court has avoided committing to an explicit test of structured proportionality. Instead, as section II explains, the Court has developed a series of different tests that apply in different contexts. This section examines the extent to which these tests can be seen to incorporate the three stages of structured proportionality. Finally, section III evaluates the current place of proportionality in Australia by examining some of the differences and reservations that continue to divide the Court. This analysis paves the way for an examination, in Chapter 6, of the place of facts within proportionality reasoning in Australia.

[1] *McCloy v New South Wales* (2015) 257 CLR 178.

## I. THE AUSTRALIAN ADOPTION OF PROPORTIONALITY

In the landmark case of *Commonwealth v Tasmania*, in the course of considering the application of the external affairs power in section 51(xxix) of the *Australian Constitution*,[2] Deane J remarked:

> Implicit in the requirement that a law be capable of being reasonably considered to be appropriate and adapted to achieving what is said to provide it with the character of a law with respect to external affairs is a need for there to be a *reasonable proportionality* between the designated purpose or object and the means which the law embodies for achieving or procuring it.[3]

In this passage Deane J appears to equate the language of 'appropriate and adapted'[4] – which has long been used to determine constitutional validity – with the concept of 'proportionality'. From here, proportionality has gained a foothold in Australian constitutional law, and both courts and commentators have tended to trace the introduction of proportionality as a distinct concept to Deane J's judgment in the *Tasmanian Dam Case*.[5] It is now widely acknowledged that proportionality reasoning *of some form* has a role in two distinct areas of constitutional law: first, in relation to the characterisation of laws with respect to certain heads of Commonwealth legislative power; and, second, in determining the limits of express and implied constitutional guarantees.[6] Until recently, however, the Court has preferred to frame its tests by using the language of 'appropriate and adapted', and there has been considerable division and uncertainty around the extent to which these existing tests are analogous to, or incorporate, elements of the tripartite test of proportionality.[7]

When Deane J used the expression 'reasonable proportionality' in the *Tasmanian Dam Case*, it was by no means clear that he was seeking to import the structured formula of proportionality into Australian law. The actual test

[2] *Commonwealth of Australia Constitution Act 1900* (Imp) 63 & 64 Vict, c 12, s 9 (hereinafter '*Australian Constitution*').

[3] *Commonwealth v Tasmania* (1983) 158 CLR 1, 260 (emphasis added) (hereinafter '*Tasmanian Dam Case*').

[4] The language of 'appropriate and adapted' is generally considered to have been borrowed from the US case of *McCulloch v Maryland* 17 US 159 (1819); see *Mulholland v Australian Electoral Commission* (2004) 220 CLR 181, 199 [39] (Gleeson CJ).

[5] See, eg, *Minister for Resources v Dover Fisheries* (1993) 43 FCR 565, 576 (Gummow J) (hereinafter '*Dover Fisheries*'); J Kirk, 'Constitutional Guarantees, Characterisation and the Concept of Proportionality' (1997) 21 *Melbourne University Law Review* 1, 2.

[6] HP Lee, 'Proportionality in Australian Constitutional Adjudication' in G Lindell (ed), *Future Directions in Australian Constitutional Law: Essays in Honour of Professor Leslie Zines* (Sydney, Federation Press, 1994).

[7] See further the discussion in section II.B below.

endorsed by Deane J, and a majority of the Court, was that in order for a law to be supported by the external affairs power, it must be 'capable of being reasonably considered to be appropriate and adapted to achieving what is said to impress it with the character of a law with respect to external affairs'.[8] Rather than seeking to modify the 'appropriate and adapted' test, it appears that Deane J was using 'proportionality' in a more general sense. When used in this more general sense, proportionality seeks to evaluate legislative ends in light of their *fit* with the means adopted to pursue those ends. It does not involve discrete stages or tiers of analysis. Justice Deane illustrated this more general use of proportionality by what he termed an 'extravagant example': a hypothetical law that required all sheep in Australia to be killed to prevent the spread of disease.[9] Such a law, he considered, could not be characterised as a law with respect to external affairs simply because Australia had an international obligation requiring it to take measures to safeguard against the spread of sheep disease.[10] The hypothetical law went too far, meaning that there would be a lack of 'reasonable proportionality' between the law and the objective.[11] Although Deane J highlighted the need to examine the relationship between the law and its purpose – a relationship which, as explained in Chapter 2, is central to proportionality reasoning – the inquiry was not broken down into separate or sequential stages. So, while Deane J may have introduced the language of proportionality in the constitutional context, he did not seek to change the existing test or to introduce a structured formula of proportionality.

Second, Deane J's reference to proportionality, in the sense of directing an inquiry into the connection between a law and its purpose, was not a novel one in Australian law in 1983. The High Court had already adopted a somewhat similar test in the context of reviewing delegated legislation.[12] In 1933 in *Williams v Melbourne Corporation*, when considering whether a

[8] *Tasmanian Dam Case* (n 3) 259. A majority of the Court held that the *National Parks and Wildlife Conservation Act 1983* (Cth) and regulations made pursuant to this Act could be characterised as laws with respect to 'external affairs' pursuant to s 51(xxix) of the *Australian Constitution* (Mason, Murphy, Brennan and Deane JJ; Gibbs CJ, Wilson and Dawson JJ dissenting). Note that it had long been recognised that for a law to be authorised under the external affairs power, it must conform to the treaty being implemented; see *R v Burgess; Ex parte Henry (No 2)* (1936) 55 CLR 608, 645–46, 659–60, 674–75, 688; *R v Poole; Ex parte Henry* (1939) 61 CLR 634, 644, 647–48, 655–56; *Airlines of NSW Pty Ltd v New South Wales (No 2)* (1965) 113 CLR 54, 86, 125–26, 136. In some of these cases there are signs of the emergence of the language of 'appropriate and adapted', which is now a central part of the test of validity.

[9] *Tasmanian Dam Case* (n 3) 260.

[10] ibid.

[11] ibid.

[12] Note that in the context of reviewing the validity of delegated legislation, the concept of proportionality has often arisen in combination with a requirement of 'reasonableness'; see D Pearce and S Argument, *Delegated Legislation in Australia*, 5th edn (Sydney, LexisNexis Butterworths, 2017) 351 [21.1]; M Aronson, M Groves and G Weeks, *Judicial Review of Administrative Action and Government Liability*, 6th edn (Sydney, Thomson Reuters, 2017) 376 [6.490]. For a detailed account, see *Vanstone v Clark* (2005) 147 FCR 299, 337 [141]ff (Weinberg J).

by-law was within power, Dixon J noted that in some cases the 'true character' of the by-law may reveal that 'it could not reasonably have been adopted as a means of attaining the ends of the power'.[13] Although Dixon J did not use the language of 'appropriate and adapted' or 'proportionality', in later cases the Court has sought to draw parallels between these expressions and Dixon J's formulation. In *South Australia v Tanner*, for instance, the test of validity for delegated legislation was described as the 'reasonable proportionality' test enunciated in the *Tasmanian Dam Case*: 'whether the regulation is capable of being considered to be reasonably proportionate to the pursuit of the enabling purpose'.[14] The substance of this test was considered to be '[t]he same' as that articulated by Dixon J in *Williams*, notwithstanding the differences in wording.[15] Therefore, there appears to be some merging of the tests of 'reasonable proportionality' and 'capable of being reasonably considered appropriate and adapted'. This conflation of the two expressions was noted by French CJ in *Attorney-General (South Australia) v Adelaide City Corporation*, who described the 'proportionality test' as being 'formulated by Dixon J in *Williams*, adopted by Deane J in the *Tasmanian Dam Case*, and accepted in *Tanner*'.[16] Despite this degree of convergence, it has also been observed that the approach to be taken with respect to delegated legislation is not identical to that used when determining constitutional validity.[17]

It is also not apparent that in the *Tasmanian Dam Case* Deane J was intending to transplant the particular, European version of structured proportionality into Australian law when he used the term 'proportionality'. He did not cite any European cases to support his reference to proportionality and he did not appear to draw specifically upon the concept as it is used in other jurisdictions.[18] It is in

[13] *Williams v Melbourne Corporation* (1933) 49 CLR 142, 155. See also *Shanahan v Scott* (1957) 96 CLR 245, 250 (Dixon CJ, Williams, Webb and Fullagar JJ); *Dover Fisheries* (n 5), 577–78 (Gummow J). Dixon J's formulation in *Williams* has been described as a 'rudimentary form of proportionality review', but one that extends into the substance of delegated legislation: A Edgar, 'Judicial Review of Delegated Legislation: Why Favour Substantive Review over Procedural Review?' in J Bell, M Elliott, JNE Varuhas and P Murray (eds), *Public Law Adjudication in Common Law Systems: Process and Substance* (Oxford, Hart Publishing, 2016) 201.

[14] *South Australia v Tanner* (1989) 166 CLR 161, 165 (Wilson, Dawson, Toohey and Gaudron JJ) (hereinafter '*Tanner*'). There was, as Allars notes, no suggestion in *Tanner* that the concept had been transplanted from Europe: M Allars, 'Proportionality, Tradition and Constitutional Framework: Borrowing Foreign Legal Notions in Australian Public Law' in G Doeker-Mach and KA Ziegert (eds), *Law and Legal Culture in Comparative Perspective* (Stuttgart, Franz Steiner Verlag, 2004) 294, 298.

[15] *Tanner* (n 14) 165 (Wilson, Dawson, Toohey and Gaudron JJ).

[16] *Attorney-General (South Australia) v Adelaide City Corporation* (2013) 249 CLR 1, 40 [60] (hereinafter '*Adelaide City Corporation*').

[17] See, eg, *Dover Fisheries* (n 5) 577; *Tanner* (n 14) 173–74 (Brennan J).

[18] It may be that Deane J's introduction of proportionality was influenced by his commitment to the protection of individual liberty: H Roberts, 'A Mirror to the Man – Reflecting on Justice William Deane: A Private Man in Public Office' (2011) 32 *Adelaide Law Review* 17, 32, 37–40. See also Allars (n 14) 299.

both later cases[19] and in the academic commentary[20] that Deane J's use of the term has been attributed to the European concept of proportionality, including some reference to cases from other jurisdictions.[21] These acknowledgements of the European origins of proportionality have, however, typically not been cast in a positive light. Justice Dawson in particular was critical of adopting the concept in the Australian setting, expressing concern that proportionality required judges to make quasi-legislative judgments that descended into merits review.[22]

As this brief historical survey indicates, from at least the 1980s onwards, the specific language of proportionality has been part of Australian constitutional law. Its development is intertwined with a parallel development in the context of determining the validity of delegated legislation. In the constitutional context, after Deane J's reference to 'reasonable proportionality' in the *Tasmanian Dam Case*, similar language was picked up in the implied rights jurisprudence that emerged in the 1990s.[23] In these early iterations, however, the term was still used in a general sense of interrogating the relationship between legislative means and ends. Although the existing tests arguably incorporated some aspects of the three-part formula of proportionality,[24] there remained some caution about developing a more structured test of proportionality.

## II. THE DEVELOPMENT OF PROPORTIONALITY

### A. The Development of Different Tests

As indicated above, it is now widely accepted that *some form* of proportionality arises in two distinct areas of constitutional law: the characterisation of laws with respect to certain heads of Commonwealth legislative power and in determining the limits of express and implied constitutional guarantees.[25] In relation to the first category, proportionality only has a recognised role where characterisation depends on purpose (such as in relation to the defence power

[19] For instance, in *Dover Fisheries*, Gummow J noted that the concept of '"reasonable proportionality" as a criterion for assessment of validity in constitutional and administrative law appears to have entered the stream of the common law through Europe and, in particular, from the jurisprudence of the Court of Justice of the European Communities and the European Court of Human Rights': *Dover Fisheries* (n 5) 575.

[20] See, eg, Kirk (n 5); Lee (n 6); B Selway, 'The Rise and Rise of the Reasonable Proportionality Test in Public Law' (1996) 7 *Public Law Review* 212.

[21] See, eg, *Cunliffe v Commonwealth* (1994) 182 CLR 272, 356–57 (Dawson J); *Leask v Commonwealth* (1996) 187 CLR 579, 594 (Brennan CJ), 600–601 (Dawson J). As pointed out in ch 1, proportionality has a longer history in the common law than is often recognised; see ch 1, n 10.

[22] *Cunliffe* (n 21) 356–57; *Leask* (n 21) 600–05; *Victoria v Commonwealth* (1996) 187 CLR 416, 572 (hereinafter '*Industrial Relations Act Case*'). For some discussion, see Allars (n 14) 303ff.

[23] See, eg, *Nationwide News Pty Ltd v Wills* (1992) 177 CLR 1, 29, 94; *Australian Capital Television Pty Ltd v Commonwealth* (1992) 177 CLR 106, 143–44, 157–58 (hereinafter '*ACTV*').

[24] This is discussed further below.

[25] See, eg, Kirk (n 5); Lee (n 6).

and the treaty implementation aspect of the external affairs power). In relation to the second category, questions of proportionality arise most prominently in the context of section 92 of the *Australian Constitution*, the implied freedom of political communication and the implied right to vote.[26] As foreshadowed earlier, in all of these areas, the High Court has traditionally framed the test of validity by using the language of 'appropriate and adapted' rather than 'proportionality'. While most of the existing literature on this topic is organised in terms of discrete areas of constitutional law,[27] this section analyses the various different tests that have been developed by the Court across a range of areas. It focuses on the differences between the various tests and the degree to which each formulation might be seen to import varying levels of scrutiny.

### *i. Reasonably Capable of Being Considered Appropriate and Adapted*

In the context of constitutional characterisation, the Court has so far rejected any general role for proportionality. The majority of the heads of power in section 51 of the *Australian Constitution* are 'subject-matter' powers and the dominant view is that proportionality does not arise when determining whether a law is made 'with respect' to one of these subject matters.[28] However, it has been acknowledged that proportionality plays a role in respect of the characterisation of purposive powers (such as the defence power),[29] powers that have a purposive element (such as the implementation of treaties under the external affairs power)[30] and, more controversially, the incidental aspects of a power.[31]

[26] As noted in ch 1 (at n 43), although a number of other areas of constitutional law contain nascent elements of proportionality reasoning, in these fields proportionality has not yet been as developed as it is in the areas under consideration in this book.

[27] See, eg, BF Fitzgerald, 'Proportionality and Australian Constitutionalism' (1993) 12 *University of Tasmania Law Review* 263; Lee (n 6); Kirk (n 5); A Mason, 'The Use of Proportionality in Australian Constitutional Law' (2016) 27 *Public Law Review* 109; S Chordia, *Proportionality in Australian Constitutional Law* (Sydney, Federation Press, 2020).

[28] The test to be applied for subject-matter powers is one of 'sufficient connection'; see *Re Dingjan; Ex parte Wagner* (1995) 183 CLR 323, 369; *Grain Pool of Western Australia v Commonwealth* (2002) 202 CLR 479, 492.

[29] Note that in a series of cases during the Second World War, Starke J (in dissent) held that defence was a subject-matter power; see, eg, *Victorian Chamber of Manufacturers v Commonwealth* (1943) 67 CLR 347, 381; *Australian Woollen Mills v Commonwealth* (1944) 69 CLR 476, 490–91. However, the dominant view is that the defence power is a purposive power: *Thomas v Mowbray* (2007) 233 CLR 307, [135] 359 (Gummow and Crennan JJ), [221] 384 (Kirby J), [425] 453 (Hayne J).

[30] See, eg, *Tasmanian Dam Case* (n 3) 260; *Richardson v Forestry Commission* (1988) 164 CLR 261, 311–12, 346; *Industrial Relations Act Case* (n 22) 487–88.

[31] Note, however, that this has been the subject of considerable debate and disagreement within the Court. See, eg, *Nationwide* (n 23) 30–31 (Mason CJ), *cf* 88–89 (Dawson J); *Cunliffe* (n 21) 296–97 (Mason CJ), 320–21 (Brennan J), *cf* 351 (Dawson J); *Leask* (n 21) 591–93 (Brennan CJ), 605 (Dawson J), 616–17 (McHugh J); *Plaintiff S156/2013 v Minister for Immigration and Border Protection* (2014) 254 CLR 28, 45 [36] (French CJ, Hayne, Crennan, Kiefel, Bell and Keane JJ). Most recently in *Spence v Queensland* (2019) 93 ALJR 643, the majority noted that the use of proportionality in the context of characterisation has been criticised and seemed to endorse a more limited use of proportionality (at 665 [63]). See also J Stellios, *Zines's The High Court and the Constitution*, 6th edn (Sydney, Federation Press, 2015) 56–63; Chordia (n 27) 130.

Although the Court has not always been consistent with its language, when dealing with the characterisation of purposive powers, it has tended to frame the relevant test as whether the law is 'reasonably capable of being considered appropriate and adapted'.[32] A similar formulation has been used when assessing the validity of delegated legislation.[33] In the constitutional sphere, there has been some acknowledgement that this formulation is different from the alternative formulation of 'reasonably appropriate and adapted' (which tends to be used in the context of constitutional guarantees).[34] As Mason CJ observed in *Cunliffe v Commonwealth*:

> In the case of the implication, as with a constitutional guarantee, this question is simply whether the burden or restriction is reasonably appropriate and adapted, in the court's judgment, to the legitimate end in view. In the context of whether a law is within power, the question is whether the law is capable of being reasonably considered to be appropriate and adapted to the end sought to be achieved.[35]

This view, that there is a distinction between the two expressions, has been explained in terms of the level of scrutiny that is involved. For instance, when applying the 'capable of' formulation, the Court has emphasised that it is not entitled simply to substitute its own view of what is appropriate. In *Richardson v Forestry Commission*, Deane J explained:

> In my view, it is not necessary for this Court to be persuaded that the particular provisions are, in fact, appropriate and adapted to the designated purpose or object. That is a matter for the Parliament. Obviously, the relevant requirement will be satisfied if the Court is so persuaded. As I have indicated however, it will, in my view, suffice if it appears to the Court that the relevant provisions are capable of being reasonably considered to be so appropriate and adapted.[36]

Similarly, in *Coleman v Power*, McHugh J appeared to accept that this test was 'more deferential to the judgment of the legislature' than the test of 'reasonably appropriate and adapted'.[37] In the *Adelaide City Corporation* case, which concerned whether certain by-laws made by the City of Adelaide were within the relevant by-law-making power *and* whether they contravened

[32] See, eg, *Polyukhovich v Commonwealth* (1991) 172 CLR 501, 697 (Gaudron J); *Industrial Relations Act Case* (n 22) 487 (Brennan CJ, Toohey, Gaudron, McHugh and Gummow JJ). Note that at times the test has been phrased as whether the law is 'capable of being reasonably considered to be appropriate and adapted'. See, eg, *Tasmanian Dams Case* (n 3) 260 (Deane J); *Cunliffe* (n 21) 300 (Mason CJ).

[33] See the discussion in section I, above.

[34] Whether or not these different formulations make a practical difference in terms of outcomes has been doubted: S McDonald, 'Involuntary Detention and the Separation of Judicial Power' (2007) 35 *Federal Law Review* 1, 28.

[35] *Cunliffe* (n 21) 300.

[36] *Richardson* (n 30) 312.

[37] *Coleman v Power* (2004) 220 CLR 1, 48 [87]. See also Gummow and Hayne JJ at 78 [196] who also rejected the submission that the second *Lange* question should be 'weakened' by being framed as 'reasonably capable of being seen as appropriate and adapted'.

the implied freedom of political communication, French CJ explicitly recognised that the different tests entailed different levels of judicial scrutiny.[38] In the context of delegated legislation made in furtherance of a purposive power, French CJ followed the approach of *Tanner* and confirmed a test of 'reasonable proportionality'.[39] This test required an assessment of whether the by-law 'is, or is capable of being, a reasonable and proportionate … exercise of the by-law making power'.[40] This test was described as 'a development of the of the high threshold "unreasonableness" test derived from the nineteenth century English authorities'.[41] In other words, this test involved a low level of judicial scrutiny, requiring only a 'rational relationship between the purpose for which the power is conferred and the laws made in furtherance of that purpose'.[42]

In the context of assessing the validity of delegated legislation, there are some signs of a more structured test of proportionality emerging.[43] As explained above, the High Court has traditionally expressed the test in terms of whether the delegated legislation is 'capable of being considered to be reasonably proportionate' to achieve the purpose of the enabling legislation.[44] The High Court has not, when applying this test, typically applied a structured or tiered form of proportionality analysis. However, in the case of *Brett Cattle Co Pty Ltd v Minister for Agriculture, Fisheries and Forestry*, Rares J in the Federal Court introduced the elements of 'suitability', 'necessity' and 'adequacy of balance' when assessing the validity of a ministerial ban on live exports made pursuant to Commonwealth legislation.[45] In doing so, he followed the approach of the High Court developed in *McCloy*,[46] notwithstanding the different settings involved.[47] Whether or not this approach, which involves a higher level of judicial scrutiny, is appropriate when reviewing delegated legislation remains the subject of debate.[48]

[38] *Adelaide City Corporation* (n 16) 40–42 [59]–[62].

[39] ibid 39 [58]. The other members of the Court adopted slightly different formulations of the relevant test: see 59 [123] (Hayne J), 69 [155] (Heydon J, in dissent), 83–84 [198]–[201] (Crennan and Kiefel JJ), 90 [224] (Bell J).

[40] ibid 32 [43] (French CJ).

[41] ibid 39 [58]. See also *Tajjour v New South Wales* (2014) 254 CLR 508, 549 [35] (French CJ).

[42] *Adelaide City Corporation* (n 16) 39–40 [58]. This was distinguished from the test of 'reasonably appropriate and adapted' (applicable in the context of the implied freedom), which was described by French CJ as a 'lower threshold' test (at 41 [62]).

[43] For example, in *Adelaide City Corporation* (n 16), Crennan and Kiefel JJ appeared to conflate the test for delegated legislation with that for laws burdening the implied freedom (at 84 [201]).

[44] See, eg, *Tanner* (n 14) 165 (Wilson, Dawson, Toohey and Gaudron JJ).

[45] *Brett Cattle Co Pty Ltd v Minister for Agriculture, Fisheries and Forestry* (2020) 274 FCR 337, 418–25 [327]–[362].

[46] *McCloy* (n 1).

[47] ibid 411 [300].

[48] Although the ministerial ban in question was thought, unlike traditional delegated legislation cases, to engage rights, Boughey argues that Rares J dramatically extended the protection that the principle of legality usually gives to rights: J Boughey, 'Brett Cattle: New Limits on Delegated Law-Making Powers' (2020) 31 *Public Law Review* 347, 350–54.

### *ii. Reasonably Appropriate and Adapted*

In the context of constitutional limitations or guarantees, the Court has until recently preferred the expression 'reasonably appropriate and adapted'.[49] This test has been used to determine limitations on the implied freedom of political communication,[50] and a similar formulation has been used in the cases dealing with the implied right to vote.[51] This test was set out by a unanimous High Court in *Lange v Australian Broadcasting Corporation*:

> First, does the law effectively burden freedom of communication about government or political matters either in its terms, operation or effect? Second, if the law effectively burdens that freedom, is the law reasonably appropriate and adapted to serve a legitimate end the fulfilment of which is compatible with the maintenance of the constitutionally prescribed system of representative and responsible government and the procedure prescribed by s 128 for submitting a proposed amendment of the Constitution to the informed decision of the people.[52]

In *Coleman v Power*, the second question was modified by replacing the phrase 'the fulfilment of' with 'in a manner', clarifying that both the end and the manner of its achievement must be compatible with the system of representative and responsible government.[53] In contrast to the 'reasonably capable of being considered' formulation, the 'reasonably appropriate and adapted' test appears to involve a higher level of scrutiny.[54] The wording of this test suggests that the Court itself has to form a view about whether the law is a reasonable way of achieving the particular purpose. As noted above, various members of the High Court have recognised that there is a substantive as opposed to a merely semantic difference between the different formulations. There has been some indication that the 'appropriate and adapted' standard is less 'deferential to the judgment of the legislature'[55] than the weaker 'capable of' formulation. However, at the

[49] See B Challenor, 'The Balancing Act: A Case for Structured Proportionality under the Second Limb of the *Lange* Test' (2015) 40 *University of Western Australia Law Review* 267, 276ff, who notes that in the context of the implied freedom of political communication, some justices have preferred a 'weaker' formulation than 'reasonably appropriate and adapted'.

[50] Note the introduction of structured proportionality testing in *McCloy* (n 1), which is discussed in section II.C below.

[51] *Roach v Electoral Commissioner* (2007) 233 CLR 162, 174 [7] (Gleeson CJ), 199 [85] (Gummow, Kirby and Crennan JJ); *Rowe v Electoral Commissioner* (2010) 243 CLR 1, 20 [23]–[24] (French CJ), 59 [161] (Gummow and Bell JJ), 65 [184] (Hayne J), 118 [374] (Crennan J), 126 [404] (Kiefel J); *Murphy v Electoral Commissioner* (2016) 261 CLR 28, 49 [31] (French CJ and Bell J), 67 [85] (Gageler J), 94 [204] (Keane J), 107 [244] (Nettle J), 121–22 [293] (Gordon J).

[52] *Lange v Australian Broadcasting Corporation* (1997) 189 CLR 520, 567 (footnotes omitted) (Brennan CJ, Dawson, Toohey, Gaudron, McHugh, Gummow and Kirby JJ).

[53] *Coleman* (n 37) 50–51 [93]–[96] (McHugh J), 78 [196] (Gummow and Hayne JJ). See also recent restatements: *Unions NSW v New South Wales* (2013) 252 CLR 530, 553 [35], 556 [44] (French CJ, Hayne, Crennan, Kiefel and Bell JJ); *McCloy* (n 1) 200–01 [23] (French CJ, Kiefel, Bell and Keane JJ), 230–32 [125]–[131] (Gageler J), 258 [220] (Nettle J), 280–81 [306] (Gordon J).

[54] Boughey (n 48) 352.

[55] *Coleman* (n 37) 48 [87] (McHugh J). See also *Adelaide City Corporation* (n 16) 40–43 [59]–[65] (French CJ).

same time, the Court has been conscious of the proper limits of its role and has emphasised that 'reasonably appropriate and adapted' does not mean 'essential' or 'unavoidable'.[56]

### *iii. Reasonably Necessary*

While the above analysis indicates that it is possible to discern some difference between the 'reasonably appropriate and adapted' and 'reasonably capable of being considered' tests, a question remains as to whether the test applied in the context of the guarantee in section 92 of the *Australian Constitution* involves an additional standard. In respect of the 'trade and commerce' limb of section 92, in *Cole v Whitfield* a unanimous High Court framed the relevant test in terms of whether the provision constitutes a discriminatory burden of a protectionist kind,[57] thus ending decades of uncertainty that had dogged the section.[58] Although the new test brought some much-needed clarity to section 92, the extent of permissible regulation remained less clear. In *Cole* itself, the parties agreed that the prescribed minimum size regulations were needed in order to ensure the conservation of crayfish stock in Tasmania.[59] These agreed facts enabled the Court to conclude that 'the extension of the prohibitions against sale and possession to imported crayfish is a *necessary* means of enforcing the protection against the catching of undersized crayfish in Tasmanian waters'.[60] There was no need, on the facts of *Cole*, for the Court to elaborate further upon the extent of permissible regulation.

In subsequent cases, this issue was more squarely before the Court. In *Castlemaine Tooheys Ltd v South Australia*, for instance, the Court had to determine whether regulations made under the *Beverage Container Amendment Act 1986* (SA), which imposed different deposits for refillable and non-refillable glass bottles, infringed section 92.[61] The Court confirmed that the freedom from discriminatory burdens of a protectionist kind did not prevent a State from legislating either to protect the community from a real danger or to enhance the welfare of the community.[62] In determining the extent of permissible restrictions, the majority described the relevant test as being whether the

[56] In the context of electoral regulation, see *Roach* (n 51) 199 [85] (Gummow, Kirby and Crennan JJ), citing *Mulholland* (n 4) 199–200 [39]–[40] (Gleeson CJ).

[57] *Cole v Whitfield* (1988) 165 CLR 360, 394 (Mason CJ, Wilson, Brennan, Deane, Dawson, Toohey and Gaudron JJ).

[58] Michael Coper, *Freedom of Interstate Trade under the Australian Constitution* (Sydney, Butterworths, 1983); Stellios (n 31) chs 6–8.

[59] *Cole* (n 57) 362, 382.

[60] ibid 409 (emphasis added).

[61] *Castlemaine Tooheys Ltd v South Australia* (1990) 169 CLR 436. Note that the deposits were refundable on return of the bottles.

[62] ibid 472 (Mason CJ, Brennan, Deane, Dawson and Toohey JJ). Note that Gaudron and McHugh JJ reached the same result, but favoured a broader test based on discrimination.

regulation was 'necessary or appropriate and adapted' to such purposes.[63] In defining the test in this way, the majority referred to the Court's previous use of the 'appropriate and adapted' test in the context of the external affairs power.[64] There was, in the majority's view, a 'compelling case' for adopting a similar approach in the context of section 92.[65]

There are a couple of things to note about the framing of the relevant test in *Castlemaine Tooheys*. First, when referring to the Court's previous approach, the majority described the test in terms of a law being 'appropriate and adapted', omitting the qualification 'capable of being reasonably considered' that was used in some of the earlier cases.[66] In this way, the majority appears to conflate the two standards, simply noting that a 'similar' approach should be adopted in the context of section 92.[67] In addition, the test in *Castlemaine Tooheys* was described in terms of the law being 'necessary or appropriate and adapted'.[68] Although the majority noted that the prohibitions in *Cole* 'were in fact necessary', it considered that a standard of actual necessity was too onerous:

> [I]t would place the Court in an invidious position if the Court were to hold that only such regulation of interstate trade *as is in fact* necessary for the protection of the community is consistent with the freedom ordained by s 92.[69]

So, while the Court in *Castlemaine Tooheys* introduced the language of 'necessity' into the relevant test, it appeared to treat this expression as equivalent to the 'appropriate and adapted' test. In other words, it was not clear whether the Court intended to introduce a higher level of scrutiny than that conveyed by the traditional 'appropriate and adapted' formulation.

In *Betfair v Western Australia*, after an almost 20-year hiatus, the test for the trade and commerce limb of section 92 was again refashioned.[70] Although the High Court confirmed the 'discriminatory protectionism' approach of *Cole v Whitfield*, its precise formulation was expressed in slightly different terms. By this stage, the Court had been toying with the language of proportionality in

[63] ibid. Note that this two-part approach to s 92 has sometimes been described in terms of an 'invalidity test' and a 'savings test'. See G Villalta Puig, *The High Court of Australia and Section 92 of the Australian Constitution* (Sydney, Lawbook Co, 2008) ch 5; N Oreb, 'Betting across Borders – *Betfair Pty Limited v Western Australia*' (2009) 31 *Sydney Law Review* 607.

[64] *Castlemaine Tooheys* (n 61) 473. Note that here the majority uses the language of 'appropriate and adapted', citing *Tasmanian Dam Case* (n 3) and *Richardson* (n 30). However, in those cases, as explained above, the precise formulation was expressed as 'capable of being reasonably considered appropriate and adapted'.

[65] *Castlemaine Tooheys* (n 61) 473 (Mason CJ, Brennan, Deane, Dawson and Toohey JJ).

[66] ibid 472. This point has also been made by D Rose, '*Cole v Whitfield*: "Absolutely Free" Trade?' in HP Lee and G Winterton (eds), *Australian Constitutional Landmarks* (Cambridge, Cambridge University Press, 2003) 341.

[67] *Castlemaine Tooheys* (n 61) 473.

[68] ibid.

[69] ibid (emphasis added).

[70] *Betfair Pty Ltd v Western Australia* (2008) 234 CLR 418.

other contexts, and counsel for the plaintiffs and for Tasmania submitted that the 'appropriate and adapted' test in *Castlemaine Tooheys* involved considering the 'proportionality' between the differential burden imposed on out-of-state and in-state producers and the competitively neutral objective which it is designed to achieve.[71] The majority, appearing to accept this submission, noted that such 'proportionality' must give significant weight to the considerations of a national economy and defined the relevant test as 'a criterion of "reasonable necessity"'.[72] In articulating the test in this way, the majority considered that it was acting consistently with previous authority, including *Cole*.[73] It did, however, express a number of reservations about aspects of the reasoning in *Castlemaine Tooheys*.[74] While the majority did not explicitly acknowledge any shift in the relevant standard, its use of the language of 'reasonable necessity' and its emphasis on its own responsibility for determining constitutional validity[75] seem to suggest a higher standard of scrutiny.[76]

In *Palmer v Western Australia*, the Court again revisited the test to be applied in the section 92 context.[77] The Court sought to align the 'trade and commerce' and the 'intercourse' limbs of section 92 by focusing on whether the impugned law imposed unjustified discriminatory burdens.[78] For the majority, 'protectionism' was no longer a necessary element of the test, though it was acknowledged that it would often be relevant to the trade and commerce limb.[79]

[71] ibid 422 (summary of plaintiffs' argument), 476–77 [101] (Gleeson CJ, Gummow, Kirby, Hayne, Crennan and Kiefel JJ).

[72] ibid 477 [102] (Gleeson CJ, Gummow, Kirby, Hayne, Crennan and Kiefel JJ), citing Gleeson CJ in *Thomas v Mowbray* (n 29) 331–33 [20]–[26]. This approach was confirmed in *Betfair Pty Ltd v Racing New South Wales* (2012) 249 CLR 217, 269 [52] (French CJ, Gummow, Hayne, Crennan and Bell JJ), 295 [136] (Kiefel J), but in that case (as in *Sportsbet Pty Ltd v New South Wales* (2012) 249 CLR 298, handed down on the same day) the impugned provisions were found not to constitute a discriminatory burden of a protectionist kind, and so there was no need to consider the 'savings test' aspect of s 92.

[73] *Betfair* (n 70) 477 [102]–[103] (Gleeson CJ, Gummow, Kirby, Hayne, Crennan and Kiefel JJ). Note that the Court cited the discussion by Gleeson CJ in *Thomas v Mowbray* (n 29) 331–36 [20]–[26], and also quoted Mason J in *North Eastern Dairy Co Ltd v Dairy Industry Authority of NSW* (1975) 134 CLR 559, 608.

[74] In particular, the emphasis in *Castlemaine Tooheys* (n 61) on the power of a State to legislate for the well-being of its own people was qualified to emphasise the national nature of the new economy: *Betfair* (n 70) 453 [18], 474 [89]–[90] (Gleeson CJ, Gummow, Kirby, Hayne, Crennan and Kiefel JJ).

[75] *Betfair* (n 70) 476 [99]. *cf Castlemaine Tooheys* (n 61) 473 (Mason CJ, Brennan, Deane, Dawson and Toohey JJ).

[76] See *Palmer v Western Australia* (2021) 92 ALJR 299, 257 [137] (Gageler J).

[77] ibid.

[78] ibid 241–42 [47] (Kiefel CJ and Keane J), 249 [97] (Gageler J), 265 [181] (Gordon J), 273 [218] (Edelman J). See also JK Kirk, 'Section 92 in its Second Century' in J Griffiths and J Stellios (eds), *Current Issues in Australian Constitutional Law: Tributes to Professor Leslie Zines* (Sydney, Federation Press, 2020) 277–79.

[79] *Palmer* (n 76) 241 [47] (Kiefel CJ and Keane J), 278 [239] (Edelman J). Gageler J took the view that the trade and commerce limb guarantees freedom from discriminatory burdens of a protectionist kind, whereas the intercourse limb guarantees freedom from discriminatory burdens of any kind (at 253 [114]). Similarly, Gordon J was of the view that the nature of the discrimination differs between the two limbs (at 266 [184]).

Importantly, the Court confirmed that even if the law is relevantly discriminatory, it might nonetheless be valid if it is 'reasonably necessary' to achieve some other purpose.[80] There was some divergence about whether this test involved structured proportionality testing of the kind now applied in the context of the implied freedom.[81] While Kiefel CJ and Keane J, and Edelman J separately, all endorsed a structured approach – incorporating the three elements of suitability, necessity and adequate balance – there was some difference in terms of whether this was the *only* method of justification that might be applied. For Kiefel CJ and Keane J, structured proportionality was seen as a means of elaborating, or giving content to, the test of reasonable necessity.[82] Justice Edelman was more explicit, holding that structured proportionality was *the* method for assessing whether burdens on trade, commerce or intercourse could be justified.[83] Justice Gageler and Gordon J, in contrast, each rejected the use of structured proportionality and preferred the previous formulation of 'reasonable necessity'.[84] Justice Gageler again expressed strong resistance to the idea of structured proportionality, rehearsing some of his earlier criticisms.[85] The upshot of *Palmer* is that while the test remains one of 'reasonable necessity', structured proportionality may – at least according to three justices – be used to assess whether a discriminatory burden can be justified.

### B. 'Appropriate and Adapted' versus 'Proportionality'?

Until the introduction of a structured test of proportionality in 2015, the Court had – as explained above – adopted a number of differently worded tests that applied in different contexts. While the Court preferred the language of 'appropriate and adapted', at times the language of proportionality crept in and there was considerable uncertainty about the extent to which these different tests might incorporate elements of the tripartite formula of proportionality.

In relation to the first formulation – reasonably capable of being considered appropriate and adapted – the relevant inquiry is whether the law is *capable* of being considered to advance a particular purpose. It does not involve the Court forming a direct judgment about whether the measure is reasonable or necessary. When described in this way, this test begins to look very

[80] ibid 242 [50] (Kiefel CJ and Keane J), 249 [97] (Gageler J), 268 [192] (Gordon J), 286 [273] (Edelman J). Note that for Edelman J, 'reasonable necessity' was considered as part of the three-stage test of structured proportionality. As explained above, the language of 'necessity' was introduced in *Castlemaine Tooheys*: see nn 68ff and accompanying text.

[81] Discussed in section II.C below.

[82] *Palmer* (n 76) 242–44 [51]–[58].

[83] ibid 284–85 [261]–[265].

[84] ibid 258–60 [141]–[151] (Gageler J), 269–70 [198]–[199] (Gordon J).

[85] ibid 258–60 [140]–[151].

similar to the first stage of proportionality – that of suitability. As explained in Chapter 2, at this stage of proportionality analysis, a court interrogates the link between a law and its purpose. In this way, the suitability inquiry is sometimes seen as a device to ascertain the real or true purpose of a law. This understanding of the 'capable of' test, as analogous to the suitability limb of proportionality, is consistent with comments from various justices that this test does not entitle the Court to substitute its view for that of the legislature.[86]

The second formulation – reasonably appropriate and adapted – takes the inquiry one step further. As with the 'reasonably capable of being considered' test, the first task is to determine whether the law is capable of being considered to advance the purpose it is designed to achieve. In other words, the relevant starting point is once again the connection between a law and its purpose. As explained above, this inquiry can be seen as broadly analogous to the 'suitability' limb of the proportionality inquiry. However, the 'reasonably appropriate and adapted' test goes further than the 'reasonably capable' test, as it requires the Court itself to form a view of whether the measure reasonably advances the purpose. That is, it involves the Court considering the effectiveness of the measure and whether it is likely to actually advance the particular purpose. This includes, at times, a consideration of alternatives.[87] This suggests that some aspects of the 'necessity' limb of proportionality also enter the analysis at this stage. However, as will be explained below, the scope of the necessity inquiry remains less developed than it is in other jurisdictions.

In the context of section 92, for some time there had been debate about the extent to which the test of 'reasonable necessity' incorporates aspects of the tripartite proportionality formula. Academic commentators diverged on this question, with some, such as Jeremy Kirk, suggesting that all three levels of proportionality were already implicitly being applied by the Court.[88] Others have been more cautious, suggesting that the discussion of what was necessary in *Betfair* was 'fleeting' and, on the facts of the case, quite straightforward.[89] There was thus considerable uncertainty about whether the test of reasonable necessity introduced a heightened level of scrutiny. This uncertainty was exacerbated by the subsequent development, in the context of the implied freedom, of a test of structured proportionality, with speculation mounting about whether a similar test would be adopted for section 92.[90] As explained above, three justices

[86] See, eg, *Adelaide City Corporation* (n 16) 40 [60] (French CJ).

[87] The question of necessity, as explained in ch 2, involves considering whether any hypothetical alternatives might achieve the same purpose. See also *Monis v The Queen* (2013) 249 CLR 92, 214 [347] (Crennan, Kiefel and Bell JJ), who referred to *Betfair* (n 70) 479 [110].

[88] Kirk (n 5) 14, cited by the High Court in *Palmer* (n 76) 243–44 [57] (Kiefel CJ and Keane J), 284 [264] (Edelman J). See also Villalta Puig, who suggested the Court was now 'only one level away' from adopting a three-tiered approach to proportionality: Villalta Puig (n 63) 190.

[89] Oreb (n 63) 617.

[90] Note that a number of commentators resisted such a development: Chordia (n 27) 149–51; A Simpson, 'Section 92 as a Transplant Recipient?' in Griffiths and Stellios (n 78) 288–94.

of the High Court have now endorsed the use of structured proportionality in this context. However, the continuing dissent, along with changes to the composition of the Court,[91] means that its foothold is not yet secure.

Although it is possible to see the existing tests of validity as incorporating various aspects of proportionality reasoning, the reality is more complex. As is apparent from the comparative jurisdictions considered in the previous chapter, the three stages of the proportionality inquiry often overlap. Moreover, judges do not always clearly articulate the different steps that inform their reasoning process. Some commentators have long suggested that the Court's existing tests were in many ways equivalent to structured proportionality, and involved the same types of considerations and the making of similar evaluative judgments.[92] While there is some force in these observations, when applying the three different formulations set out above, the Court has until recently refrained from describing its inquiry in terms of proportionality and has avoided structuring its analysis into discrete stages or sub-tests. Prior to 2015, the dominant view emerging from the Court was that the expressions 'proportionality' and 'appropriate and adapted' were largely interchangeable and were simply alternative ways of describing the same test. This view was confirmed in *Lange*, where the unanimous Court noted that the test for assessing limitations on the implied freedom had been expressed in various ways in the past, and it did not consider it necessary to distinguish between the two concepts.[93] Indeed, in a footnote, the Court observed that there was 'little difference' between the formulations of 'reasonably appropriate and adapted' and 'proportionality'.[94]

Against this degree of consensus, however, there were signs of division. These were most apparent in the context of the implied freedom of political communication, which has been the subject of considerable litigation. Some members of the Court advocated abandoning the language of 'appropriate and adapted' altogether, claiming it is both opaque and unwieldy. Justice Kirby, for instance, critiqued the phrase as being 'inappropriate and ill-adapted to perform the constitutional function repeatedly assigned to it by members of this Court'.[95] In *Monis v The Queen*, Crennan, Kiefel and Bell JJ made similar criticisms

[91] Note that Steward J was appointed to the Court in December 2020 and Gleeson J was appointed to the Court in March 2021.

[92] In relation to the implied freedom, see A Stone, 'The Limits of Constitutional Text and Structure: Standards of Review and the Freedom of Political Communication' (1999) 23 *Melbourne University Law Review* 668; A Stone, 'The Limits of Constitutional Text and Structure Revisited' (2006) 29 *University of New South Wales Law Journal* 842; A Stone, 'Constitutional Orthodoxy in the United Kingdom and Australia: The Deepening Divide' (2014) 38 *Melbourne University Law Review* 836, 842; A Stone, 'Proportionality and its Alternatives' (2020) 48 *Federal Law Review* 123, 140. In relation to s 92, see also Kirk (n 5) 14, 20, 63; *cf* A Simpson: 'Grounding the High Court's Modern Section 92 Jurisprudence: The Case for Improper Purpose as the Touchstone' (2005) 33 *Federal Law Review* 445, 459–62.

[93] *Lange* (n 52) 562 (Brennan CJ, Dawson, Toohey, Gaudron, McHugh, Gummow and Kirby JJ).

[94] ibid 567 fn 272.

[95] *Mulholland* (n 4) 266 [247]. See also *Levy v Victoria*, (1997) 189 CLR 579, 645–46 (Kirby J).

of the 'appropriate and adapted' terminology and queried whether this 'more cumbersome and inexact phrase' should be continued.[96] Led by Kiefel J, as she then was, there was a preference emerging for a more structured form of proportionality testing.[97] There were also divisions emerging in terms of the substance of the *Lange* test and the nature of the inquiries that it involved. These included debates about the extent to which elements of proportionality were already involved in the *Lange* analysis, and whether such inquiries were appropriate for the Court at all.[98]

### C. *McCloy* and the Advent of Structured Proportionality

These uncertainties and divisions within the Court culminated in late 2015 with the Court's decision in *McCloy*, which concerned the implied freedom of political communication.[99] In this decision, four of the seven members of the Court reformulated the second limb of the *Lange* test to include a structured, three-part proportionality analysis.

The case concerned the validity of the *Election Funding, Expenditure and Disclosures Act 1981* (NSW), which imposed restrictions on political donations.[100] The joint judgment of French CJ, Kiefel, Bell and Keane JJ, while confirming that the two-part *Lange* test remains authoritative, observed that as a unanimous decision of the Court, the decision 'may be expected to reflect some compromise'.[101] The reference in *Lange* to a legislative measure being 'appropriate and adapted' was not, their Honours explained, to be understood as a 'complete statement of what is involved'.[102] In order to give content to, and elaborate upon, the requirements of the *Lange* test, the joint judgment identified three key questions:

> Does the law effectively burden the freedom in its terms, operation or effect? …
>
> If 'yes' to question 1, are the purpose of the law and the means adopted to achieve that purpose legitimate, in the sense that they are compatible with the maintenance

[96] *Monis* (n 87) 195 [283]. See also Edelman J in *Clubb v Edwards; Preston v Avery* (2019) 267 CLR 171, 329–30 [461].

[97] Chief Justice Kiefel has written extra-judicially about proportionality on a number of occasions. See, eg, S Kiefel, 'English, European and Australian Law: Convergence or Divergence?' (2005) 79 *Australian Law Journal* 220; S Kiefel, 'Section 92: Markets, Protectionism and Proportionality-Australian and European Perspectives' (2010) 36 *Monash University Law Review* 1; S Kiefel, 'Proportionality: A Rule of Reason' (2012) 23 *Public Law Review* 85.

[98] See, eg, *Tajjour* (n 41) 570–571 [110]–[113], 575 [133] (Kiefel, Crennan and Bell JJ), *cf* 579–80 [149]–[150] (Gageler J); *Unions NSW* (n 53) 576–78 [129], [134] (Keane J).

[99] *McCloy* (n 1).

[100] A majority of the Court (French CJ, Kiefel, Bell and Keane JJ in a joint judgment, and Gageler J and Gordon J each writing separately) rejected the plaintiffs' challenge in its entirety. Nettle J dissented in relation to the prohibited donor provisions, holding that these arbitrarily discriminated against property developers and were not sufficiently justified to satisfy the second limb of the *Lange* test: *McCloy* (n 1) 272 [266].

[101] *McCloy* (n 1) 214–15 [71].

[102] ibid.

> of the constitutionally prescribed system of representative government? This question reflects what is referred to in these reasons as 'compatibility testing' ...
>
> If 'yes' to question 2, is the law reasonably appropriate and adapted to advance that legitimate object? This question involves what is referred to in these reasons as 'proportionality testing'.[103]

As this passage makes clear, the first of the two traditional *Lange* questions remains the same. The major change is that the second *Lange* question is broken down into the stages of 'compatibility testing' and 'proportionality testing'. The testing of compatibility (question two) first involves identifying whether the law pursues a legitimate aim. Clarifying an area of previous uncertainty, the joint judgment explained that a legitimate aim 'is one which is compatible with the system of representative government provided for by the *Constitution*; which is to say that the purpose does not impede the functioning of that system and all that it entails'.[104] This aspect of the compatibility test is consistent with forms of proportionality applied elsewhere, as the inquiry usually commences with the identification of a legitimate aim.[105] In the subsequent case of *Brown v Tasmania*, the Court clarified that 'compatibility testing' is directed purely towards the question of whether the purpose of the law is legitimate, and it does not involve evaluating the means adopted to achieve the purpose.[106]

Most significantly for present purposes, the third question articulated in *McCloy* introduced a sequential proportionality test to determine whether the law was reasonably appropriate and adapted to advancing the legitimate object. The joint judgment agreed with the plaintiffs' submission that proportionality analysis 'of some kind' formed part of the *Lange* test, but emphasised that this did not simply involve a 'matter of impression'.[107] The three stages identified by the joint judgment mirror the traditional approach to proportionality that was analysed in Chapter 2 and is applied in the comparative jurisdictions.[108] The first question is that of suitability or '"appropriateness" or "fit"', which assesses whether there is a rational connection between the legislative provision in question and the legitimate purpose which is pursued by the legislation.[109] This involves assessing whether the measure is capable of

[103] ibid 193–94 [2].

[104] ibid 203 [31] (citation omitted).

[105] See ch 2, section I.A.

[106] *Brown v Tasmania* (2017) 261 CLR 328, 363–64 [104] (Kiefel CJ, Bell and Keane JJ), 375–76 [155]–[156] (Gageler J), 416 [277] (Nettle J), 478 [481] (Gordon J). This aspect of 'compatibility testing' had been unclear in *McCloy* as it appeared to countenance an assessment of both the legislative ends and means: *McCloy* (n 1) 193–94 [2], 203 [31], 212–13 [67] (French CJ, Kiefel, Bell and Keane JJ).

[107] *McCloy* (n 1) 212–13 [67].

[108] As explained in the previous chapter, the approach in South Africa is less structured and the Court instead considers a list of factors: see ch 4, text accompanying n 28.

[109] *McCloy* (n 1) 217 [80] (French CJ, Kiefel, Bell and Keane JJ), citing A Barak, *Proportionality: Constitutional Rights and Their Limitations* (Cambridge, Cambridge University Press, 2012) 303.

contributing to the legitimate purpose rather than whether it actually achieves this purpose. According to the joint judgment, this does not involve any value judgment about whether the purpose could have been achieved in a different way.[110] The second stage of the majority's 'proportionality testing' is defined in terms of 'necessity', and it involves asking whether there are any 'obvious and compelling' alternatives that have a less-restrictive effect on the freedom.[111] These first two questions, in the joint judgment's reasons, do not involve any examination of the importance of the legislative purpose or the extent of the effect on the implied freedom.[112] The final question is expressed in terms of whether the law is 'adequate in its balance'.[113] According to the joint judgment, this represents:

> [A] criterion requiring a value judgment, consistently with the limits of the judicial function, describing the balance between the importance of the purpose served by the restrictive measure and the extent of the restriction it imposes on the freedom.[114]

Aspects of the joint judgment's revised approach to proportionality will be returned to below, but at present it suffices to note that the other three members of the Court in *McCloy* rejected this reformulation of the *Lange* test. Justice Nettle and Gordon J both noted that in recent cases some differences had emerged in relation to the second stage of the *Lange* test,[115] but did not consider that it was necessary to alter the existing test. For Gordon J, the traditional *Lange* test had been applied 'without apparent difficulty' since the *Lange* decision itself[116] and there was no need to depart from the 'known questions and tools'.[117] The most strident criticism came from Gageler J, who considered that the case did not 'warrant consideration of the benefits and detriments of the wholesale importation into our constitutional jurisprudence, under the rubric of proportionality, of a particular and prescriptive form of proportionality analysis'.[118]

Despite its somewhat tentative beginnings and some changes to the composition of the Court, since the decision in *McCloy*, structured proportionality has continued to be endorsed by a (growing) majority in the context of the implied freedom of political communication. In 2017 in *Brown v Tasmania*, the Court was expressly invited to overrule the *McCloy* test of

[110] *McCloy* (n 1) 217 [80].
[111] ibid 217 [81].
[112] ibid 218 [83]. This can be contrasted with Gageler J's approach, which is discussed below.
[113] ibid 217 [79].
[114] ibid 193–94 [2].
[115] ibid 281 [309] (Gordon J), 258–59 [221] (Nettle J).
[116] ibid 282 [310].
[117] ibid 282 [311]. Similarly, for Nettle J, it was not necessary to resolve the differences that had emerged in previous cases (at 269 [255]).
[118] ibid 234 [140].

proportionality.[119] Chief Justice Kiefel, Bell and Keane JJ confirmed the three stages of 'proportionality testing' that were developed in *McCloy*, and held that the impugned provisions of the *Workplaces (Protection from Protesters) Act 2014* (Tas) imposed a significant burden on the implied freedom that had not been justified.[120] Justice Nettle, in separate reasons, also applied structured proportionality to assess the second *Lange* question, relying on the 'adequate balance' limb of the test.[121] In the subsequent decisions of *Clubb v Edwards; Preston v Avery*[122] and *Comcare v Banerji*,[123] the structured approach to proportionality has been further cemented. In *Clubb*, the majority of Kiefel CJ, Bell and Keane JJ rejected a submission that full proportionality analysis was not required where the burden imposed by the law was slight. Instead, according to their Honours, the *McCloy* test required that '*any* effective burden on the freedom must be justified'.[124] Justice Nettle also confirmed the use of structured proportionality testing in *Clubb* and refined the approach to the necessity question he had developed in *Brown*.[125] Finally, Edelman J also endorsed structured proportionality testing for the first time, noting that while it was a 'tool' of analysis, it was not 'dispensable'.[126]

Beyond the context of the implied freedom of political communication, the use of structured proportionality remains unclear. As explained above, three members of the Court have recently endorsed its use in the context of assessing whether burdens on trade, commerce and intercourse will infringe section 92.[127] Similarly, a single judge of the Federal Court has adopted structured proportionality in the context of reviewing delegated legislation.[128] In other contexts, however, the High Court has resisted its use. In *Murphy v Electoral Commissioner*, which was decided less than a year after *McCloy*, six members of the Court declined to apply structured proportionality.[129] The case concerned the validity of the 'suspension period' in the *Commonwealth Electoral Act 1918* (Cth), which precluded claims for enrolment or transfer from being considered during the period from the closing of the Electoral Rolls and the end of polling. The plaintiffs argued that the suspension period was contrary to the requirements of sections 7 and 24 of the *Australian Constitution* and that

[119] Both the State of Tasmania (the defendant) and Attorney-General for the State of Queensland (intervening) submitted that *McCloy* should be reconsidered, and the Commonwealth submitted that a modified version of *McCloy* should be adopted: see *Brown* (n 106) 368–69 [124]–[127].
[120] ibid 374 [152].
[121] ibid 422–23 [290].
[122] *Clubb* (n 96).
[123] *Comcare v Banerji* (2019) 267 CLR 373 (hereinafter '*Banerji*').
[124] *Clubb* (n 96) 199 [64].
[125] ibid 264–66 [266]–[269].
[126] ibid 332 [468].
[127] See the text accompanying nn 77ff above.
[128] See the text accompanying n 45 above.
[129] *Murphy* (n 51).

the law was invalid unless the disqualification was for a 'substantial reason'.[130] While the Court unanimously upheld the legislation, only Kiefel J applied a structured proportionality test.[131] The other justices, some of whom held there was no burden imposed by the provisions,[132] considered that the proportionality analysis developed in *McCloy* was not appropriate in this case.[133]

Proportionality also remains subject to strident criticism from a minority of the Court. Justices Gageler and Gordon, in a series of judgments, have each developed their critique of proportionality. This critique contains a number of distinct strands. First, proportionality is said to be too 'rigid', in that it demands a standardised set of questions for every law that burdens the freedom.[134] This 'one size fits all' approach, according to Gageler J, fails to take account of 'varying degrees of latitude' that might be afforded to government action.[135] Second, the requirement for a court the assess whether a law is 'adequate in its balance' is characterised as being too 'open-ended'; it does not reflect the reasons underpinning the implied freedom and provides insufficient guidance for how courts are to reconcile incommensurable interests.[136] For both Gageler J and Gordon J, proportionality, with its European origins, is inconsistent with the common law's case-specific method of adjudication.[137]

## III. EVALUATING PROPORTIONALITY

The adoption of structured proportionality in Australia brings the High Court's approach, at least in the context of the implied freedom of political communication, closer to the approach of other jurisdictions. However, the Court remains cautious about mirroring the approach used elsewhere, and it has endeavoured to develop some distinctively Australian features. In addition, some key areas of uncertainty remain: the role of balancing and the level of scrutiny.

[130] Anthony John Murphy, 'Plaintiff's Annotated Submissions', Submission in *Murphy v Electoral Commissioner*, M247/2015, 11 April 2016, [8], [23]–[26].

[131] *Murphy* (n 51) 61–62 [64]–[65].

[132] ibid 54–55 [40]–[42] (French CJ and Bell J), 94 [204] (Keane J), 125 [308] (Gordon J).

[133] ibid 53 [38]–[39] (French CJ and Bell J), 72 [101] (Gageler J), 94 [202] (Keane J), 107 [244]–[245] (Nettle J), 122 [297] (Gordon J). Note that French CJ and Bell J considered that whether structured proportionality was relevant would depend on 'the character of the law' in question, whereas Keane J declined to apply structured proportionality as he held there was no burden. Justice Gordon, who rejected the use of proportionality at all, considered there was a 'critical difference' between the implied freedom of political communication and Parliament's power to regulate elections, as in the latter context Parliament is 'effectively under an obligation to maintain laws of that kind': see 123 [300], [301].

[134] *Brown* (n 106) 477 [477] (Gordon J); *Clubb* (n 96) 305 [391] (Gordon J).

[135] *McCloy* (n 1) 235 [142]–[143].

[136] *Brown* (n 106) 377 [160] (Gageler J); see also 465–66 [432] (Gordon J).

[137] See, eg, *Brown* (n 106) 477 [476]–[477] (Gordon J); *Clubb* (n 96) 224 [159] (Gageler J), 305 [391] (Gordon J). But see A Carter, 'Moving Beyond the Common Law Objection to Structured Proportionality' (2021) 49 *Federal Law Review* 73.

The 'proportionality testing' developed in *McCloy*, which forms part of the second limb of the *Lange* test, is expressed in almost identical terms to the conventional proportionality formula. The three steps of 'suitability', 'necessity' and 'adequate … balance' require, importantly, a sequential application.[138] Articulating the inquiry in this way has the potential to lead to a more structured and transparent approach to assessing limitations.[139] In addition, in *McCloy* the joint judgment's open reliance on some form of balancing, which expressly acknowledges the need to make 'value judgments',[140] represents a shift away from the 'legalism' that has dominated Australian constitutional adjudication.[141] In several important respects, then, the adoption of structured proportionality testing represents an analytical shift towards the methodological approach applied in other jurisdictions, including Germany, Canada and South Africa.[142]

However, against this degree of similarity, there remain some differences compared to the global model of proportionality. The Court has sought to confine the necessity stage to a consideration of those alternatives that are 'obvious and compelling'.[143] It is also wary about drawing too heavily on the approaches used in other jurisdictions. The joint judgment in *McCloy*, for instance, sought to fashion a domestic version of proportionality that reflected the Australian constitutional setting. While acknowledging that '[a]nalogous criteria' were used in other jurisdictions, particularly in Europe,[144] the joint judgment emphasised that utilising such criteria in Australia did not 'involve acceptance of the application of proportionality analysis by other courts as methodologically correct'.[145] In *McCloy* and the cases which have followed it, the Court has tended to draw mostly on cases from the UK, Canada and the US, perhaps indicating a greater comfort with common law modes of reasoning.[146] In addition, it continues to reject distinctly European concepts such as the 'margin of appreciation' as having any application in Australia.[147]

[138] *McCloy* (n 1) 194–95 [2] (French CJ, Kiefel, Bell and Keane JJ).

[139] Transparency is one of the benefits of proportionality reasoning espoused by the joint judgment: ibid 215–16 [74].

[140] ibid 216 [76]. See also *Clubb* (n 96) 202 [74] (Kiefel CJ, Bell and Keane JJ).

[141] See the discussion in ch 1, section III.B.

[142] For further analysis, see A Carter, 'Proportionality in Australian Constitutional Law: Towards Transnationalism' (2016) 76 *Heidelberg Journal of International Law* 951.

[143] *McCloy* (n 1) 211 [58] (French CJ, Kiefel, Bell and Keane JJ). See also *Clubb* (n 96) 265–66 [267]–[269] (Nettle J), 337 [479] (Edelman J).

[144] *McCloy* (n 1) 195 [3] (French CJ, Kiefel, Bell and Keane JJ).

[145] ibid 195–96 [4].

[146] See, eg, *McCloy* (n 1) 207 [44], 217 [78] (French CJ, Kiefel, Bell and Keane JJ); *Unions NSW v New South Wales (No 2)* (2019) 264 CLR 595, 617–18 [48]–[52] (Kiefel CJ, Bell and Keane JJ), 627 [82] (Gageler J) (hereinafter '*Unions (No 2)*'); *Clubb* (n 96) 345–49 [502]–[508] (Edelman J); *Banerji* (n 123) 422 [98] (Gageler J).

[147] *Unions NSW* (n 53) 553 [34], 556 [45] (French CJ, Hayne, Crennan, Kiefel and Bell JJ); *McCloy* (n 1) 220 [92] (French CJ, Kiefel, Bell and Keane JJ). See also *Unions (No 2)* (n 146) 617 [51] (Kiefel CJ, Bell and Keane JJ); *Clubb* (n 96) 262 [263] (Nettle J).

## A. Balancing

Despite some convergence with the approach to proportionality used in other jurisdictions, some differences emerge at the third stage. The majority continues to describe the third stage as '*adequate* in its balance', again preferring not to replicate the precise formula used elsewhere.[148] In *McCloy*, for instance, the joint judgment attempted to confine the task of balancing, claiming that it 'does not entitle the courts to substitute their own assessment for that of the legislative decision-maker'.[149] The process of balancing, it observed:

> must proceed upon an acceptance of the importance of the freedom and the reason for its existence. This stands in contrast to the basic rule of balancing as applied to human rights, which has been subject to criticism for failing to explain the reasons underlying the creation of the right in order to put the reasons for its protection, or which justify its limitation, in perspective.[150]

In this way, the Court sought to emphasise that the task of balancing was consistent with the Court's constitutional role and would not intrude upon the legislative function.[151]

In *McCloy* itself, although the joint judgment spent some time espousing the benefits of the new approach to proportionality, when it came to applying the relevant test, the majority's reasoning was rather conclusory. The joint judgment sought to downplay the significance of the balancing inquiry[152] and simply concluded that the restriction on the implied freedom was 'more than balanced by the benefits sought to be achieved'.[153] While the revised test more openly acknowledges the role of value judgments, it may be that in practice there is some reluctance to embrace an explicitly value-laden approach. The *Australian Constitution*, unlike the constitutions of Germany or South Africa,[154] does not contain an express statement of values.[155] While certain values can be inferred from the text and structure of the *Constitution*,[156]

[148] *McCloy* (n 1) 193–95 [2] (French CJ, Kiefel, Bell and Keane JJ). See M Wesson, 'Crafting a Concept of Deference for the Implied Freedom of Political Communication' (2016) 27 *Public Law Review* 101, 106.

[149] *McCloy* (n 1) 219–20 [89]. This claim is far from self-evident and raises questions about the appropriate role of the Court vis-a-vis the legislature.

[150] ibid 219 [88].

[151] ibid 219–20 [89]–[91].

[152] ibid 219 [88].

[153] ibid 221 [93].

[154] See the discussion in ch 1, section III.C. Note that such statements of values were a common feature of constitutions following the post-war model: LE Weinrib, 'The Postwar Paradigm and American Exceptionalism' in S Choudhry (ed), *The Migration of Constitutional Ideas* (Cambridge, Cambridge University Press, 2006).

[155] C Saunders and M Donaldson, 'Values in Australian Constitutionalism' in D Davis, A Richter and C Saunders (eds), *An Inquiry into the Existence of Global Values: Through the Lens of Comparative Constitutional Law* (Oxford, Hart Publishing, 2015).

[156] ibid.

an overt balancing inquiry presents challenges for the Court's traditional approach to constitutional adjudication.

In subsequent cases, the majority has attempted to clarify the nature of the balancing inquiry in the Australian context. In *Brown*, for instance, Nettle J indicated that while the European concept of proportionality asks where 'the balance should lie', the *McCloy* formulation of 'adequate in its balance' was to be understood as an 'outer limit'.[157] Only those measures that were 'manifestly excessive' or 'grossly disproportionate' would fall foul of the balancing test.[158] In that case Nettle J held that a number of the restrictions on protest activity in the Tasmanian legislation went 'far beyond' the legislative purpose and were therefore disproportionate.[159] In *Clubb* this approach was adopted by other members of the majority, with Kiefel CJ, Bell and Keane J emphasising that it is for the legislature, not the Court, to determine the 'correct balance' of the law.[160] The Court will only intervene where the lack of balance is 'such as to manifest irrationality'.[161] Similarly, Edelman J has indicated that the balance will only be inadequate 'if it involves gross or manifest lack of balance between, on the one hand, the foreseeable magnitude and likelihood of the burden upon freedom of political communication and, on the other hand, the importance of the purpose'.[162] In *Banerji*, Edelman J indicated that the need to respect parliamentary policy required the courts to exercise 'great latitude' in conducting the balancing inquiry.[163]

This caution surrounding the nature of balancing reflects deeper concerns about the limits of the judicial role.[164] The types of evaluative judgments that proportionality compels sit uncomfortably with the traditional understanding of the judicial role that has dominated constitutional interpretation in Australia. As explained in Chapter 1, the Court's conception of its role has been heavily influenced by its insistence on a strict separation of judicial power. These concerns also infiltrate the 'necessity' stage of proportionality testing, and the consideration of alternatives has been limited to those that are 'obvious and compelling'.[165] Such concerns about proportionality are nothing new in Australia,[166] and they have also emerged in other contexts where proportionality tests are applied.[167]

[157] *Brown* (n 106) 422–23 [290].
[158] ibid.
[159] ibid 423 [291].
[160] *Clubb* (n 96) 200 [66].
[161] ibid. See also *Banerji* (n 123) 404–05 [42] (Kiefel CJ, Bell, Keane and Nettle JJ).
[162] *Clubb* (n 96) 344 [497] (footnote omitted). See also *Banerji* (n 123) 457 [205] (Edelman J).
[163] *Banerji* (n 123) 442 [165].
[164] See the discussion on the nature of the judicial role in ch 1, section III.B.
[165] See n 143 above.
[166] See the discussion in the text accompanying n 22 above.
[167] See *Momcilovic v The Queen* (2011) 245 CLR 1, 44 [36] (French CJ), 171 [430] (Heydon J), 220 [575] (Crennan and Kiefel JJ). Stone suggests that while these passages do not address proportionality analysis directly, 'they do indicate that the High Court is uncomfortable about elements of that form of analysis': Stone, 'Constitutional Orthodoxy' (n 92) 855. See also *Aurukun Shire Council v Chief Executive Officer, Office of Liquor Gaming and Racing in the Department of Treasury* (2012) 1 Qd R 1, 71 [162] (Keane JA).

As will be explored in the next chapter, this judicial unease extends to the Court's approach to questions of fact that underpin proportionality reasoning.

## B. Levels of Scrutiny

In other jurisdictions, the courts have made it clear that proportionality is a variable standard that can be applied with different degrees of intensity. In Germany, for instance, the Federal Constitutional Court has developed different standards of scrutiny that apply in different contexts.[168] In Canada and South Africa, by contrast, while there is a single standard of proportionality, it is applied flexibly depending on the circumstances of the case.[169]

In Australia, there has, to date, been some uncertainty over whether structured proportionality ought to be further refined into different categories or standards of review. In *Tajjour v New South Wales*, which was an important precursor to the development of structured proportionality testing, Crennan, Kiefel and Bell JJ rejected the application in Australia of different 'categories of scrutiny', such as those applied in the US.[170] The *Lange* test, they observed, 'does not involve differing levels of scrutiny'.[171] In *McCloy* itself, where structured proportionality was first adopted, the joint judgment rejected the importation into Australian law of the 'scrutiny of compelling government interests applied in United States constitutional jurisprudence'.[172]

In subsequent cases, the majority has continued to resist the development of a more defined approach to levels of scrutiny. In *Brown*, for instance, the joint judgment rejected the adoption of any 'general rule' about levels of justification, suggesting a preference for a flexible standard of proportionality.[173] Nevertheless, the joint judgment's observation that justification should be 'commensurate' with the nature of the burden[174] suggests there may be some leeway for the development of different standards of scrutiny in future cases. In *Clubb* the joint judgment continued to acknowledge the nature and extent of the burden will be relevant to assessing whether a law is justified under the *McCloy* test.[175] While other members of the majority agreed, they cautioned

[168] See ch 4, n 33 and accompanying text.

[169] See ch 4, nn 34 and 35 and accompanying text.

[170] *Tajjour* (n 41) 575 [131].

[171] ibid 575 [132]; see also 551 [37] (French CJ), *cf* 580–81 [151] (Gageler J). See also *Monis* (n 87) 130 [64] (French CJ), 212 [342] (Crennan, Kiefel and Bell JJ).

[172] *McCloy* (n 1) 215 [72] (French CJ, Kiefel, Bell and Keane JJ).

[173] *Brown* (n 106) 369 [128] (Kiefel CJ, Bell and Keane JJ). The plaintiffs had submitted that the legislation required a 'compelling justification' as it was directed to the content of political communications, but the joint judgment rejected this submission, observing that neither the terms nor the purpose of the legislation 'seeks to affect the content of the opinion which a protester may seek to voice': see 368 [122].

[174] ibid 369 [128]. See also 367 [118] (Kiefel CJ, Bell and Keane JJ), 423 [291] (Nettle J).

[175] *Clubb* (n 96) 194 [43], 202 [75] (Kiefel CJ, Bell and Keane JJ).

against any rigid or rule-based system. Justice Nettle, for instance, rejected submissions from Victoria and the Commonwealth that where the burden was 'slight', the degree of justification could be 'calibrated' according to the burden.[176] In particular, he considered that such submissions were 'conclusory' and might shortcut a 'more thorough assessment of appropriateness and adaptedness'.[177] Justice Edelman also took the view that the balancing inquiry 'should not involve rigid categories of review', but should be '"properly attuned" to the nature of the freedom' and the seriousness of the impact on the 'systemic integrity of the constitutional system of representative and responsible government'.[178]

In contrast, other members of the Court have expressed a preference for a more structured approach to the question of scrutiny. Justice Gordon, for instance, has indicated that there are elements of the US 'categorical' approach to constitutional review evident within the Court's existing 'appropriate and adapted' jurisprudence.[179] Justice Gageler has developed what he describes as an approach of 'precedent-based calibrated scrutiny', which operates within the traditional 'appropriate and adapted test'.[180] Under this approach, as the name suggests, the level of scrutiny is adjusted depending on the circumstances of the case. Importantly, the nature and intensity of the burden on political communication are 'calibrated' according to the risk placed on the maintenance of the constitutionally prescribed systems of government.[181] In *McCloy*, for instance, where the law in question restricted political communication in the conduct of elections for political office, Gageler J considered that the appropriate standard of scrutiny was that of 'compelling justification'.[182] Again in *Brown* and *Clubb*, Gageler J adopted a standard of 'close scrutiny'.[183] While both Gordon J and Gageler J have stopped short of endorsing a strict tiered approach to review, such as that applied in the US, their approaches appear to be a step towards a more defined approach.

## IV. CONCLUSION

The introduction of a structured test of proportionality can be seen as part of a broader evolution of proportionality-style reasoning in Australian constitutional law. As this chapter has demonstrated, over several decades, the Court has applied various tests in different contexts: 'reasonably capable of being

[176] ibid 261–63 [261], [264].
[177] ibid 263 [265].
[178] ibid 344 [498] (citation omitted).
[179] *Brown* (n 106) 477 [477].
[180] *Clubb* (n 96) 225 [161]. See also *Brown* (n 106) 377–79 [162]–[166].
[181] *Clubb* (n 96) 225 [162].
[182] ibid 232 [183]. This standard was applied by Mason CJ in *ACTV* (n 23) 143.
[183] *Brown* (n 106) 390 [203]; *Clubb* (n 96) 232 [183], *cf* 304 [386]–[387] (Gordon J).

considered appropriate and adapted', 'reasonably appropriate and adapted' and 'reasonably necessary'. These tests contain various elements of suitability, necessity and balancing, but it is only since 2015 that the Court has explicitly applied all three elements as part of a structured proportionality test. Questions remain as to the extent to which this test will be applied in contexts beyond the implied freedom of political communication. Against this background, the following chapter seeks to clarify the relationship between facts and proportionality by examining the role of facts within each of these different formulations.

# 6

# *The Factual Basis of Proportionality in Australia*

THE HIGH COURT has long acknowledged that, '[h]ighly inconvenient as it might be', questions of constitutional validity will 'sometimes depend on facts, facts which somehow must be ascertained by the court responsible for deciding the validity of the law'.[1] Yet, the Court has, on the whole, not adequately grappled with the importance of questions of fact that arise under proportionality analysis. As explained in Chapter 2, a court's conclusion about whether a measure is proportionate is best characterised as a question of law. Underpinning this conclusion, however, there are various factual propositions. This chapter explores the correlation between facts and proportionality in Australia by investigating whether, and how, the framing of constitutional tests affects the need for factual inquiry. It begins with a brief introduction to the High Court's traditional approach to facts in constitutional adjudication, before examining the extent to which facts have been recognised as relevant to the various formulations of proportionality-style reasoning that were identified in the previous chapter. Overall, this chapter demonstrates that the High Court's treatment of facts remains inconsistent and the introduction of a structured test of proportionality has not necessarily increased the role of facts.

## I. RECOGNISING FACTS

The notion that facts may be relevant to, or even determinative of, questions of constitutional validity presents something of a conundrum. On the one hand, the common law is predicated on the idea of determining disputes in their particular setting. A court's jurisdiction is only triggered on the application of a party, and the parties themselves are, on the whole, expected to furnish the court with appropriate evidentiary material. In Australia, at least, the High Court can only determine concrete controversies and it is

[1] *Commonwealth Freighters Pty Ltd v Sneddon* (1959) 102 CLR 280, 292 (Dixon CJ). More recently, see *Unions NSW v New South Wales (No 2)* (2019) 264 CLR 595, 631 [94] (Gageler J) (hereinafter '*Unions (No 2)*').

precluded from issuing advisory opinions.[2] On the other hand, when it comes to constitutional questions, the Court has been hesitant to develop standards that depend on findings of fact.[3] Yet this apparent conundrum makes sense in light of the distinction, discussed in Chapter 3, between adjudicative and non-adjudicative facts. The facts relevant to constitutional validity are non-adjudicative in nature and it is these facts about which the Court has traditionally been cautious. The history of this attitude stretches back to the Court's early years, when, as Susan Kenny has observed, 'wherever possible, such standards were deliberately avoided by the early Court in its attempt to minimise the need for factual determinations in constitutional adjudications'.[4] Instead, the Court has preferred an abstract style of analysis, which has meant that the underlying factual aspects of its decisions are often concealed.[5]

There are a number of factors that help explain the Court's reluctance to embrace fact-dependent standards. First, as explained in Chapter 1, for many years the Court's dominant interpretive approach has been one of 'legalism', which at least claims to minimise the need for judges to rely on extra-legal sources.[6] This is reinforced by the Court's particular understanding of judicial power, which circumscribes the functions that can be performed by courts.[7] As a consequence, the Court has long expressed the view that factual questions relating to social, political or economic matters are beyond the proper limits of its role. As early as 1908, for example, Isaacs J commented that Parliament was 'infinitely more capable than the Court' of determining such issues.[8] Similarly, the Court's landmark decision in *Amalgamated Society of Engineers v Adelaide Steamship Co Ltd* to overhaul the implied immunities doctrine reflected, in part, a concern that the judicial branch was not equipped to determine 'political necessities'.[9]

Coupled with these institutional concerns, there are concerns that fact-dependent constitutional standards will lead to uncertainty and unpredictability.[10] In *Murphy v Electoral Commissioner*, for instance, Keane J

[2] *In re Judiciary and Navigation Acts* (1921) 29 CLR 257. *cf* the situation in Canada: see ch 1, text accompanying n 90.

[3] S Kenny, 'Constitutional Fact Ascertainment' (1990) 1 *Public Law Review* 134, 149; J Lennan, 'How to Find Facts in Constitutional Cases' (2011) 30 *Civil Justice Quarterly* 304.

[4] Kenny (n 3) 149. See also G Sawer, *Australian Federalism in the Courts* (Melbourne, Melbourne University Press, 1967) 56.

[5] P Brazil, 'The Ascertainment of Facts in Australian Constitutional Cases' (1970) 4 *Federal Law Review* 65, 71.

[6] See ch 1, section III.B. But note that even in the 'heyday' of legalism, there were signs that policy considerations played a role: C Saunders, 'Interpreting the Constitution' (2004) 15 *Public Law Review* 289, 291.

[7] See the discussion in ch 1, text accompanying nn 59ff.

[8] *Jumbunna Coal Mine NL v Victorian Coal Miners' Association* (1908) 6 CLR 309, 376.

[9] *Amalgamated Society of Engineers v Adelaide Steamship Co Ltd* (1920) 28 CLR 129, 151 (Knox CJ, Isaacs, Rich and Starke JJ) (hereinafter '*Engineers' Case*').

[10] As Zines observed, '[t]o accept that rules of law can depend on facts is to invite a degree of instability': L Zines, *The High Court and the Constitution*, 5th edn (Sydney, Federation Press, 2008) 650. See now J Stellios, *Zines's The High Court and the Constitution*, 6th edn (Sydney, Federation Press, 2015) 687.

rejected an argument that 'changes in the milieu in which the Act operates', such as advances in technology, could result in the impugned provisions becoming invalid.[11] It was not the Court's role, according to Keane J, to respond to changing factual circumstances in this way:

> It is the function of Parliament to make laws in order to change the world. To assert that changes in the world may unmake laws made by Parliament is to assert the existence of an exception to this understanding of the role of Parliament.[12]

In addition, the procedures by which cases conventionally reach the High Court influence the Court's approach to facts. While these procedural questions are dealt with in more detail in Chapter 7, it is important to note that whether exercising appellate or original jurisdiction, the Court rarely engages directly with fact-finding. In addition, amicus interventions remain rare.[13] The Court is often able to rely on statements of fact agreed between the parties or findings of fact made by lower courts.[14] Although, at least in the case of constitutional facts, it appears open to the Court to make additional findings of fact, in practice the Court often avoids any extensive engagement with factual questions.

Despite the Court's traditional reluctance to engage with facts, since the 1940s the Court has acknowledged that *at times*, facts will be relevant to questions of constitutional validity.[15] These constitutional facts, as they have become known, have been distinguished from the ordinary facts that arise between the parties.[16] The recognition of constitutional facts has been most prominent in the Court's jurisprudence dealing with the defence power and section 92 of the *Australian Constitution*.[17] In both these areas, as the previous chapter has explained, the Court has adopted tests that involve elements of proportionality reasoning.[18] While others have documented the Court's approach to constitutional facts more generally,[19] there has been little specific analysis of such facts in the context of proportionality reasoning.

[11] *Murphy v Electoral Commissioner* (2016) 261 CLR 28, 91 [194].

[12] ibid 93 [199]. This issue was considered but not resolved by Edelman J in *Clubb v Edwards; Preston v Avery* (2019) 267 CLR 171, 333–35 [470]–[471]. Note, however, that when considering the meaning of constitutional terms, certain members of the Court have at times been prepared to accept that these may change over time. See, eg, *Attorney-General (Cth); Ex rel McKinlay v Commonwealth* (1975) 135 CLR 1, 36 (McTiernan and Jacobs JJ); *Roach v Electoral Commissioner* (2007) 233 CLR 162, 174 [7] (Gleeson CJ), *cf* 219 [161] (Hayne J).

[13] See ch 7, n 22.

[14] See the discussion in ch 7, section I.A.

[15] In comparison with other jurisdictions, the High Court's recognition of such facts is relatively recent; see Kenny (n 3) 149; Stellios (n 10) 683–84.

[16] See, eg, *Stenhouse v Coleman* (1944) 69 CLR 457, 469 (Dixon J); *Breen v Sneddon* (1961) 106 CLR 406, 411 (Dixon CJ). See also the discussion of constitutional facts in ch 3, section II.A.

[17] *Commonwealth of Australia Constitution Act 1900* (Imp) 63 & 64 Vict, c 12, s 9 (hereinafter '*Australian Constitution*').

[18] See ch 5, section II.A.

[19] See, eg, JD Holmes, 'Evidence in Constitutional Cases' (1949) 23 *Australian Law Journal* 235; PH Lane, 'Facts in Constitutional Law' (1963) 37 *Australian Law Journal* 108; Brazil (n 5); E Campbell, 'Fact Finding in Constitutional Cases' in Constitutional Commission, *Final Report of the Constitutional Commission*, vol 2 (Australian Government Publishing Service, 1988);

## II. FACTS AND THE FRAMING OF CONSTITUTIONAL TESTS

As Chapter 5 has established, the High Court has developed a range of different tests of constitutional validity that incorporate various aspects of proportionality reasoning. These tests can be viewed along a spectrum ranging from 'reasonably capable of being considered appropriate and adapted' to 'structured proportionality'. Given the conceptual similarities between the different tests, it might perhaps be expected that the Court would adopt a consistent attitude towards facts. The following section of this chapter examines the role of facts within each of these tests in order to assess whether the shift towards a more structured form of proportionality testing has increased the need for the courts to undertake factual inquiry.

### A. Reasonably Capable of Being Considered Appropriate and Adapted

The first variant of proportionality that emerges in the Australian context is the test of 'reasonably capable of being considered appropriate and adapted'.[20] This formulation has been applied in relation to the characterisation of laws with respect to certain heads of power, and a similar test has been applied to assess the validity of delegated legislation.[21] As argued in the previous chapter, this test can be seen as broadly analogous to the 'suitability' limb of the proportionality test and it imposes a relatively low level of judicial scrutiny.[22] In Australia, however, it forms the beginning and end of the inquiry, as the Court does not, under this test, proceed to examine the subsequent stages of proportionality.

In terms of facts, Chapter 2 has established that under the suitability sub-test, a court must rely on certain facts or assumptions about the empirical world. At this stage, a court only has to find that the law is capable of advancing the particular purpose. It is not required to determine whether the law *actually* advances the purpose, nor will it generally be required to assess any alternative measures. Therefore, when assessing suitability, a court will generally be able to

Kenny (n 3); B Selway, 'The Use of History and Other Facts in the Reasoning of the High Court of Australia' (2001) 20 *University of Tasmania Law Review* 129; Lennan (n 3); JD Heydon, *Cross on Evidence*, 12th Australian edition (Sydney, LexisNexis Butterworths, 2020) ch 2.

[20] As explained in ch 5, this test is sometimes expressed as whether the law is 'capable of being reasonably considered to be appropriate and adapted'; see ch 5, n 32.

[21] See ch 5, section II.A.i.

[22] However, in the context of the judicial review of delegated legislation, it has been noted that this test is more intense than the traditional *Wednesbury* standard of unreasonableness: A Edgar, 'Judicial Review of Delegated Legislation: Why Favour Substantive Review over Procedural Review?' in J Bell et al (eds), *Public Law Adjudication in Common Law Systems: Process and Substance* (Oxford, Hart Publishing, 2016) 203.

avoid the more difficult questions of prognosis.[23] As Chapter 3 has explained, the issues of both purpose and connection may be able to be answered by reference to the text and structure of the legislation itself, or the relevant facts may be within the general knowledge of the courts.[24] At other times, however, courts may need to refer to empirical materials to establish the relevant facts.

The High Court, when applying the 'reasonably capable of being considered appropriate and adapted' test, has displayed some willingness to acknowledge the factual aspects of the inquiry. For instance, in the context of the characterisation of laws under heads of Commonwealth legislative power, facts have been recognised as relevant where the power in question is purposive or contains a purposive element. Most prominently, this can be seen in the context of the defence power in section 51(vi) of the *Australian Constitution*. In a series of cases during the Second World War, the Court developed an approach to the defence power that was dependent upon the factual circumstances in which the law operated.[25] It held that the scope of the defence power is not fixed but 'elastic', meaning that it can contract or expand depending on the circumstances.[26] As explained in Chapter 5, the defence power is engaged when the legislation in question furthers the 'purpose' of defence,[27] and this test can be understood as incorporating aspects of proportionality reasoning.[28] Although the manner in which the test is expressed has varied, the inquiry involves ascertaining, first, the purpose of the law (and whether it is a defence purpose) and, second, whether the law is capable of advancing that purpose.

In answering these questions, the Court has explicitly acknowledged the relevance of facts. As Dixon J explained in *Andrews v Howell*, the application of the defence power 'depends upon facts, and as those facts change so may its actual operation'.[29] These facts, according to Dixon J, may concern 'the nature and dimensions of the conflict ... actual and apprehended dangers, exigencies and course of the war, and ... the matters that

[23] Note that in the typical formulation of proportionality, as explained in ch 2 and applied in the comparative jurisdictions, the suitability stage does not involve the assessment of alternative measures.

[24] In this case, they would fall within the accepted bounds of judicial notice. See further the discussion in ch 7, section I.B.ii.

[25] See Brazil (n 5) 68.

[26] *Stenhouse* (n 16) 472. Note that the Court has held that the scope of the defence power does not immediately contract after the cessation of hostilities; see *R v Foster* (1949) 79 CLR 43.

[27] As discussed in ch 2, section II.B.i, the identification of the legislative purpose may be viewed as an empirical question, and so ascertaining the scope of the 'defence' threat in a given case can be understood to involve questions of fact.

[28] See the discussion in ch 5, section II.A.i.

[29] *Andrews v Howell* (1941) 65 CLR 255, 278. This understanding of the defence power has been confirmed in later cases, and the Court has had regard to various facts to determine questions of validity. See, eg, *Stenhouse* (n 16) 469; *Sloan v Pollard* (1947) 75 CLR 445, 469; *Jenkins v Commonwealth* (1947) 74 CLR 400, 402. Note, however, that the Court has not always agreed on whether such facts must be ascertained to determine constitutional validity. See, eg, *Thomas v Mowbray* (2007) 233 CLR 307, 363 [146] (Gummow and Crennan JJ), 324–26 [6]–[9] (Gleeson CJ), 446 [403] (Hayne J), 512 [612] (Heydon J), 481–88 [523]–[534] (Callinan J), 411 [296] (Kirby J).

are incident thereto'.[30] In that case, the Court held that the prosecution of the war meant that it was necessary for the government to decide how refrigerated shipping space should be used,[31] and so regulations empowering the Commonwealth to acquire apples and pears were held to be within the scope of the defence power. Similarly, in *Stenhouse v Coleman*, the Court upheld an order that restricted the manufacturing and sale of bread.[32] Justice Dixon noted that determining whether the measure was incidental or conducive to the operation of the war depended upon 'a correct ascertainment of the true nature and operation of the provisions impugned and of their bearing upon the prosecution of the war'.[33]

While the Court has clearly recognised the relevance of facts in the context of the defence power, there has been some suggestion that the defence power is exceptional in this regard. In *Murphy*, for instance, Keane J rejected any general link between facts and proportionality.[34] The plaintiffs in that case argued that changes in technology meant there was no longer a 'substantial reason' to justify the suspension period on enrolments in the *Commonwealth Electoral Act 1918* (Cth).[35] Justice Keane dismissed this argument, taking the view that constitutional validity could not be dependent on changing factual circumstances.[36] In particular, Keane J sought to distinguish the Commonwealth Parliament's power to make laws regulating elections from both the operation of the defence power and section 92 (where, he acknowledged, changing factual circumstances may be relevant).[37]

Yet, Keane J's claim about the 'exceptional' nature of the defence power seems to be cast too strongly. In other contexts where the Court has applied a similar test, facts have been acknowledged as relevant to the Court's inquiry. In relation to the external affairs power, for instance, the Court needs to assess the connection between the law and a particular purpose (namely, the treaty obligations in question).[38] When applying the 'reasonably capable of being considered appropriate and adapted' test, the Court has acknowledged that facts might be relevant. In *Richardson v Forestry Commission*, the Court had

[30] *Andrews* (n 29) 278.
[31] ibid 278.
[32] *Stenhouse* (n 16).
[33] ibid 469.
[34] *Murphy* (n 11) 93 [199].
[35] Anthony John Murphy, 'Plaintiff's Annotated Submissions', Submission in *Murphy v Electoral Commissioner*, M247/2015, 11 April 2016 [8]. See also Transcript of Proceedings, *Murphy v Electoral Commissioner* [2016] HCATrans 108 (11 May 2016) 580–715, 789–946; Transcript of Proceedings, *Murphy v Electoral Commissioner* [2016] HCATrans 111 (12 May 2016) 1805–2799.
[36] *Murphy* (n 11) 91 [194]. See further the discussion in ch 7, nn 142ff and accompanying text.
[37] ibid 92–93 [199]–[200].
[38] See, eg, *Richardson v Forestry Commission* (1988) 164 CLR 261, 289 (Mason CJ and Brennan J); *Victoria v Commonwealth* (1996) 187 CLR 416, 487 (Brennan CJ, Toohey, Gaudron, McHugh and Gummow JJ).

the benefit of an interlocutory hearing in which the relevant evidence was set out.[39] The issue for the Full Court was whether Commonwealth legislation enacted to protect certain areas of Tasmanian wilderness was supported by the external affairs power. Chief Justice Mason and Brennan J, in upholding the legislation in its entirety, acknowledged that the Court would often have to be satisfied of the facts that provided a constitutional basis for the legislation. They referred to the Court's established jurisprudence on constitutional facts in both the defence power and section 92 contexts.[40] They were satisfied that the evidence heard before Mason CJ established '[b]roadly speaking, that … there are particular stands of rare timber, aboriginal cave dwellings and archaeological sites' and also that one of the areas may possess important world heritage characteristics that had not yet been identified.[41] This enabled them to conclude that there was a reasonable 'basis for a legislative judgment' that substantial parts of the areas may possess world heritage characteristics.[42] In contrast, Deane J and Gaudron J, in separate and partially dissenting judgments, were not satisfied that there was enough evidence to support the validity of the entire Act.[43] While the Court divided on the sufficiency of the evidence, the case demonstrates that facts were considered to be *relevant* to the application of the constitutional test.

The Court has also, as discussed in Chapter 5, applied a similar formulation of the test in the context of reviewing delegated legislation.[44] In this setting, the Court has again been willing to take account of the factual circumstances in which the delegated legislation operates.[45] In *Williams v Melbourne Corporation*, for instance, in order to assess the validity of the by-law in

[39] *Richardson* (n 38). The matter came before the High Court by way of questions reserved pursuant to s 18 of the *Judiciary Act 1903* (Cth). Chief Justice Mason had before him a number of affidavits filed by the plaintiff and the defendant. These included an affidavit from the Chief Commissioner of Forests for Tasmania, as well as affidavits from conservation and archaeological experts. The plaintiff's submissions to the Full Court also included a number of appendices which included information relating to the World Heritage Convention process. See Graham Frederick Richardson, 'Appendices to Plaintiff's Submissions', Submission in *Richardson v Forestry Commission*, C4/1987, 12 October 1987.

[40] *Richardson* (n 38) 294 (Mason CJ and Brennan J), citing *Australian Communist Party v Commonwealth* (1951) 83 CLR 1, *Hughes and Vale Pty Ltd v New South Wales (No 2)* (1955) 93 CLR 127 and *Commonwealth Freighters* (n 1).

[41] *Richardson* (n 38) 294.

[42] ibid 295.

[43] ibid 318 (Deane J), 347–48 (Gaudron J).

[44] As discussed in ch 5, in *Brett Cattle Co Pty Ltd v Minister for Agriculture, Fisheries and Forestry* (2020) 274 FCR 337, Rares J introduced a test of structured proportionality in this context. In finding the minister's ban on live exports to be invalid, Rares J had the benefit of extensive evidence.

[45] In the context of reviewing the 'reasonableness' of delegated legislation, the courts have been willing to inquire into facts in circumstances where the regulations themselves depend on matters of fact. See, eg, *Austral Fisheries Pty Ltd v Minister for Primary Industries and Energy* (1992) 37 FCR 462; *Bienke v Minister for Primary Industries and Energy* (1996) 63 FCR 567; *Melbourne Pathology Pty Ltd v Minister for Human Services and Health* (1996) 40 ALD 565; *Visa International Service Association v Reserve Bank of Australia* (2003) 131 FCR 300. As a result, it is perhaps not surprising that the courts have been willing to undertake factual inquiry when applying a form of proportionality reasoning to review delegated legislation.

question, Dixon J took account of various facts concerning the nature of sale-yards, the operation of the slaughter industry and the transportation of cattle.[46] Similarly, in *South Australia v Tanner*, the majority justices observed that it was necessary for the Court to 'form a view as to the existence and dimensions of the actual or threatened pollution or deterioration of water in the Watershed' to determine whether the regulations were within power.[47] Furthermore, in *Tanner*, the majority observed that these 'matters of fact' were ones that needed to be ascertained by evidence rather than judicial notice.[48]

It is worth noting that when applying the 'reasonably capable of being considered' test, the Court has tended to refrain from considering alternatives. This approach is consistent with the view that this test is broadly analogous to the suitability limb of structured proportionality and that it represents a low level of judicial scrutiny. In the context of the defence power, Dixon J indicated in *Sloan v Pollard* that it was not relevant that other measures might have been adopted to achieve the same purpose.[49] The Court was only concerned with 'the appropriateness of the means to the end', and it would not inquire further into the 'the choice of means'.[50] A similar approach has been taken in the context of reviewing delegated legislation. For instance, in *Attorney-General (South Australia) v Adelaide City Corporation*, which concerned the validity of by-laws that prohibited street preaching without a permit, there was also some reluctance to consider alternatives.[51] Chief Justice French, for example, acknowledged that the availability of alternative modes of regulation 'may be relevant' with respect to delegated legislation, but cautioned against '[c]ounterfactual explorations' as they would risk 'second-guessing' the merits of the delegated legislation.[52] Justice Hayne was even more reluctant to accept the role of alternatives, preferring to define the task of determining validity as one of characterisation.[53]

From the above analysis, it is clear that facts have sometimes been considered relevant to the 'reasonably capable of being considered appropriate and adapted' test. The Court has been willing to take account of facts that concern the background context in which the law operates as well as the practicalities of how the law actually works in order to establish the relevant connection between the law and its purpose. In *Richardson*, for instance, the Court considered

[46] *Williams v Melbourne Corporation* (1933) 49 CLR 142, 153–55 ('*Williams*').

[47] *South Australia v Tanner* (1989) 166 CLR 161, 165 (Wilson, Dawson, Toohey and Gaudron JJ) (hereinafter '*Tanner*').

[48] ibid.

[49] *Sloan v Pollard* (1947) 75 CLR 445, 472.

[50] ibid.

[51] *Attorney-General (South Australia) v Adelaide City Corporation* (2013) 249 CLR 1.

[52] ibid 43 [65].

[53] ibid 59 [123]. Justices Crennan and Kiefel did not expressly address the question of alternatives in this context, but suggested (at 84 [201]) that the test bore an 'obvious affinity' with a test of proportionality and that similar questions would arise. In this way, their Honours appeared to merge the two tests together. When considering alternatives under the *Lange* test, they noted (at 86 [207]) that none had been identified.

empirical material relating to the Tasmanian wilderness areas to determine whether the legislation was a valid exercise of the external affairs power.[54] Similarly, the Court has relied on evidence to ascertain facts about, inter alia, the cattle industry and road use,[55] and the extent of water pollution[56] in order to assess the validity of delegated legislation. The Court has appeared relatively comfortable with relying on empirical material in this context, though it has stopped short of considering alternatives.

### B. Reasonably Appropriate and Adapted

The next formulation developed by the Court is the 'reasonably appropriate and adapted' test. This test is predominantly used in relation to the implied freedom of political communication, and a modified variation (which requires the existence of a 'substantial reason') has been applied in cases concerning voting rights.[57] Although – as I will explain below – both stages of the two-part *Lange* test[58] involve empirical questions, the High Court has not always relied on evidence or even acknowledged the relevance of facts. In its implied freedom jurisprudence, the Court has often stated that it will take account of a law's practical operation, but until recently there has been little explicit discussion of facts in this context. This can be contrasted with section 92 of the *Australian Constitution*, where the Court has long acknowledged the relevance of facts. This disparity is also reflected in the existing scholarship, with the issue of constitutional facts largely absent from the extensive academic literature on the implied freedom, and commentary on constitutional fact-finding often omitting the implied freedom altogether.[59]

Under the first *Lange* question, the Court asks whether the law effectively burdens the freedom to communicate about government or political matters either in its terms, operation or effect. By focusing on the practical operation of a law and its effects, this part of the inquiry would appear to invite questions of fact. Yet when it comes to the question of burden, the Court seldom engages in a detailed factual inquiry. For a start, the Court has repeatedly insisted that the implied freedom is not a personal right and that the assessment of the burden

[54] *Richardson* (n 38). See also the text accompanying n 39 above.

[55] *Williams* (n 46). See also the text accompanying n 46 above.

[56] *Tanner* (n 47). See also the text accompanying n 47 above.

[57] See *Murphy* (n 11) 49 [31] (French CJ and Bell J) 67 [85] (Gageler J), 107 [244] (Nettle J), 121–23 [293] (Gordon J).

[58] *Lange v Australian Broadcasting Corporation* (1997) 189 CLR 520, 567 (citations omitted), as modified in *Coleman v Power* (2004) 220 CLR 1, 50–51 [93]–[96], 78 [196]. See also ch 5, nn 52 and 53 and accompanying text, where the test is set out in full.

[59] Note that the following accounts of constitutional facts do make some reference to the implied freedom of political communication, but do not consider the issue in any detail: S Gageler, 'Fact and Law' (2009) 11 *Newcastle Law Review* 1, 10–11; C Tran, 'Facts and Evidence in Litigation under the *Charter of Human Rights and Responsibilities Act 2006* (Vic) and the *Human Rights Act 2004* (ACT)' (2012) 36 *Melbourne University Law Review* 287, 291; Stellios (n 10) 694.

in a particular case is only relevant as part of considering the law's effect on political communication as a whole.[60] Second, the question of burden is usually relatively easily established and the Court has held that even 'slight' burdens need to be justified.[61] Finally, in a number of cases, the Court has assumed a burden and proceeded to examine the second *Lange* question.[62]

It is the second limb of the *Lange* test, where the Court must ask whether the law is 'reasonably appropriate and adapted' to serve a legitimate end, which is most often determinative. This limb of the test, which incorporates the suitability limb of proportionality as well as some aspects of the necessity limb,[63] also invites empirical questions. Given that this test requires the Court itself to form a view about whether the law is likely to actually advance the purpose, a greater emphasis on facts might perhaps be expected under this part of the test. In the early implied freedom case of *Cunliffe v Commonwealth*, Mason CJ noted the relevance of facts to the question of justification:

> In the context of an implication of freedom of communication, in order to justify the imposition of some burden or restriction on that right, it is generally not enough simply to assert the existence of facts said to justify the imposition of that burden or restriction. The relevant facts must either be agreed or proved or be such that the Court is prepared to take account of them by judicial notice or otherwise.[64]

In that case, the impugned provisions of the *Migration Act 1958* (Cth) restricted giving immigration assistance or providing representation to aliens. Mason CJ took the view that the scope and extent of the mischief to which the provisions were directed, insofar as they imposed additional requirements on legal practitioners, had not been established by evidence, judicial notice or legislative findings.[65] He referred to a Joint Standing Committee report, but concluded that it contained 'no relevant findings or conclusions' on this question.[66] This failure to establish 'the scope and extent of the alleged mischief' contributed to Mason CJ's conclusion (in dissent) that the provisions were not appropriate and adapted to the legitimate end.[67]

Despite this early recognition of the role of facts in determining whether a burden is justified, the Court has often not engaged directly with questions of fact. In many cases there is no detailed discussion of the factual basis of the

[60] See, eg, *Wotton v Queensland* (2012) 246 CLR 1, 31 [80] (Kiefel J); *Unions NSW v New South Wales* (2013) 252 CLR 530, 553–554 [35]–[36] (French CJ, Hayne, Crennan, Kiefel and Bell JJ); *Brown v Tasmania* (2017) 261 CLR 328, 1110 [90] (Kiefel CJ, Bell and Keane JJ).

[61] *Clubb* (n 12) [64] (Kiefel CJ, Bell and Keane JJ).

[62] For instance, in *Comcare v Banerji*, the plurality noted that a law which 'prohibits or limits political communication to any extent will generally be found to impose an effective burden on the implied freedom': *Comcare v Banerji* (2019) 267 CLR 373, 398–99 [29] (Kiefel CJ, Bell, Keane and Nettle JJ) (hereinafter '*Banerji*'). See also *Unions NSW v New South Wales* (2013) 252 CLR 530, 555 [40] (French CJ, Hayne, Crennan, Kiefel and Bell JJ).

[63] See the discussion in ch 5, section II.A.ii.

[64] *Cunliffe v Commonwealth* (1994) 182 CLR 272, 304.

[65] ibid 304.

[66] ibid.

[67] ibid.

legislative provisions and, until recently, the Court has rarely discussed the issue of constitutional facts in this context. This reluctance to engage with facts can be seen in *Levy v Victoria*, another early implied freedom case, which concerned the validity of regulations prohibiting access to wetland areas.[68] The plaintiff argued that without evidence about the nature of the hunting activities, the question of whether the regulation was appropriate and adapted to achieve a claimed safety aim was 'one of speculation'.[69] The Court rejected this submission, with Brennan CJ observing that while it was 'possible' that validity might depend on facts, 'questions of fact seldom have to be resolved'.[70] While he referred to the distinction between constitutional facts and ordinary facts in issue between the parties,[71] he considered that only in 'rare instances' would it be impossible to determine a question of validity upon a demurrer.[72] In *Levy* itself, Brennan CJ took the view that *even if* the facts asserted by the plaintiff about the safety of duck shooting could be established,[73] this did not mean that the opinion of the Governor in Council could not properly have been formed.[74]

In other implied freedom cases, the Court appears to act on the basis of reason or logic, supplemented by its own general knowledge or assumption.[75] In the seminal case of *Lange*, for instance, it is clear that in developing the common law defence of qualified privilege, the Court was acting on the basis of certain assumptions about the world.[76] These included, for example, assumptions about

[68] *Levy v Victoria* (1997) 189 CLR 579.

[69] ibid 590 (summary of the plaintiff's argument). Note that counsel referred to *Castlemaine Tooheys Ltd v South Australia* (1990) 169 CLR 436, but this was not referred to in any of the judgments.

[70] *Levy* (n 68) 598.

[71] ibid. Note that Brennan CJ referred to the Court's jurisprudence on constitutional facts in other areas, including *Tanner* (n 47) and *Commonwealth Freighters* (n 1).

[72] *Levy* (n 68) 598.

[73] As Brennan CJ noted, the plaintiff submitted that evidence at a trial 'would show, inter alia, that there was no risk to life or limb by entry upon a proclaimed area while duck shooting was proceeding since the shooting of ducks occurs when they are on the wing and the gun is lifted above the level of any human intruder': ibid 599.

[74] ibid; see also 649 (Kirby J).

[75] As explained earlier in the book, this does not mean that the relevant inquiry is not factual in nature. However, in such instances, the Court might not explicitly acknowledge that the inquiry is factual (for example, by relying on evidence to support its claims or by explicitly invoking the doctrine of judicial notice).

[76] *Lange* (n 58). Note that *Lange* proceeded by way of a case stated under s 18 of the *Judiciary Act 1903* (Cth) and the stated case included a summary of the facts giving rise to the plaintiff's defamation proceedings against the Australian Broadcasting Corporation: see 'Case Stated Book', *Lange v Australian Broadcasting Corporation*, S109/1996, 10 December 1996. The Court in *Lange* (which was heard together with *Levy*) had before it a large volume of affidavits that had been adduced by a number of media organisations, an industrial organisation and the Australian Press Council, all of whom sought to intervene in the proceedings. Much of this evidence was directed towards the effects of the decisions of *Theophanous v Herald & Weekly Times* (1994) 182 CLR 104 and *Stephens v West Australian Newspapers Ltd* (1994) 182 CLR 211, and the likely consequences for defamation actions if these decisions were to be overturned. The Court permitted all but one of the bodies to intervene, but held that the affidavits filed in support of the application for leave could not be relied upon in the hearing of the substantive proceedings; see *Levy* (n 68) 587. See also Transcript of Proceedings, *Lange v Australian Broadcasting Corporation* [1997] HCATrans 85 (3 March 1997) 30–31 (Brennan CJ).

the way public powers are exercised and the nature of the modern bureaucratic State,[77] the operation of the law of defamation and the practicalities of the Australian political system,[78] including the types of discussions that might affect electoral choice.[79] In assessing whether the common law and the New South Wales statutory law of defamation were 'reasonably appropriate and adapted' to serve the legitimate end of protecting personal reputation,[80] the Court's understanding of defamation law and modern political conditions[81] enabled it to conclude that the common law doctrine 'must now be seen as imposing an unreasonable restraint' on the freedom of political communication.[82] The Court had no difficulty in making a prognosis about the degree of damage, concluding that where a publication had thousands of recipients, the damage was 'obviously so much greater'.[83]

In other cases there are signs that the Court is prepared to supplement its assumptions with reference to additional empirical material, but with little acknowledgement that it is engaged in a fact-finding exercise. For instance, in *Australian Capital Television Pty Ltd v Commonwealth*,[84] the Court's own understanding of the electoral system was supplemented by a number of reports prepared by Parliamentary Committees.[85] The case concerned various provisions in the *Broadcasting Act 1942* (Cth), which prohibited broadcasting during an election period and also allocated 'free time' to political parties based on their performance at the previous election. In concluding that the challenged provisions were invalid,[86] various members of the Court referred to these reports. For Mason CJ, for instance, the reports confirmed that the law's purpose was to safeguard the integrity of the political system by reducing the need to raise significant funds, and also indicated that similar restrictions had been introduced in other countries.[87] However, Mason CJ cautioned against attempts to

[77] In particular, the Court noted that social and political conditions had changed, and it endorsed McHugh J's depiction in *Stephens v West Australian Newspapers* (1994) 182 CLR 211, 264: *Lange* (n 58) 565, 570.

[78] *Lange* (n 58) 565, 572.

[79] ibid 576.

[80] ibid 569.

[81] ibid 571.

[82] ibid 570.

[83] ibid 572.

[84] *Australian Capital Television Pty Ltd v Commonwealth* (1992) 177 CLR 106 (hereinafter '*ACTV*').

[85] These materials included a Joint Standing Committee Report and a Select Committee report. Note that *ACTV* proceeded to the High Court by way of demurrer. These reports were provided to the Court by the Commonwealth Solicitor-General as part of four volumes of materials; see Transcript of Proceedings, *Australian Capital Television Pty Ltd v Commonwealth* (High Court of Australia, S5/1992, 17 March 1992) 89–91. See the discussion of *ACTV* in D Meagher, 'The Brennan Conception of the Implied Freedom: Theory, Proportionality and Deference' (2011) 30 *University of Queensland Law Journal* 119, 123–26.

[86] *ACTV* (n 84) 147 (Mason CJ), 175–76 (Deane and Toohey JJ), 224 (Gaudron J).

[87] ibid 129–131. In making these comments, Mason CJ referred to information contained in the Senate Select Committee Report that was before the Court. In addition, the Commonwealth filed supplementary submissions detailing the restrictions on political broadcasts in other jurisdictions: Commonwealth of Australia, 'Commonwealth Supplementary Submissions – 4 Political

restrict the implied freedom by way of 'some imagined necessity'.[88] He ultimately concluded that it was 'obvious' that the law gave preferential treatment to existing political parties[89] and that the free time provisions failed to provide meaningful access to new and independent candidates.[90] Therefore, the parliamentary reports do not appear to have been critical to the ultimate outcome of the case, and assumptions continued to play a role.[91] Moreover, the Court undertook little detailed empirical analysis of current political practices and instead adopted an abstract style of analysis.[92] As a result, the assumptions on which the Court acted have been subjected to considerable criticism.[93]

More recently, the Court has displayed a greater recognition of the relevance of facts within the 'reasonably appropriate and adapted' test. While a majority of the Court has now adopted a structured test of proportionality (discussed further in section II.D below), the minority justices have preferred the traditional 'appropriate and adapted' formulation.[94] In *McCloy* itself,[95] the Court had before it various reports prepared by the Independent Commission Against Corruption (ICAC) and other bodies.[96] These reports were referred to in order to illustrate the background circumstances in which the legislation operated and the nature of the problem Parliament was trying to address,[97] but it was the minority justices (who did not subscribe to the new proportionality test) who engaged more explicitly with the issues of fact.[98] Justice Gordon, for example, referred to the comparative practices of other jurisdictions to strengthen her conclusion that the suggested alternatives would not achieve the same purpose as the challenged provisions.[99] Justice Nettle also referred to the reports before

Broadcasting – The Practice of the United Kingdom, Ireland and Canada', Submission in *Australian Capital Television Pty Ltd v Commonwealth*, S5/1992, 18 March 1992. See also R Dixon, 'Proportionality and Comparative Constitutional Law versus Studies' (2018) 12 *Law & Ethics of Human Rights* 203, 215.

[88] *ACTV* (n 84) 145.

[89] ibid 132.

[90] ibid 146.

[91] See also ibid 175 (Deane and Toohey JJ).

[92] GN Rosenberg and JM Williams, 'Do Not Go Gently into That Good Right: The First Amendment in the High Court of Australia' (1997) *Supreme Court Law Review* 439.

[93] See the extensive empirical analysis conducted by Rosenberg and Williams (n 92), which demonstrates the flawed nature of many of the Court's assumptions. See also DZ Cass, 'Through the Looking Glass: The High Court and the Right to Speech' (1993) 4 *Public Law Review* 229, 239–40, 244–46.

[94] In *McCloy v New South Wales* (2015) 257 CLR 178, Gageler J, Nettle J and Gordon J all continued to apply the 'reasonably appropriate and adapted' test, but in subsequent cases, Nettle J has joined the majority in endorsing structured proportionality. Note that Gageler J has developed an approach of 'calibrated scrutiny'; see ch 5, nn 180ff and accompanying text.

[95] *McCloy* (n 94).

[96] These reports, or extracts thereof, were included in the special case book: see 'Special Case Book', *McCloy v New South Wales*, S211/2014, 28 January 2015. See also ch 7, text accompanying n 96.

[97] *McCloy* (n 94) 250 [194] (Gageler J), 261–62 [233] (Nettle J), 292–93 [359] (Gordon J).

[98] For a discussion of the majority justices, see section II.D below.

[99] *McCloy* (n 94) 286 [330].

the Court, but queried whether such evidence was always necessary. He noted, for instance, that the public concern over the influence of property developers was based more on 'inference than direct evidence', but suggested that it was 'not illogical or unprecedented for Parliament to enact legislation in response to inferred legislative imperatives'.[100] Indeed, he observed that often this was the only way that Parliament could deal with matters 'prophylactically'.[101] In relation to the question of alternatives, he appears to have proceeded on the basis of assumption, noting that the question of whether the prohibited donor provisions had a significant effect on corruption or undue influence was 'essentially irrelevant'.[102] However, he went on to find the prohibited donor provisions invalid because they discriminated against property developers, indicating that there was 'no direct evidence or sufficient basis for inference' that all donations from property developers would be of a 'corrupt or unduly influential character'.[103]

The most explicit recognition of the importance of facts within the 'appropriate and adapted' test was in the 2019 case of *Unions NSW v New South Wales (No 2)*.[104] In this case, which concerned the validity of expenditure caps on 'third-party' campaigning in State elections, facts were considered pivotal to the question of justification.[105] Justice Gageler, for instance, explicitly acknowledged the relevance of constitutional facts in determining whether the burden on the implied freedom could be justified:

> The State's justification for the burden on political communication imposed by s 29(10) of the EF Act therefore cannot succeed unless the Court can be satisfied of the existence of facts on which that justification depends.[106]

While the special case before the Court contained details about the practical operation of the expenditure caps and of the relevant legislative history, Gageler J held that on the 'critical question' of the amount of the cap, there was a 'gap in the factual substratum'.[107] In particular, as Gageler J noted, the Joint Standing Committee on Electoral Matters had indicated in 2016 that there was an 'unanswered question of fact' as to whether a cap of $500,000 would be sufficient to allow third-party campaigners with an opportunity to present its case.[108] According to Gageler J, Parliament had failed to undertake

[100] ibid 261–62 [233].
[101] ibid 262 [233].
[102] ibid 272 [265].
[103] ibid 273 [268].
[104] *Unions (No 2)* (n 1).
[105] Note that six members of the Court held that New South Wales had failed to justify the burden on the freedom, but they were divided on whether this should be assessed by using the traditional 'appropriate and adapted' formula or structured proportionality. Justice Edelman invalided that provision on the basis that it pursued an additional, illegitimate purpose.
[106] *Unions (No 2)* (n 1) 632 [96].
[107] ibid 633 [99].
[108] ibid.

the necessary inquiries as recommended by the Joint Standing Committee and so the cap imposed by the legislation could not be justified.[109] Justice Gordon agreed, holding that she was not satisfied that the expenditure cap was reasonably appropriate and adapted to achieve its constitutionally permissible end.[110] In particular, she held that New South Wales had failed to discharge its 'onus' of demonstrating that the burden was justified, including by adducing sufficient evidence.[111]

In the subsequent decisions of *Clubb v Edwards; Preston v Avery*,[112] where Gordon J and Gageler J again preferred the traditional 'appropriate and adapted' formulation, there was some acknowledgement of facts. As it had not been shown that Mrs Clubb engaged in political communication, both justices addressed the substance of the *Preston* appeal only.[113] Justice Gageler engaged more overtly with the question of facts, noting that evidence that was adduced in *Clubb* could be taken into account on questions of legislative or constitutional fact in the *Preston* case.[114] In assessing the question of justification, Gageler J noted that the reason that the Tasmanian Parliament had applied a protest prohibition throughout the 150 m safe access zone was not apparent either from the Second Reading speech or from the legislative history or evidence.[115] Critical for Gageler J, however, was the finding from the magistrate below which detailed a number of specific locations beyond the 150 m radius from which protesters remained able to protest.[116] This finding of constitutional fact was 'decisive'[117] in Gageler J's ultimate conclusion that – as there was 'enough opportunity for protests to be held at other locations meaningfully proximate to the premises' – that the burden on the freedom was not undue.[118] Justice Gordon, who agreed with the result, was less explicit about the factual justification. Her analysis focused on the construction of the legislation, but when discussing the purpose of the protest prohibition, Gordon J acknowledged that her conclusion was 'reinforced' by the parliamentary debates and publicly available materials cited in the debates.[119]

[109] ibid 633–34 [101]–[102].
[110] ibid 649–50 [150]–[151].
[111] ibid 650 [151].
[112] *Clubb* (n 12).
[113] ibid 221–22 [149]–[153] (Gageler J), 292–93 [349] (Gordon J).
[114] ibid 228 [172]. This was accepted by the parties.
[115] ibid 239–40 [209]. In particular, he noted that: 'Perhaps the idea of having an access zone of that dimension was simply borrowed from Victoria without it being thought to make any difference that the Tasmanian protest prohibition was to be more restrictive of political communication than its Victorian equivalent.'
[116] ibid 240 [211].
[117] ibid.
[118] ibid 241 [213].
[119] ibid 302 [380].

## C. Reasonably Necessary

A third variation of proportionality-type reasoning adopted by the High Court is that of 'reasonable necessity', which is employed in the context of the guarantee in section 92.[120] First, to determine whether section 92 is engaged, the Court asks whether the law discriminates against interstate trade, commerce or intercourse.[121] Second, even if the law is relevantly discriminatory, it will nonetheless be valid if it is 'reasonably necessary' to achieve some other purpose.[122] In *Palmer v Western Australia*, the Court considered whether this test of justification involved structured proportionality testing.[123] Chief Justice Kiefel and Keane J took the view that the three stages of structured proportionality could give content to, or explicate, the test of reasonable necessity,[124] but suggested it might not be the only method of justification.[125] Justice Edelman seemed to go further, holding that structured proportionality was *the* method to be applied when determining whether a law which burdens section 92 can be justified.[126] Justice Gageler and Justice Gordon, in contrast, rejected the use of structured proportionality in the context of assessing 'reasonable necessity'.[127] So, while three justices have now endorsed the use of structured proportionality in this context, whether or not this remains the majority position remains to be seen.

Facts have long been recognised as relevant in the context of section 92, even before the landmark decision of *Cole v Whitfield*.[128] In 1949, for instance, in *Bank of New South Wales v Commonwealth*, the Privy Council noted that in section 92 cases, the 'problem to be solved will often be not so much legal as political, social or economic'.[129] Despite the long recognition of facts in this context, the actual emphasis placed on facts has shifted over time, in part reflecting changes in the framing of the relevant test.[130] The revised approach to

[120] Note that in *Palmer v Western Australia*, the High Court held that the 'trade and commerce' limb and the intercourse limb of s 92 should be aligned: (2021) 95 ALJR 229, 242 [48] (Kiefel CJ and Keane J), 249 [97] (Gageler J), 265 [181] (Gordon J), 279 [241] (Edelman J).

[121] Note that by aligning the two limbs of s 92, the majority of the High Court in *Palmer* held that protectionism was not the only form of discrimination that may enliven s 92, though it was acknowledged that it would most often be relevant to the trade and commerce limb; see ibid 242 [47] (Kiefel CJ and Keane J), 278 [239] (Edelman J).

[122] As explained in ch 5, the language of 'necessity' was introduced in *Castlemaine Tooheys* (1990) 169 CLR 436. See also *Betfair Pty Ltd v Western Australia* (2008) 234 CLR 218.

[123] *Palmer* (n 120).

[124] ibid 242–44 [51]–[58].

[125] ibid 243 [56].

[126] ibid 284– 85 [261]–[265].

[127] ibid 258–60 [141]–[151] (Gageler J), 269–70 [198]–[199] (Gordon J).

[128] *Cole v Whitfield* (1988) 165 CLR 360.

[129] *Bank of New South Wales v Commonwealth* (1949) 79 CLR 497, 639 (Lord Porter). But see J Stone, 'A Government of Laws and Yet of Men' (1948) 1 *University of Western Australia Law Review* 461, 498ff.

[130] For example, under the 'criterion of operation' test, the emphasis given to factual questions was inconsistent: M Coper, *Freedom of Interstate Trade under the Australian Constitution* (Sydney, Butterworths, 1983) 126.

section 92 ushered in by *Cole* clarified not only the relevant test for section 92, but also the centrality of facts to this test. In *Cole* the questions of both 'discrimination' and 'protectionism' were acknowledged by the Court to raise 'issues of fact and degree'.[131] In addition, the Court's ultimate conclusion that the prohibitions in question were a '*necessary* means' of ensuring the protection of crayfish in Tasmanian waters[132] was also dependent on the facts. While the agreed facts in *Cole* meant that the Court was able to reach this conclusion without any detailed consideration of the facts, in later cases the factual aspects became more acute.

In *Castlemaine Tooheys Ltd v South Australia*, the Court had before it a detailed statement of agreed facts that contained information and statistics about the market share of beer in South Australia, the use of refillable and non-refillable bottles, and the deposit system that operated in South Australia.[133] In applying its reformulated test of 'necessary or appropriate and adapted', the Court held that neither of the proffered objectives (the need to protect the environment from the litter problem or the need to conserve energy resources) provided 'an acceptable explanation or justification for the differential treatment'.[134] In reaching this conclusion, it relied on concessions made by South Australia that a refund of 6 cents per non-refillable bottle for the first 12 months[135] would have been sufficient to achieve the same purpose. Accordingly, the 15 cents that was fixed by regulation exceeded what was necessary to ensure the same rate of return for both refillable and non-refillable bottles.[136] As others have observed, this concession in relation to the facts ultimately 'damaged [South Australia's] defence of the impugned legislation as a necessary or proportionate regulatory measure'.[137]

Nearly two decades later, in *Betfair Pty Ltd v Western Australia*, the Court confirmed the relevance of facts to the refashioned section 92 test of 'reasonable necessity'.[138] The Court had before it considerable evidence regarding the nature of the existing betting market in Western Australia, the nature of the betting industry and its value, and the development of an Australia-wide market for telephone and internet wagering services.[139] This evidence enabled

[131] *Cole* (n 128) 409.
[132] ibid 409 (emphasis added).
[133] *Castlemaine* (n 122) 437ff.
[134] ibid 477 (Mason CJ, Brennan, Deane, Dawson and Toohey JJ).
[135] Which would then reduce to 4 cents: ibid 474.
[136] ibid; see also 463.
[137] G Williams, S Brennan and A Lynch, *Blackshield and Williams Australian Constitutional Law and Theory: Commentary and Materials*, 7th edn (Sydney, Federation Press, 2018) 1286 [28.49]. See also A Simpson, 'Grounding the High Court's Modern Section 92 Jurisprudence: The Case for Improper Purpose as the Touchstone' (2005) 33 *Federal Law Review* 445, 480 fn 203.
[138] *Betfair* (n 122) 477 [102] (Gleeson CJ, Gummow, Kirby, Hayne, Crennan and Kiefel JJ).
[139] Note that *Betfair* came before the High Court by way of a special case stated under r 27.08 of the *High Court Rules 2004* (Cth). This evidence was included in the Special Case Book filed by the parties, which included a three-volume 'Book of Documents': see 'Special Case Book', *Betfair v Western Australia*, C2/2007, 5 October 2007.

the Court to find that there was a 'close substitutability' between various methods of wagering,[140] meaning there was a 'cross-elasticity of demand'.[141] Based on these findings, the Court was able to conclude that both of the challenged provisions operated to protect the local Western Australian operators and so conferred a discriminatory burden of a protectionist kind.[142] When considering whether the regulation was nonetheless permissible, the Court acknowledged that this involved 'an attempt at an evidentiary level to measure something of an imponderable'.[143] In applying the test of reasonable necessity, it relied on the alternative legislative choice taken by Tasmania. This provided some empirical support to enable the Court to conclude that the Western Australian choice was not necessary to achieve the propounded object.[144]

More recently, in *Palmer*, facts were again relevant to the Court's application of section 92. In that case, which concerned a challenge to the COVID-19 border restrictions imposed by Western Australia, the parties were unable to reach agreement on the facts.[145] As a result, the matter was remitted to a judge of the Federal Court to make the necessary findings of fact. Various expert witnesses gave evidence before the Federal Court and Rangiah J made detailed findings about the 'reasonable need for and efficacy of the community isolation measures'.[146] The High Court was able to draw upon these findings in concluding that the burden imposed by the *Emergency Management Act 2005* (WA) was justified. Chief Justice Kiefel and Keane J, for instance, considered that Rangiah J's findings about the risk of community transmission left 'little room' for debate about effective alternatives.[147] Therefore, they held there was no effective alternative which would achieve the same purpose.

*Betfair* and *Palmer* confirm that, as foreshadowed in both *Cole* and *Castlemaine*, the assessment of whether discriminatory burdens on trade, commerce or intercourse can be justified is underpinned by questions of fact. The relevance of alternatives, in particular, invites an inquiry into questions of fact. The nature of these facts, concerning technical and economic concepts, will often involve specialised knowledge. While the Court has alluded to the difficulty of measuring these empirical questions,[148] in practice it often relies on agreement between the parties or will remit the matter to a lower court.

[140] *Betfair* (n 122) 480 [115] (Gleeson CJ, Gummow, Kirby, Hayne, Crennan and Kiefel JJ).
[141] ibid 481 [122].
[142] ibid 481–82 [118]–[122].
[143] ibid 479 [110].
[144] ibid.
[145] *Palmer* (n 120) 237 [15].
[146] *Palmer v State of Western Australia (No 4)* [2020] FCA 1221 [5].
[147] *Palmer* (n 120) 247 [80]; see also 272 [208] (Gordon J).
[148] *Betfair* (n 122) 479 [110].

### D. Structured Proportionality

The final test developed by the Court is structured proportionality. As explained in the previous chapter, in *McCloy v New South Wales*, a slim majority of the Court adopted a three-part test of proportionality within the second limb of the *Lange* test.[149] While this test has been subject to considerable criticism from other members of the Court, it has now been endorsed by five justices.[150] This raises the question of whether this turn towards proportionality will, or should, trigger a greater focus on facts.

In *McCloy*, it will be recalled, the issue for the Court was whether restrictions on political donations were compatible with the implied freedom of political communication. As explained above, the Court had before it various reports[151] which were used to demonstrate that a problem of corruption existed in New South Wales and that the challenged legislation was designed to reduce the risk of corruption or undue influence. For instance, the joint judgment referred to the 'difficulties associated with uncovering and prosecuting corruption of this kind' and observed that the reports revealed 'the reality of the risk of corruption and the loss of public confidence which accompanies the exposure of acts of corruption'.[152] However, when it came to applying the later elements of the new 'proportionality testing', there was less emphasis on the empirical material. Even though the inclusion of the 'necessity' limb meant that the question of alternatives was squarely before the Court,[153] the joint judgment's engagement with questions of fact was slim. As Gabrielle Appleby has observed, the Court's consideration of alternative measures was 'largely … uninformed' by facts or evidence.[154] The joint judgment did note that the plaintiffs had identified two potential alternatives, but considered that these had not been adequately explained.[155] So, although it was held that the alternative measures identified by the plaintiffs had not been shown to be equally effective, there was no specific discussion of whether evidence would be required for this task.[156]

Similarly, at the 'balancing' stage of the new proportionality test, there was little engagement with questions of fact. The assessment of the 'adequacy' of the balance was brief, with the joint judgment concluding that the restriction

[149] *McCloy* (n 94) 193–95 [2] (French CJ, Kiefel, Bell and Keane JJ).

[150] See, eg, *Clubb* (n 12) 202 [74] (Kiefel CJ, Bell and Keane JJ), 264–65 [266] (Nettle J), 332–33 [468] (Edelman J); *Banerji* (n 62) 400 [32] (Kiefel CJ, Bell, Keane and Nettle JJ), 451 [188] (Edelman J).

[151] See the text accompanying n 96, above.

[152] *McCloy* (n 94) 209 [51] (French CJ, Kiefel, Bell and Keane JJ).

[153] ibid 211 [58].

[154] G Appleby, 'Functionalism in Constitutional Interpretation: Factual and Participatory Challenges: Comment on Dixon' (2015) 43 *Federal Law Review* 493, 494. While Appleby has suggested that the plaintiffs in *McCloy* failed to discharge an 'onus' of proof, the joint judgment did not describe the obligation on the plaintiffs as specifically as this.

[155] *McCloy* (n 94) 211 [61].

[156] Appleby (n 154) 494.

on the implied freedom was 'more than balanced' by the law's benefits.[157] In reaching this conclusion, the joint judgment noted that the effect of the impugned provisions on the implied freedom was 'indirect' and also that the 'public interest in removing the risk and perception of corruption is evident'.[158]

Therefore, in the *McCloy* decision, the adoption of a test of structured proportionality did not, in itself, propel those members of the Court further into a fact-finding exercise. Although there was considerable empirical material before the Court, this was mainly used to bolster the conclusion that there was a legitimate problem to be addressed and that the legislation was related to this problem. In this way, the empirical material can be seen as directed to the question of legitimate purpose and also to the suitability limb. It is not clear whether this material was essential to the Court's conclusion, and the same result may well have been reached even if the reports had not been available. In addition, during the later stages of the proportionality testing, where facts might be expected to play a greater role, there was little engagement with empirical questions, perhaps reflecting a view that this was an obvious or clear-cut case.

In the cases since *McCloy*, the Court has displayed a growing recognition of the relevance of facts to structured proportionality testing. In *Brown v Tasmania*, for instance, which concerned whether the *Workplaces (Protection from Protesters) Act 2014* (Tas) (hereinafter 'the *Protesters Act*') impermissibly burdened the implied freedom of political communication, the Court again made reference to various factual material.[159] The facts agreed[160] in the special case[161] contained an account of the history of political protests in Tasmania,[162] and the Court also had before it a 'Fact Sheet' relating to the draft Bill.[163] One of the questions raised by the parties was whether these agreed facts and materials provided a sufficient factual basis to resolve the dispute, as the plaintiffs argued there was a lack of evidence about the extent of the financial impact on Tasmanian business activity.[164]

[157] *McCloy* (n 94) 220–21 [93] (French CJ, Kiefel, Bell and Keane JJ).

[158] ibid 221 [93].

[159] *Brown* (n 60).

[160] Note that if the parties did not agree on the relevant facts they faced the prospect of remittal; see Transcript of Proceedings, *Brown v Tasmania* [2016] HCATrans 271 (14 November 2016) 140 (Gordon J).

[161] 'Special Case Pursuant to Rule 27.08', *Brown v Tasmania*, H3/2016, 9 December 2016. Note that many of the annexures to the special case related to the specific protest activities of the plaintiffs. This reflects the history of the litigation, where the first question stated by the parties was whether the plaintiffs had standing to seek relief, but this question was later conceded; see *Brown* (n 60) 340 [5] (Kiefel CJ, Bell and Keane JJ). In addition, note that the Court's reasons were limited to the validity of the *Workplaces (Protection from Protesters) Act 2014* (Tas) as it applied to forestry land or business access areas in relation to forestry land.

[162] 'Special Case Pursuant to Rule 27.08', *Brown v Tasmania*, H3/2016, 9 December 2016 [57]–[72].

[163] See *Brown* (n 60) 347 [36] (Kiefel CJ, Bell and Keane JJ). Note that this was a public document, extracts of which were supplied to the Court by the plaintiffs: Transcript of Proceedings, *Brown v Tasmania* [2017] HCATrans 093 (2 May 2017) 3790, 3802.

[164] Robert James Brown and Jessica Anne Willis Hoyt, 'Plaintiffs' Submissions', Submission in *Brown v Tasmania*, H3/2016, 27 February 2017, [62].

Consistently with *McCloy*,[165] the material about the history of protests in Tasmania was predominantly used to support the Court's reasoning at the earlier stages of analysis rather than at the necessity or balancing stages. This material was considered relevant to determining, first, whether the legislation imposed a burden on the implied freedom and, second, in ascertaining the purpose of the legislation. In terms of the question of burden, the joint judgment of Kiefel CJ, Bell and Keane JJ referred to the facts of the special case as part of an extensive review of the operation and effect of the statute.[166] While noting that the burden on the freedom was not to be answered by reference to how a statute operated in an individual case, the joint judgment considered such evidence may provide 'useful examples of the statute's practical effect'.[167] Justice Nettle, similarly, engaged in a detailed discussion of the history of political protests against forestry activities in Tasmania[168] in order to conclude that the legislation imposed an effective burden, in that it had a 'real or actual effect' on the implied freedom.[169] When it came to the assessing the purpose of the legislation, there was also some acknowledgement that the context in which the legislation was enacted was relevant. In particular, while the starting point was the ordinary processes of statutory construction,[170] the background extrinsic material provided relevant context that confirmed the mischief to which the legislation was directed.[171]

When it came to the question of suitability, there was little engagement with the questions of fact. The inquiry at this stage was described as one of 'rational connection'[172] and it was primarily seen as a task of reason or logic (that is, not one that needed to be supported by evidence). The joint judgment, for instance, followed the majority in *McCloy* in describing the test as 'an inquiry which logic requires'.[173] In undertaking this inquiry, however, the joint judgment was informed by its previous analysis of the history and operation of the legislation.[174] Justice Nettle, similarly, had little difficulty concluding that the *Protesters Act* 'evidently' had a rational connection to the purpose of the law.[175]

At the necessity stage of analysis, although acknowledging that this involved some assessment of the effectiveness of the legislation, there was some reluctance to undertake a detailed factual analysis. The consideration

[165] *McCloy* (n 94). See the text accompanying nn 151ff, above.

[166] *Brown* (n 60) 346–47 [32]–[37], 353–59 [61]–[87]. *cf* Gordon J, who did not consider that this material was relevant to the question of burden (at 431 [316]).

[167] ibid 360 [90].

[168] ibid 398 [237]ff.

[169] ibid 413 [270]. See also Gageler J (at 387 [191]ff), who drew upon the long history of political protest to conclude that there was a substantial burden.

[170] ibid 362 [96] (Kiefel CJ, Bell and Keane JJ).

[171] ibid 363 [101], referring to Gageler J in *McCloy* (n 94). See also *Brown* (n 60) 415 [276] (Nettle J).

[172] *Brown* (n 60) 370 [132] (Kiefel CJ, Bell and Keane JJ).

[173] ibid 370 [133], quoting *McCloy* (n 94) 217 [80] (French CJ, Kiefel, Bell and Keane JJ).

[174] *Brown* (n 60) 371 [134] (Kiefel CJ, Bell and Keane JJ).

[175] ibid 418 [281].

of alternatives was confined to those that are 'obvious' and 'compelling',[176] with the joint judgment stressing that the necessity test did 'not involve a free-ranging inquiry as to whether the legislature should have made different policy choices'.[177] The joint judgment's engagement with questions of fact at this stage was slim; while passing reference was made to the history of protests in Tasmania, it did not engage in any detailed analysis of the effectiveness of the legislation or the alternative regime contained in the *Forest Management Act 2013* (Tas). According to the joint judgment, whether the *Protesters Act* would be effective in deterring the relevant protests was 'debatable' and did not need to be determined.[178] Instead, their Honours considered the legislation was too broad, holding that it was 'likely to deter protest of all kinds'.[179] The *Forest Management Act* offered an alternative solution that was 'substantially less restrictive' on the freedom,[180] meaning that the *Protesters Act* went further than was reasonably necessary.

Justice Nettle, who also applied a test of structured proportionality,[181] reached the opposite conclusion on the question of necessity. He considered the alternative legislative regimes suggested by the plaintiffs: the *Forest Management Act*,[182] and legislation or proposed legislation in Tasmania,[183] Western Australia[184] and New South Wales.[185] Like the joint judgment, then, legislation was used in an evidentiary sense to determine whether there were any less restrictive means. While Nettle J noted there was 'some force' in the plaintiffs' submission that the *Forest Management Act* offered an alternative, less restrictive legislative model, ultimately he considered this was a question for Parliament.[186] The necessity test was not, he cautioned, 'a prescription to engage in an assessment of the relative merits of competing legislative models'.[187] For Nettle J, it had not been demonstrated that there were obvious and compelling alternatives that had significantly less impact on the freedom.[188]

In terms of the balancing stage of proportionality, Nettle J was the only member of the Court who relied on this stage to find the impugned provisions invalid. His conclusion in relation to balancing, namely that the provisions were

[176] ibid 372 [139].
[177] ibid 371 [139].
[178] ibid 373 [145].
[179] ibid.
[180] ibid 373 [146].
[181] Note that in later cases, Nettle J has refined his approach to the question of necessity: *Clubb* (n 12) 266 [268].
[182] This was, according to Nettle J, the 'most obvious example': *Brown* (n 60) 419 [283].
[183] *Police Offences Act 1935* (Tas).
[184] Proposed amendments to the *Criminal Code* (WA).
[185] *Inclosed Lands Protection Act 1901* (NSW).
[186] *Brown* (n 60) 420 [286].
[187] ibid 418 [282].
[188] ibid 422 [289].

'grossly disproportionate', rested upon his assessment that the relevant burden was substantial.[189] As explained above, his analysis of the question of burden was informed by his consideration of the history and practical operation of the legislation.[190] This confirms, consistently with the analysis in Chapters 2 and 3, that the balancing inquiry, while predominantly a normative exercise, is not performed in isolation, but against the backdrop of the previous inquiries. In addition, the Court's tendency to confine balancing to those measures that are 'grossly disproportionate'[191] may well limit the need for it to undertake detailed factual analysis.

The most explicit recognition of facts in the context of assessing whether a burden on the implied freedom is justified appears in *Unions (No 2)*, which was decided in 2019.[192] Chief Justice Kiefel, Bell and Keane JJ, in applying structured proportionality, held that New South Wales had not justified the burden on the implied freedom as 'necessary' to prevent the 'drowning out' of other voices.[193] In reaching this conclusion, their Honours drew upon the Court's jurisprudence in the context of section 92.[194] They commented that while Parliament 'does not generally need to provide evidence to prove the basis for legislation which it enacts', the position is different in relation to laws that burden the implied freedom.[195] As with those judges who declined to apply structured proportionality, it was critical that Parliament had not undertaken any further inquiries, despite the recommendation of the Joint Standing Committee.[196] Justice Nettle agreed, noting that what is required to justify an effective burden would depend on the circumstances of each case.[197] In this case, Parliament's failure to heed the Committee's recommendation was decisive: 'It is as if Parliament simply went ahead and enacted the *Electoral Funding Act* without pausing to consider whether a cut of as much as 50 per cent was required.'[198]

In *Spence v Queensland*, which was handed down a few months after *Unions (No 2)*, there was also an acknowledgement of the need for an adequate factual foundation.[199] The plaintiffs sought to distinguish the facts of *McCloy*, arguing that Queensland did not have a recent history of corruption, and so the justification that was accepted by the Court in *McCloy* had no application in Queensland.[200] The plurality held that, unlike in *Unions (No 2)*, there

[189] ibid 422–23 [290]–[291].
[190] ibid 423–25 [292]–[295].
[191] *Clubb* (n 12) 275 [292] (Nettle J).
[192] *Unions (No 2)* (n 1).
[193] ibid 618 [53].
[194] ibid 615–16 [42]–[43].
[195] ibid 616 [45].
[196] ibid 618 [53].
[197] ibid 640 [117]. Justice Nettle observed that sometimes the need for a particular legislature measure might be 'self-evident or appear with relative clarity without the need for extensive if indeed any evidence on the point', whereas at other times expert reports may be necessary.
[198] ibid 641 [117].
[199] *Spence v Queensland* (2019) 93 ALJR 643.
[200] ibid 671 [94].

was an adequate factual foundation to justify the burden.[201] In particular, the legislative history indicated that the choice to amend the Queensland legislation was 'based on lessons learned from the experience in New South Wales'.[202] In addition, drawing on Nettle J's remarks in *McCloy*, the plurality indicated that it was open to Parliament to act 'prophylactically' in response to 'inferred legislative imperatives'.[203] Justice Edelman, in separate reasons, agreed that parliaments must be able to act 'by reference to possibilities and probabilities'.[204] He noted that any differences between the circumstances in New South Wales and Queensland could only affect the balancing stage, but there was no basis for concluding that there was any difference in the importance of the 'core underlying purpose of removing the risk and perception of corruption'.[205]

In subsequent cases the Court has relied on factual material, but its discussion has not always been explicit. In the *Clubb* appeal, which concerned the validity of Victorian legislation that prohibited protests within a 'safe access zone' around abortion clinics,[206] the Court had before it a variety of factual material, both from the magistrate's findings below and evidence adduced by amicus curiae. Chief Justice Kiefel, Bell and Keane JJ relied on this material to support their conclusion that the Victorian prohibition was justified. In terms of suitability, the joint judgment noted that the Second Reading Speech indicated that the safe access zone of 150 metres was chosen after consultation with a wide range of stakeholders, and their Honours had no difficulty in concluding that the law had a 'rational connection' with its purpose.[207] At the necessity stage, their Honours accepted the 'unchallenged evidence' that the effect of the law (in contrast to the pre-existing law) was to 'reduce the deterrent effect of anti-abortion activities near premises where abortions are provided'.[208] At the balancing stage, there was no explicit discussion of facts, but the plurality commented that, as with *McCloy*, the 'difficulties in the balancing exercise do not loom as large as they sometimes may'.[209] While the evidence seemed to confirm the Court's conclusions, there was little discussion of whether such material was necessary. In addition, in the *Preston* appeal, where there was less empirical material before the Court, the same conclusion was reached.

Both Nettle J and Edelman J were more explicit in acknowledging the role of factual questions underpinning proportionality analysis. For instance, in the *Clubb* appeal, Nettle J's conclusion on the question of suitability was expressly informed by evidence before the magistrate that the proscription on prohibited

[201] ibid 671 [95] (Kiefel CJ, Bell, Gageler and Keane JJ).
[202] ibid 671 [96].
[203] ibid 671 [96], quoting Nettle J in *McCloy* (n 94) 262 [233].
[204] *Spence* (n 199) 718 [323].
[205] ibid 719 [325].
[206] *Clubb* (n 12).
[207] ibid 205 [84].
[208] ibid 205 [86]; see also 206–07 [90].
[209] ibid 209 [101].

behaviour had had a positive effect on patient and staff well-being.[210] Moreover, when it came to the necessity limb, Nettle J considered multiple parliamentary sources to ground his conclusion that the communication prohibition was necessary.[211] There was less explicit factual analysis at the balancing stage, in part because this was framed to only capture those laws that are 'grossly disproportionate'.[212]

Justice Edelman also acknowledged the fact-dependent nature of the test, observing that there is 'no doubt that at each stage of proportionality testing, a court can consider as constitutional facts and circumstances those matters confronting Parliament at the time the challenged law was enacted'.[213] He also acknowledged the difficulty of changing facts,[214] but this did not need to be resolved in the *Preston* appeal,[215] as there was no suggestion that the material relied on by the parties and interveners, which was subsequent to the enactment of the legislation, 'reflected any change in underlying facts or circumstances'.[216] As such, Edelman J proceeded to assess the three stages of the proportionality inquiry on the basis of the constitutional facts at the time that the laws were enacted. In terms of the question of suitability, Edelman J noted that this was 'almost always satisfied since the construct of legislative purpose is based upon a legislature that is assumed to act rationally'.[217] Thus, at this stage of the inquiry, there was no need for further factual analysis. There was some reference to the underlying empirical material when assessing the depth and width of the burden for the necessity inquiry, but Edelman J noted that Parliament must 'be able to make choices about the best policies to pursue for the implementation of legislation'.[218] The question of the radius of the access zone was a judgment that was 'peculiarly within the province of Parliament as advised by stakeholders, experts and committees'.[219] As such, it appears that as long as Parliament *itself* was informed by the relevant evidentiary material, Edelman J did not consider it part of the Court's job to rewrite the legislative scheme.[220]

In *Banerji*, by contrast, there was little explicit discussion of facts or the evidentiary basis upon which the provisions were based.[221] In this case, which concerned tweets made by a member of the public service, the central question

[210] ibid 269 [276]; in relation to the *Preston* appeal, see 280 [306].
[211] ibid 271–72 [280]–[281], [283], 274–75 [289]: these included the Statement of Compatibility, experiential evidence presented to the High Court by the Castan Centre for Human Rights Law (appearing as amicus curiae), and evidence before the magistrate from a clinical psychologist.
[212] ibid 275 [292].
[213] ibid 334 [470]
[214] This issue is returned to in ch 7, section III.
[215] Note Edelman J disposed of the *Clubb* appeal, relating to the Victorian legislation, on the basis of partial disapplication: *Clubb* (n 12) 324–25 [443].
[216] ibid 334–35 [471].
[217] ibid 335 [472].
[218] ibid 337 [478].
[219] ibid 339 [484].
[220] ibid 310 [407].
[221] *Banerji* (n 62).

for the Court was whether certain provisions of the *Public Service Act 1999* (Cth) impermissibly infringed the implied freedom of political communication. The finding that the provisions were suitable, necessary and adequate in their balance to the maintenance and protection of an apolitical public service was largely unsupported by factual material. Instead, the Court was informed mainly by the construction of the legislation and the Australian Public Service (APS) guidelines.[222] For instance, in finding the law to be suitable, Kiefel CJ, Bell, Keane and Nettle JJ held that the provisions represented a 'rational means of realising [the] … objectives'.[223] Similarly, at the necessity stage, the plurality noted that where a law has a 'significant purpose consistent with the system of representative and responsible government' and is suitable, it will rarely be found to lack necessity.[224] The respondent's argument that anonymous communications ought to be excluded was rejected, and the plurality concluded that there was no 'obvious and compelling' alternative.[225] At the 'adequate balance' stage, the plurality had regard to the range of penalties available and the procedures in place, finding that the benefit was not 'manifestly outweighed' by the effect on the implied freedom,[226] but was a 'plainly reasoned and focused response' to the legitimate aim.[227] The Court in *Banerji* declined to entertain an argument that the provisions did not extend to 'anonymous' communications, but noted that had the case been presented differently before the Administrative Appeals Tribunal (AAT), it was 'not improbable' that evidence would have been needed to demonstrate damage to reputation and integrity of the APS.[228]

## III. THE CORRELATION BETWEEN PROPORTIONALITY AND FACTS?

The above analysis indicates that the High Court has not, so far, developed a consistent or explicit framework for the role of facts in tests of proportionality. While there has been a growing recognition of the factual dimensions of proportionality, there appears to be no simple correlation between facts and proportionality. Even though the conceptual structure of proportionality, which was analysed in Chapter 2, might suggest that a turn towards a more structured form of proportionality is likely to make factual questions more pressing, in practice the picture is more complex. The Australian experience shows that a more explicit reliance on proportionality reasoning, including the consideration

[222] Note that Edelman J (who applied structured proportionality) and Gageler J and Gordon J (who applied the traditional appropriate and adapted formulation) all referred to the long history of this type of regulation of the public service; see, eg, 413–16 [70]–[74] (Gageler J), 438–39 [154] (Gordon J), 456–57 [203] (Edelman J).

[223] ibid 401 [34].

[224] ibid 401 [35].

[225] ibid 401–02 [35]–[36].

[226] ibid 405 [42].

[227] ibid.

[228] ibid 396–97 [23].

of alternatives, has not always been accompanied by a greater willingness to engage with facts. The Court's willingness to engage with questions of fact does not seem to track neatly onto the choice of test, and in some cases it is the judges applying the traditional 'appropriate and adapted' test who have engaged more explicitly with facts than those in the majority.

The recent implied freedom jurisprudence indicates a growing recognition of questions of fact, and the Court has acknowledged some parallels with the section 92 context. In a number of cases, the Court has been provided with a variety of empirical material, but it is not always clear how critical this has been to the Court's overall findings. In *Brown*, for instance, although there was discussion of the history of political protests in Tasmania, this was most relevant to the analysis of the relevant burden (a question which applies regardless of whether structured proportionality testing is adopted).[229] In *Unions (No 2)*, the lack of evidence was critical, but this was in the unusual circumstance where the Joint Standing Committee itself had recommended that further inquiries be undertaken.[230] There has been some discussion of when parties will be required to produce evidence, but the Court is not always consistent, and common sense or logic continue to play a role. There has also been some recognition of the problem of changing facts, but this issue has not been resolved.[231]

Drawing upon the different categories of facts that were developed in Chapter 3, there are signs of some differences emerging at the various stages of proportionality analysis. In Chapter 3, it will be recalled, I suggested that the facts that are relevant to each sub-test of proportionality reasoning will often exhibit different characteristics, and distinguishing more clearly between the different stages might lead to a fuller understanding of the High Court's approach.

The starting point for any proportionality inquiry is, of course, legislative purpose.[232] Ascertaining the purpose or mischief to which legislation is directed is a familiar task of statutory construction, and the modern approach to statutory interpretation confirms that certain extrinsic materials, such as parliamentary and executive materials, can be used in this task.[233] In addition, the cases discussed in this chapter show that at times, the High Court has referred to extrinsic material to support its conclusion about legislative purpose. For instance, in *McCloy* and *Brown*, the Court referred to empirical materials to support its conclusion about the purpose to be achieved by the law.[234] From the cases so far, it appears likely that the Court will continue to apply its established

[229] See the discussion at text accompanying nn 166ff, above.

[230] See the discussion at text accompanying nn 107ff and 196ff, above.

[231] This is discussed further in ch 7, section III.

[232] Legislative purpose informs all the inquiries that follow: *Brown* (n 60) 362 [96] (Kiefel CJ, Bell and Keane JJ).

[233] *Bropho v Western Australia* (1990) 171 CLR 1, 20 (Mason CJ, Deane, Dawson, Toohey, Gaudron and McHugh JJ); *CIC Insurance Ltd v Bankstown Football Club Ltd* (1997) 187 CLR 384, 408 (Brennan CJ, Dawson, Toohey and Gummow JJ). See also ch 2, nn 72 and 73.

[234] See, eg, the discussion in section II.D above.

approach to statutory interpretation, and the advent of structured proportionality will not trigger particular changes in this regard.

Similarly, when assessing whether a law is capable of advancing a given purpose, the Court appears relatively comfortable with referring to empirical materials. As explained in Chapter 3, at this stage the court is concerned with the background context of the law and its practical operation. Whether the inquiry is framed in terms of 'suitability' or the more familiar language of 'reasonably capable of being considered appropriate and adapted', there are numerous examples in Australia of where the High Court has referred to empirical materials and acknowledged the relevance of facts in determining the connection between a law and its purpose.[235] For instance, in the context of the defence power, the external affairs power and the review of delegated legislation, the Court has referred to evidence to enable it to establish the requisite connection. When applying structured proportionality testing, it has often relied on reason or logic, and has described the inquiry at this stage as one of 'rational connection'.[236] As Edelman J noted in *Clubb v Edwards; Preston v Avery*, the suitability test is 'almost always satisfied since the construct of legislative purpose is based upon a legislature that is assumed to act rationally'.[237] Therefore, the way in which the test of suitability is framed means that there is often little need for factual inquiry.

In terms of the necessity stage of proportionality reasoning, the Court has confined the inquiry to those alternatives that are 'obvious and compelling'.[238] In framing the test in this way, it has sought to limit the scope of the necessity inquiry and to reduce the need for factual inquiry. It has, for example, been loath to delve into counterfactuals or hypotheticals and has cautioned that it is not its role to 'remodel public policy'.[239] Where the Court has invalidated legislation by relying on the necessity limb, it has done so without having to undertake a detailed empirical analysis of the effectiveness of particular measures. For instance, in *Unions (No 2)*, it was the explicit recommendation of the Standing Committee – and Parliament's failure to heed this recommendation – which led the Court to find that the burden on the freedom had not been justified.[240] In other cases, the Court has been able to rely on the existence of alternative legislative schemes to demonstrate the availability of alternatives, though quite how it reaches a conclusion about the effectiveness of alternatives is not always clearly demonstrated.[241] Proponents of structured proportionality have also

[235] See the discussion in section II.A above.

[236] See, eg, *Brown* (n 60) 370 [132] (Kiefel CJ, Bell and Keane JJ); *Clubb* (n 12) 205 [84] (Kiefel CJ, Bell and Keane JJ).

[237] *Clubb* (n 12) 335 [472].

[238] See, eg, *McCloy* (n 94) 211 [58] (French CJ, Kiefel, Bell and Keane JJ). See also *Clubb* (n 12) 265–66 [267]–[269] (Nettle J), 337 [479] (Edelman J).

[239] *Clubb* (n 12) 310 [407] (Edelman J).

[240] See nn 196ff above and the accompanying text.

[241] See, eg, *Betfair* (n 122), where the Court was able to rely on the legislative scheme in Tasmania to support its conclusion that the Western Australian legislation was not necessary for the protection of the racing industry. See also *Brown* (n 60) 373 [146], where Kiefel CJ, Bell and Keane JJ held that the *Forest Management Act* offered an alternative solution, meaning that the *Protesters Act* went further than was reasonably necessary.

emphasised that evidence will *not* always be required at the necessity stage. In particular, it has been stressed that Parliament must be able to act 'prophylactically' and in relation to 'inferred legislative imperatives', without the need for evidentiary support.[242]

The balancing inquiry, as explained earlier, takes place against the background of the previous two inquiries. In performing this task, the Court must take into account factors such as the extent of the burden and the extent of the incursion into the right or freedom. Depending on how the inquiry is structured, these issues may already have been canvassed at an earlier stage of analysis and so may not be expressly considered as part of 'balancing'. In addition, the majority has indicated that a law will only be held to be inadequate in its balance where the law is 'grossly disproportionate'[243] or the benefit is 'manifestly outweighed' by the impact on the implied freedom.[244] By framing the inquiry in this way, the Court can again limit the need to undertake detailed factual analysis.

This analysis suggests that there are some differences in the Court's treatment of facts at the different stages of proportionality analysis. While it appears that the framing of constitutional tests has a bearing on the role of facts, at the same time it is clear that constitutional tests are not the *only* factor that affects how the High Court approaches facts. In reality, as others have acknowledged, judicial assessments of facts are likely to be influenced by a multitude of factors including individual judicial styles.[245] Historically, the Court has been more prepared to recognise facts in areas where there is an express constitutional provision or guarantee, such as in the context of section 92 or the characterisation of purposive powers. In the case of implied constitutional rights, ongoing concerns about legitimacy may serve to reinforce a more abstract style of analysis. However, the increasing acceptance – both of the implied freedom[246] and of structured proportionality testing[247] – may have contributed to a growing recognition of facts.

The subject matter or content of the facts themselves may also having a bearing upon the Court's approach. For instance, the facts that inform an assessment of section 92 – namely, whether a measure is discriminatory and protectionist in its effect – often concern economic or technical questions that are likely to fall outside the Court's general expertise. In contrast, when determining the

[242] *McCloy* (n 94) 261–62 [233] (Nettle J); *Spence* (n 199) 671 [96] (Kiefel CJ, Bell, Gageler and Keane JJ), 718 [323] (Edelman J).

[243] *Clubb* (n 12) 275 [292] (Nettle J).

[244] See, eg, *Clubb* (n 12) 200 [69] (Kiefel CJ, Bell and Keane JJ); *Banerji* (n 62) 402 [38] (Kiefel CJ, Bell, Keane and Nettle JJ).

[245] See, eg, Simpson (n 137) 481; K Burns, 'Judicial Use and Construction of Social Facts in Negligence Cases in the Australian High Court' (PhD thesis, Griffith University, 2011) chs 7–8.

[246] The implication now appears settled, but see *Monis v The Queen* (2013) 249 CLR 92, 181–84 [243]–[251] (Heydon J).

[247] It is now supported by five justices; see n 150.

application and limits of the implied freedoms, the Court is required to assess how a given law affects political speech or the capacity to vote. Although these inquiries also contain empirical aspects, the subjects with which they deal (such as the nature of speech, the political landscape in Australia and the electoral system) are perhaps more likely to fall within the Court's perception of its own knowledge or understanding. The Court's traditional legalistic approach to interpretation and rigid approach to the separation of powers has contributed to its general unwillingness to make overtly political, hypothetical or polycentric judgments.[248]

## IV. CONCLUSION

This chapter has sought to develop a more detailed picture of the place of facts within proportionality reasoning in Australian constitutional adjudication. It has endeavoured to understand how facts have been approached within each of the tests of constitutional validity developed by the Court. While the High Court has recognised that facts may be relevant to proportionality analysis, the emphasis given to factual questions has varied. In addition, the assumption that a turn towards a more structured form of proportionality will increase the role of facts has not, so far, been borne out by the Australian experience. Although there has been a growing recognition of the relevance of facts, the Court has not adopted an explicit or consistent approach to such facts. As the discussion in this chapter illustrates, it is possible to discern some differences in terms of how facts are used to inform the various stages of proportionality analysis. Identifying more clearly *where* and *how* facts are used to support the Court's reasoning contributes to a better understanding of the correlation between facts and proportionality reasoning. It also has implications, as will be explored in the next chapter, for the procedures by which such facts should be ascertained.

[248] Stellios (n 10) ch 17. For some discussion of 'polycentricity', see JA King, 'Institutional Approaches to Judicial Restraint' (2008) 28 *Oxford Journal of Legal Studies* 409.

# 7

# *Procedural Implications*

HAVING ESTABLISHED IN the previous chapters that facts *are* relevant to proportionality reasoning, and having identified where such facts arise and the nature of these facts, this chapter is concerned with issues of procedure.[1] It considers the procedural implications that might emerge from the revised framework for thinking about facts that has been developed in this book. The chapter is developed in three main sections. Section I critiques the High Court's current approach to fact-finding. It identifies some of the limitations of the Court's existing processes and also explains a number of key issues that remain unresolved by the Court: (i) the burden and standard of proof for constitutional facts; (ii) the scope of the doctrine of judicial notice; and (iii) the role of deference or restraint in relation to questions of fact. Against this background, section II considers how a more nuanced understanding of facts, as developed in the earlier chapters of the book, might inform the Court's approach to these three key issues. It suggests, ultimately, that a greater recognition of facts, and of the differences that arise at the three stages of proportionality analysis, offers the potential to improve the degree to which judicial assessments of proportionality are justified. Finally, given the relevance of facts to proportionality, section III considers the problem of changing facts and the implications this has in terms of the doctrine of precedent.

## I. THE HIGH COURT'S EXISTING APPROACH: LIMITATIONS AND UNRESOLVED ISSUES

### A. High Court Procedures and their Limitations

The nature of the facts underpinning proportionality reasoning mean that such facts will not always be able to be established with the same degree of certainty as other facts, and the ordinary evidentiary processes will not always be appropriate. In Australia, the particular dynamics of constitutional litigation have contributed to a lack of certainty for litigants, as the High Court has not always

[1] While the meaning of 'procedural' law has been the subject of considerable debate, in this chapter I use the term broadly to encompass a variety of questions about the methods by which the High Court finds facts. For some critique of the procedural-substantive dichotomy, see TO Main, 'The Procedural Foundation of Substantive Law' (2010) 87 *Washington University Law Review* 801.

clearly identified the facts that underpin its decisions or the processes by which these facts have been ascertained. In addition, as this section illustrates, the very procedures by which cases reach the Court have often served to facilitate the avoidance of facts.

Whether exercising its original[2] or appellate[3] jurisdiction, the Court will rarely hear factual disputes itself. For example, when hearing appeals, the Court is, on the whole, limited to the evidentiary record from the lower court.[4] When exercising its original jurisdiction,[5] which is where the majority of the Court's constitutional matters have arisen,[6] it has also generally avoided engaging in fact-finding. Although the Court *could* make determinations of fact itself, as Bradley Selway explained:

> Where issues of disputed fact arise the Court would usually remit the proceedings to another appropriate court for that court to deal with the factual issues. Apart from the specialised jurisdiction when the High Court sits as a Court of Disputed Returns, it will rarely, if ever, be involved in determining factual issues. This means that proceedings instituted in original jurisdiction will only be heard at first instance by the High Court if the facts are not in dispute or if they have been agreed.[7]

Although in the past it was not uncommon for single justices of the Court to determine the relevant facts and then formally state a case to be considered by the Full Court,[8] this practice is now seldom used.[9]

[2] *Commonwealth of Australia Constitution Act 1900* (Imp) 63 & 64 Vict, c 12, s 9 (hereinafter '*Australian Constitution*') ss 75, 76; *Judiciary Act 1903* (Cth), s 30.

[3] *Australian Constitution*, s 73; *Judiciary Act 1903* (Cth), pt V.

[4] See, eg, *Mickelberg v The Queen* (1989) 167 CLR 259; *Eastman v The Queen* (2000) 203 CLR 1, 11–13 [10]–[19] (Gleeson CJ), 23–26 [67]–[78] (Gaudron J), 32–41 [103]–[133] (McHugh J), 59–65 [181]–[197] (Gummow J). Note that there is some uncertainty as to whether the position is the same for constitutional facts: see *Mickelberg v The Queen* (1989) 167 CLR 259, 271 (Mason CJ); *Eastman v The Queen* (2000) 203 CLR 1, 76–77 [232]–[233] (Kirby J).

[5] In terms of the Court's original jurisdiction, there are three procedural routes by which matters can reach the Court. First, a party may file a 'demurrer', under which one party claims that the other party's case is untenable as a matter of law: *High Court Rules 2004* (Cth), r 27.07. Second, a case may proceed by way of a 'special case', whereby the parties state questions of law to be determined by the Full Court: *High Court Rules 2004* (Cth), r 27.08. Finally, a case may be removed from a lower court pursuant to s 40 of the *Judiciary Act 1903* (Cth). As Rosalind Dixon notes, such removal occurs 'before any final judgment is reached, or conclusive finding of fact can be made by a trial judge as to the relevant factual background or matrix for particular legislation': R Dixon, 'The Functional Constitution: Re-reading the 2014 High Court Constitutional Term' (2015) 43 *Federal Law Review* 455, 470.

[6] See ch 1, n 55.

[7] B Selway, 'The Use of History and Other Facts in the Reasoning of the High Court of Australia' (2001) 20 *University of Tasmania Law Review* 129, 133. The situation is different when the Court sits as the Court of Disputed Returns, as it did in *Re Day (No 2)* (2017) 263 CLR 201, where evidence was heard before Gordon J: *Re Day* (2017) 91 ALJR 262.

[8] See, eg, *Armstrong v Victoria (No 2)* (1957) 99 CLR 28, 37 (Dixon CJ), noting that evidence was received by Taylor J; *Attorney-General (Vic); Ex rel Black v Commonwealth* (1981) 146 CLR 559, 561, noting that evidence was received by Murphy J. See also M Leeming, 'Fact Finding' in T Blackshield, M Coper and G Williams (eds), *The Oxford Companion to the High Court of Australia* (Melbourne, Oxford University Press, 2001) 268.

[9] FWD Jones, 'High Court Procedure under the *Judiciary Act*' (1994) 68 *Australian Law Journal* 442, 443. For a more recent account of the High Court's procedures, see WestlawAU,

Instead, the Court more often confines itself to statements of fact prepared by the parties. Under the demurrer procedure, for instance, a party objects to the other party's pleading on legal grounds only,[10] and the Court will generally restrict itself to the facts identified by the parties.[11] Although in this context the Court has acknowledged that constitutional facts are distinct from ordinary facts, it has taken the view that '[o]nly in rare instances would it be impossible to determine the validity of … a law on demurrer'.[12] Similarly, under the special case procedure, the Court usually relies on the facts that are agreed between the parties. Under this procedure, the parties must agree upon the relevant facts and documents to enable the Court to decide the questions of law contained in the special case.[13] Again, while it appears to be open to the Court to refuse to accept the agreed facts[14] or to supplement these facts,[15] in practice it tends not to depart from the agreed facts.

The Court's use of these procedural mechanisms gives rise to a number of difficulties. For a start, there is the possibility that the parties will not be able to reach agreement,[16] although in practice the threat of remittal appears to offer a strong incentive.[17] There is also the difficulty that the agreed facts may not always offer a comprehensive factual foundation. As Michael Coper has observed in the context of section 92 of the *Australian Constitution*, there is 'no guarantee that the agreed facts … [will be] the true facts'.[18] In addition, while it has become relatively common for the parties to annex various extrinsic materials to their submissions or special case documents,[19] the role of this material

*The Laws of Australia* (online at 15 February 2019) 19 Government, '19.7 Practice and Procedure' [19.7.720]–[19.7.760].

[10] *High Court Rules 2004* (Cth), r 27.01.

[11] *Levy v Victoria* (1997) 189 CLR 579, 597 (Brennan CJ); *Kathleen Investments (Australia) Ltd v Australian Atomic Energy Commission* (1977) 139 CLR 117, 135 (Gibbs J); *South Australia v Commonwealth* (1962) 108 CLR 130, 142 (Dixon CJ).

[12] *Levy* (n 11) 598 (Brennan CJ).

[13] *High Court Rules 2004* (Cth), r 27.08.4. Rule 27.08.5 provides that: 'The Court may draw from the facts stated and documents identified in the special case any inference, whether of fact or law, which might have been drawn from them if proved at a trial.' For some discussion of when inferences may be drawn, see *Plaintiff M47/2018 v Minister of Home Affairs* (2019) 265 CLR 285.

[14] JD Heydon, *Cross on Evidence*, 12th Australian edn (Sydney, LexisNexis Butterworths, 2020) 264 [3165]; J Lennan, 'How to Find Facts in Constitutional Cases' (2011) 30 *Civil Justice Quarterly* 304, 323; *cf* P Brazil, 'The Ascertainment of Facts in Australian Constitutional Cases' (1970) 4 *Federal Law Review* 65, 86.

[15] *Thomas v Mowbray* (2007) 233 CLR 307, 517 [629] (Heydon J).

[16] This has been pointed out particularly in the s 92 context: see, eg, AS Bell, 'Section 92, Factual Discrimination and the High Court' (1991) 20 *Federal Law Review* 240, 246; Justice S Kiefel, 'Section 92: Markets, Protectionism and Proportionality – Australian and European Perspectives' (2010) 36 *Monash University Law Review* 1, 15.

[17] A recent example is *Brown v Tasmania* (2017) 261 CLR 328; see ch 6, n 160.

[18] M Coper, 'Section 92 of the Australian Constitution Since *Cole v Whitfield*' in HP Lee and G Winterton (eds), *Australian Constitutional Perspectives* (Sydney, Law Book Co, 1992) 146.

[19] This practice appears to date at least from the *Tasmanian Dams* case in 1983, where the Commonwealth filed material measuring approximately 48 cm in height: see *Commonwealth v Tasmania* (1983) 158 CLR 1, 50 (summary of argument); Transcript of Proceedings, *Commonwealth*

remains unclear. The Court generally avoids committing itself as to the 'status of the material as facts';[20] usually this material is not formally tendered as evidence meaning that it is not tested as it would be in a lower court.[21] Further, in practice this material is often provided by the Commonwealth, State and Territory Attorneys-General, meaning that the perspective offered tends to be limited.[22]

## B. Unresolved Issues

In addition to these procedural difficulties, the Court has failed to clarify a number of issues that are central to the ascertainment of facts in constitutional adjudication. Despite some persistent academic criticism of the Court's 'haphazard' approach to constitutional and legislative facts,[23] several key questions remain unresolved: (i) the burden and standard of proof for constitutional facts; (ii) the limits of judicial notice; and (iii) the role of deference in relation to questions of fact.

### *i. The Burden and Standard of Proof*

Although the Court has long recognised the existence of constitutional facts, there has been some uncertainty about whether, and how, the burden and standard of proof apply in this context. This is not altogether surprising in light of

*v Tasmania* [1983] HCATrans 28 (10 June 1983) 737–38; Jones (n 9) 446; M Black, 'The *Tasmanian Dam Case*: An Advocate's Memoir' (2015) 24 *Griffith Law Review* 22, 37.

[20] Jones (n 9) 443. See also J Stellios, *Zines's The High Court and the Constitution*, 6th edn (Sydney, Federation Press, 2015) 693–94.

[21] As Dixon has commented, 'the assumption is there will be no need to test the evidence because it has been agreed to by the parties': Dixon (n 5) 471.

[22] G Appleby, 'Functionalism in Constitutional Interpretation: Factual and Participatory Challenges: Comment on Dixon' (2015) 43 *Federal Law Review* 493, 500. See also P Keyzer, 'Attorneys-General, Solicitors-General and "the Public Interest" in Australian Constitutional Cases: A Case for Citizen Input into the Development of Constitutional Policy' in G Appleby, P Keyzer and J Williams (eds), *Public Sentinels: A Comparative Study of Australian Solicitors-General* (Abingdon, Routledge, 2016). Note that beyond the intervention of the Attorneys-General, which is now governed by s 78A of the *Judiciary Act 1903* (Cth), on the whole the Court has not been amenable to broad intervention. See, eg, S Kenny, 'Interveners and Amici Curiae in the High Court' (1998) 20 *Adelaide Law Review* 159; A Mason, 'Interveners and Amici Curiae in the High Court: A Comment' (1998) 20 *Adelaide Law Review* 173; E Willheim, 'Amici Curiae and Access to Constitutional Justice in the High Court of Australia' (2010) 22 *Bond Law Review* 126. In the Canadian context, it has been argued that a 'group approach' to constitutional litigation, which relies on 'epistemic communities', can enable the creation of an evidentiary record: B Perryman, 'Adducing Social Science Evidence in Constitutional Cases' (2018) 44 *Queens's Law Journal* 121, 141–45, 171–72.

[23] C Tran, 'Facts and Evidence in Litigation under the *Charter of Human Rights and Responsibilities Act 2006* (Vic) and the *Human Rights Act 2004* (ACT)' (2012) 36 *Melbourne University Law Review* 287, 332. See also S Kenny, 'Constitutional Fact Ascertainment' (1990) 1 *Public Law Review* 134; Lennan (n 14).

the procedural mechanisms discussed above which, in many cases, enable the Court to avoid having to find facts.

In terms of the burden of proof,[24] different views have emerged about which party bears the burden of persuading the Court that a particular measure infringes, or does not infringe, a constitutional limitation. The Court does not always explicitly address the question of burden and, when it does, it has divided over how the burden should be allocated. In the section 92 context, for instance, there has been some indication that the burden of proof rests with the party supporting the validity of the legislation,[25] but this has not been definitively settled.[26] Similarly, in the implied freedom jurisprudence, there have been competing views about which party bears the persuasive onus.[27] There has also been some suggestion from the High Court that the very language of 'burden' or 'onus' of proof is inapplicable when it comes to constitutional facts. The Court has indicated, for example, that constitutional facts 'cannot and do not form issues between parties to be tried like [ordinary questions of fact]'.[28] Instead, such facts are to be ascertained by the Court 'as best it can',[29] and the Court has cautioned against setting out prescriptive standards.[30] As Gageler J observed in *Unions (No 2)*, such facts could not be tried like ordinary questions of fact and they 'do not lend themselves to notions of proof or onus of proof'.[31]

In contrast, in both Canada and South Africa there has been more attention given to the allocation of the burden of proof. In both jurisdictions the general position is that the burden of establishing that an infringement of a right is justified rests on the party seeking to limit the right.[32] As explained in

[24] In common law systems, there are two different senses in which the burden of proof is used. First, there is the 'legal' or 'persuasive' burden, which is a requirement to persuade the trier of fact that the facts in issue have been established. Second, there is what is commonly referred to as the 'evidential burden', which is the obligation to adduce sufficient evidence in relation to the existence or non-existence of a fact in issue. See Heydon (n 14) 338–40 [7010]–[7015].

[25] See, eg, *Permewan Wright Consolidated Pty Ltd v Trewhitt* (1979) 145 CLR 1, 37 (Mason J); *Uebergang v Australian Wheat Board* (1980) 145 CLR 266, 287 (Barwick CJ).

[26] See, eg, *Allied Interstate (Qld) Pty Ltd v Barnes* (1968) 118 CLR 581, 594 (Windeyer J); *Hughes and Vale Pty Ltd v New South Wales (No 2)* (1955) 93 CLR 127, 194 (Williams J), *cf* 175–76 (Dixon CJ, McTiernan and Webb JJ).

[27] See, eg, *Coleman v Power* (2004) 220 CLR 1, 124 [329] (Heydon J); *Brown* (n 17) 421–22 [288] (Nettle J); *cf Unions NSW v New South Wales (No 2)* (2019) 264 CLR 595, 631 [93] (Gageler J), 650 [151] (Gordon J) (hereinafter '*Unions (No 2)*').

[28] *Breen v Sneddon* (1961) 106 CLR 406, 411 (Dixon CJ). See also *Gerhardy v Brown* (1985) 159 CLR 70, 141–42 (Brennan J): 'The validity and scope of a law cannot be made to depend on the course of private litigation.'

[29] *Commonwealth Freighters Pty Ltd v Sneddon* (1959) 102 CLR 280, 292 (Dixon CJ).

[30] As Brennan J noted in in *Gerhardy* (n 28) 142, 'it is difficult and undesirable to impose an a priori restraint on the performance of that duty'.

[31] *Unions (No 2)* (n 27) 631–32 [94].

[32] Although the concept of the burden of proof is recognised in German law, the distinction between different types of burdens is less developed than it is in the common law tradition, in part because of the largely inquisitorial nature of the proceedings: J Kokott, *The Burden of Proof in Comparative and International Human Rights Law: Civil and Common Law Approaches with Special Reference to the American and German Legal Systems* (The Hague, Kluwer Law International, 1998) 10, 224.

Chapter 4, from the early days of the *Charter*,[33] the Canadian Supreme Court has interpreted section 1 as requiring evidence of justification.[34] While a claimant must first adduce evidence that their right has been limited, the governmental party has the burden of establishing justification.[35] In South Africa the Constitutional Court has adopted a similar position, but has explained that the 'onus' is different from a conventional 'onus of proof':

> Although 'onus' is not infrequently used in this context it is, as this Court has had occasion to point out previously, an onus of a special type. It is not the conventional onus of proof as it is understood in civil and criminal trials where disputes of fact have to be resolved. It is rather a burden to justify a limitation where that becomes an issue in a s 36 analysis.[36]

There has also been some recognition that the burden of proof will not necessarily be decisive. While in private litigation a party will be unsuccessful if it fails to satisfy the relevant burden of proof, in the realm of public law the situation is different. For instance, in the South African context Mandala J has observed that if a party fails to adduce evidence of justification, the Court 'is not relieved of the obligation to conduct the justification analysis and satisfy itself as to the real status of the provisions being challenged'.[37]

When it comes to the standard of proof, similarly, the High Court of Australia has not clarified the degree of satisfaction required for constitutional facts. It is worth noting at this point that there is some confusion in the terminology: the 'standard of review' and the 'standard of proof' represent distinct concepts, but the terms are sometimes conflated or used inconsistently. As set out in Chapter 1, in this book, I am concerned with the use of proportionality as a *method* of review that is used by courts to determine conflicting interests. As a legal test, this establishes the content of the propositions to be proved; in other words, '*what* must be proved'.[38] The 'standard of review' refers to the intensity with which the method of review is applied. Proportionality analysis, as the previous chapters have demonstrated, can be applied with varying degrees of intensity.

In contrast, the standard of proof refers to the degree of satisfaction or persuasion that must be reached in order to establish the relevant facts;[39] that

[33] *Canada Act 1982* (UK) c 11, sch B pt 1 (hereinafter '*Canadian Charter of Rights and Freedoms*').

[34] See ch 4, nn 36ff and accompanying text.

[35] This general position is also reflected in other common law jurisdictions where proportionality is applied: see Tran (n 23) 316. Compare the position in Ireland: D Kenny, 'Proportionality, the Burden of Proof, and Some Signs of Reconsideration' (2014) 52 *Irish Jurist* 141.

[36] *Minister for Home Affairs v National Institute for Crime Prevention and the Re-integration of Offenders (NICRO)* [2005] 3 SA 280, [34] (Constitutional Court) (Chaskalson CJ) (footnote omitted).

[37] ibid [101]. See also P de Vos and W Freedman (eds), *South African Constitutional Law in Context* (Cape Town, Oxford University Press, 2014) 381–82.

[38] MT Grando, *Evidence, Proof, and Fact-Finding in WTO Dispute Settlement* (Oxford, Oxford University Press, 2009) 86.

[39] ibid. See also Tran (n 23) 293.

is, it directs attention to *how much* evidence is needed to establish the facts. In Australia, the classic statement of the standard of proof remains that of Dixon J in *Briginshaw v Briginshaw:*

> The truth is that, when the law requires the proof of any fact, the tribunal must feel an actual persuasion of its occurrence or existence before it can be found. It cannot be found as a result of a mere mechanical comparison of probabilities independently of any belief in its reality. No doubt an opinion that a state of facts exists may be held according to indefinite gradations of certainty … But reasonable satisfaction is not a state of mind that is attained or established independently of the nature and consequences of the fact or facts to be proved. The seriousness of any allegation made, the inherent unlikelihood of an occurrence of a given description, or the gravity of the consequences flowing from a particular finding are considerations which must affect the answer to the question whether the issue has been proved to the reasonable satisfaction of the tribunal.[40]

In *Briginshaw*, the High Court confirmed that there are only two standards of proof: proof beyond reasonable doubt for criminal matters and proof on the balance of probabilities for civil matters.[41] While the Court has specifically rejected the existence of a third, intermediate, standard,[42] it has recognised that 'the strength of the evidence necessary to establish a fact or facts on the balance of probabilities may vary according to the nature of what is sought to prove'.[43] This suggests that, although there is only one civil standard of proof, there might be some flexibility in the application of this standard.

Such flexibility is evident in the Canadian approach to section 1 of the *Charter*. Although the Supreme Court has confirmed that the relevant standard of proof is the civil standard of the balance of probabilities,[44] it has emphasised that the type of proof needed to fulfil this standard might vary depending on the context.[45] In practice, the Court has divided over the question of how much evidence will be sufficient. In *RJR-MacDonald v Canada (Attorney-General)*, for instance, La Forest J considered that the trial judge had applied the standard

[40] *Briginshaw v Briginshaw* (1938) 60 CLR 336, 361–62.

[41] Note that this is sometimes described as the 'preponderance of evidence' standard: D Hamer, 'The Civil Standard of Proof Uncertainty: Probability, Belief and Justice' (1994) 16 *Sydney Law Review* 506, 509.

[42] *Briginshaw* (n 40) 361–62 (Dixon J). See also *Cassell v The Queen* (2000) 201 CLR 189, 193 [18] (Gleeson CJ, Gaudron, McHugh and Gummow JJ).

[43] *Neat Holdings Pty Ltd v Karajan Holdings Pty Ltd* (1992) 67 ALJR 170, 171 (Mason CJ, Brennan, Deane and Gaudron JJ). See also *G v H* (1994) 181 CLR 387, 399 (Deane, Dawson and Gaudron JJ); *Shaw v Wolf* (1998) 83 FCR 113, 123–25 (Merkel J); *Cubillo v Commonwealth (No 2)* (2000) 103 FCR 1, 115 [347] (O'Loughlin J). See also A Carter, 'The Definition and Discovery of Facts in Native Title: The Historian's Contribution' (2008) 36 *Federal Law Review* 301, 309–10.

[44] *R v Oakes* [1986] 1 SCR 103, 137.

[45] *Thomson Newspapers Co* v *Canada (Attorney General)* [1998] 1 SCR 877, 942 [90], 951 [111]. Note that there has been some criticism that the Court has applied the standard of proof inconsistently; see, eg, CD Bredt, 'The Right to Equality and *Oakes*: Time for Change' (2009) 27 *National Journal of Constitutional Law* 59.

of proof too rigorously and that the Attorney-General need only demonstrate a 'rational basis' for the legislative action.[46] Justice McLachlan, in the majority, agreed that a 'flexible and realistic standard of proof' was an essential part of the section 1 analysis, but emphasised that it must 'not be attenuated' to the extent of relieving the State of the burden of justification.[47] This division reflects not only the difficulty of applying the standard of proof in relation to legislative facts, but also of distinguishing it from the standard of review.[48]

In Australia, as I have foreshadowed, although the High Court has for some time recognised the existence of constitutional facts, it has not clearly settled on a standard of proof. As Dixon J remarked in *Commonwealth Freighters Pty Ltd v Sneddon*, all that is necessary is that constitutional facts must be 'ascertained by the court as best it can'.[49] This oft-cited command suggests a desire for flexibility as well as a reluctance to set out prescriptive standards.[50] There have, however, been some hints that when it comes to determining constitutional facts, the standard of proof might not apply as strictly as it does in ordinary civil cases. In the context of section 92 of the *Australian Constitution*, for instance, the Court has acknowledged that judicial 'impression' will play a role.[51] However, the Court has not clearly distinguished between the standard of proof and the standard of review. In the context of discussing statutory charters of rights, Christopher Tran has observed that 'it might be expected that strict scrutiny of a legal claim would also entail a stricter scrutiny of the evidence establishing facts relevant to that claim, but in fact there is no necessary correlation between the two'.[52] As Tran points out, the 'reasonably appropriate and adapted' standard reveals little, if anything, about how much evidence is necessary to establish the relevant facts.[53] This difficulty is only exacerbated by the Court's tendency not to address this question explicitly.

### ii. *Judicial Notice and its Limits*

The High Court has also failed to resolve the appropriate scope of judicial notice. In its traditional conception, and at least as it applies to adjudicative facts, judicial notice operates as a shortcut to proof; that is, it is not a 'mode of proof', but instead 'narrows the scope of proof' as it relieves the trier of

[46] *RJR-MacDonald v Canada (Attorney-General)* [1995] 3 SCR 199, 284 [77].

[47] ibid 333 [138].

[48] As Tran has observed, in a number of jurisdictions the standard of proof is 'often conflated, consciously or unconsciously, with the applicable standard of review': Tran (n 23) 308.

[49] *Commonwealth Freighters* (n 29) 292.

[50] Tran (n 23) 297.

[51] *Cole v Whitfield* (1988) 165 CLR 360, 408 (Mason CJ, Wilson, Brennan, Deane, Dawson, Toohey and Gaudron JJ); *South Australia v Tanner* (1989) 166 CLR 161, 168 (Wilson, Dawson, Toohey and Gaudron JJ).

[52] Tran (n 23) 293.

[53] ibid 294.

fact from having to establish the facts via the usual evidentiary rules.[54] Judicial notice in this sense applies both to those facts that are indisputable or notorious as well as to those that can be ascertained by reference to an authoritative work or text.[55] Yet even within the realm of adjudicative fact-finding, the boundaries of judicial notice have been described as uncertain and 'erratic'.[56]

These difficulties are writ large when it comes to legislative and constitutional facts. Here, the matters to be established will very often be neither notorious nor verifiable by sources of indisputable accuracy. As such, the Court has relied on a 'loose'[57] and 'unpredictable'[58] concept of judicial notice and has failed to agree on its appropriate limits.[59] In the negligence case of *Woods v Multi-Sport Holdings*, for example, McHugh J and Callinan J differed over the appropriate scope of the doctrine in respect of legislative facts.[60] Justice McHugh adopted a liberal approach and referred to numerous reports and statistics relating to sporting injuries to support his conclusion that the standard of care should be raised.[61] In contrast, Callinan J was more circumspect, suggesting that he would 'resist any suggestion that the same degree of caution is not required when extrinsic facts are so-called legislative facts'.[62] In addition, it has been suggested that the very terminology of judicial notice is inappropriate, as '[a]n attempt to clothe legislative fact-finding in the straight-jacket which befits judicial notice of adjudicative facts is not apt and is barely meaningful'.[63]

This uncertainty has continued since the enactment of the uniform *Evidence Act 1995*.[64] Although the High Court has clarified that section 144 means that there 'would appear to be no room for the operation of the common law doctrine of judicial notice, strictly so called',[65] there remains some doubt about

[54] PB Carter, 'Judicial Notice: Related and Unrelated Matters' in E Campbell and L Waller (eds), *Well and Truly Tried: Essays on Evidence in Honour of Sir Richard Eggleston* (Sydney, Law Book Co, 1982) 89.

[55] Although the judicial notice of notorious facts after inquiry might seem 'self-contradictory', as Heydon notes, it is designed to separate legitimate from illegitimate inquiries: Heydon (n 14) 210 [3025]. In the US context, Larsen has discussed the increasing tendency of Supreme Court justices to conduct their own research (what she terms 'in-house fact finding'): AO Larsen, 'Confronting Supreme Court Fact Finding' (2013) 98 *Virginia Law Review* 1255.

[56] IR Freckelton, *Expert Evidence: Law, Practice, Procedure and Advocacy*, 6th edn (Sydney, Thomson Reuters, 2019) 155 [2.30.40]. Freckelton provides a list of examples that might be considered 'specialist' and requiring expert evidence, but about which courts have taken judicial notice.

[57] Carter (n 54) 99.

[58] Kenny (n 23) 156.

[59] P McClellan and A Doyle, 'Legislative Facts and Section 144 – A Contemporary Problem?' (2016) 12 *The Judicial Review* 421, 435ff; JJ Doyle, 'Judicial Law Making – Is Honesty the Best Policy?' (1995) 17 *Adelaide Law Review* 161, 208.

[60] *Woods v Multi-Sport Holdings* (2002) 208 CLR 460.

[61] ibid 477–81 [62]–[71].

[62] ibid 510 [163].

[63] Carter (n 54) 88.

[64] *Evidence Act 1995* (Cth), s 144.

[65] *Gattellaro v Westpac Banking Corporation* (2004) 78 ALJR 394, 397 [17] (Gleeson CJ, McHugh, Hayne and Heydon JJ).

the provision's application to non-adjudicative facts. While it appears that the Australian Law Reform Commission intended the provision to apply to *both* adjudicative and legislative facts,[66] the section itself makes no reference to different categories of fact. In addition, the High Court often overlooks section 144 when it discusses constitutional or legislative facts. In the case of *Aytugrul v The Queen*, however, a majority of the Court indicated that the section was applicable to published psychological literature, and that such material must satisfy the strict requirements of the section.[67] Accordingly, the majority held that the Court could *not* take judicial notice of the studies dealing with the persuasiveness of different modes of expressing DNA evidence for the purposes of developing a rule of inadmissibility.[68] The effect of this interpretation is that many of the facts relevant to proportionality reasoning are unlikely to meet the requirements of section 144.[69] This leaves unresolved the question of how the court should be informed of such facts.

### *iii. Deference or Restraint*

A third unresolved issue is the question of the weight to be afforded to the factual determinations made by other branches of government. As explained in Chapter 4, the comparative experience illustrates that when applying proportionality reasoning, the courts in other jurisdictions sometimes defer, in whole or in part, to findings of fact made by the legislative or executive branches. It is important to note that there are two different levels at which deference can operate.[70] First, the proportionality test itself may be framed in a way that is more or less intrusive (for instance, as explained in Chapter 5, in Australia a variety of tests have been developed that incorporate differing levels of judicial scrutiny). Second, regardless of how the legal test is framed, the courts may reduce the intensity of the inquiry by according some weight or respect to the decision-maker's view. It is this second type of deference – which arises in the course of *applying* proportionality reasoning – that is most relevant to this chapter.

[66] Law Reform Commission, *Evidence*, Interim Report No 26 (1985) vol 1, 542–47 [974]–[977]; Law Reform Commission, *Evidence*, Report No 38 (1987) 127 [227]–[228]. See also S Odgers, *Uniform Evidence Law*, 15th edn (Sydney, Thomson Reuters, 2020) 1395 [EA 144.90]; AJ Serpell, *The Reception and Use of Social Policy Information in the High Court of Australia* (Sydney, Lawbook Co, 2006) 41–43; *cf Aytugrul v The Queen* (2012) 247 CLR 170, 202–03 [73] (Heydon J).

[67] Namely, that the knowledge must be 'not reasonably open to question' and 'common knowledge' or 'capable of verification by reference to a document the authority of which cannot reasonably be questioned': *Aytugrul* (n 66) 183–84 [21] (French CJ, Hayne, Crennan and Bell JJ). This decision, along with *Gattellaro* (n 65), suggests that s 144 applies in those jurisdictions where the uniform *Evidence Act* applies; see McClellan and Doyle (n 59) 452.

[68] *Aytugrul* (n 66) 183–84 [21]–[22] (French CJ, Hayne, Crennan and Bell JJ).

[69] K Burns, 'It's Not Just Policy: The Role of Social Facts in Judicial Reasoning in Negligence Cases' (2013) 21 *Torts Law Journal* 73, 95; Odgers (n 66) 1396 [EA 144.90].

[70] M Elliott, 'Proportionality and Deference: The Importance of a Structured Approach' in C Forsyth et al (eds), *Effective Judicial Review: A Cornerstone of Good Governance* (Oxford, Oxford University Press, 2010) 269.

Within this second type of deference, there are two main grounds upon which courts may give weight to the other branches of government: legitimacy and expertise.[71] Under the first, which is sometimes described as *normative deference*,[72] a judge might choose to defer because of the decision-maker's superior democratic legitimacy.[73] In other words, there are normative reasons why a court may give respect to the decisions of another branch of government. Under the second type of deference, which is sometimes described as *empirical deference*,[74] a judge might choose to defer because of the decision-maker's superior institutional competence or expertise.[75] For instance, another branch of government may, in comparison to a court, be better suited to make the type of judgment required on a particular issue.[76]

In contrast to the lively debate in other jurisdictions,[77] in Australia the question of deference has been largely avoided. The High Court's understanding of the judicial role, and its strict interpretation of the separation of powers,[78] has meant that the Court has tended to reject any explicit notion of deference. In *McCloy v New South Wales*, for instance, the majority rejected the application of deference, or a 'margin of appreciation', in the Australian context:

> The courts acknowledge and respect that it is the role of the legislature to determine which policies and social benefits ought to be pursued. This is not a matter of deference. It is a matter of the boundaries between the legislative and judicial functions.
>
> Deference to legislative opinion, in the sense of unquestioning adoption of the correctness of these choices, does not arise for courts.[79]

[71] ibid 269. See also Gageler, who distinguishes between 'regard for the judgment or opinion of another' and 'respectful acknowledgement of the authority of another': S Gageler, 'Deference' (2015) 22 *Australian Journal of Administrative Law* 151.

[72] R Alexy, *A Theory of Constitutional Rights*, reprinted edn (J Rivers trans, Oxford, Oxford University Press, 2010) 393, 414–15. Alexy uses the language of 'discretion', but in the context of proportionality reasoning, the terms 'discretion' and 'deference' are often used interchangeably: J Rivers, 'Proportionality and Variable Intensity of Review' (2006) 65 *Cambridge Law Journal* 174, 191. See also C Henckels, *Proportionality and Deference in Investor-State Arbitration: Balancing Investment Protection and Regulatory Autonomy* (Cambridge, Cambridge University Press, 2015) 35–36.

[73] Elliott (n 70) 269.

[74] Alexy (n 72) 414–15.

[75] A Kavanagh, *Constitutional Review under the UK Human Rights Act* (Cambridge, Cambridge University Press, 2009) 183ff; ADP Brady, *Proportionality and Deference under the UK Human Rights Act: An Institutionally Sensitive Approach* (Cambridge, Cambridge University Press, 2012) 69ff.

[76] Henckels (n 72) 39; Brady (n 75) 21.

[77] In the UK, the debate over deference has been particularly extensive: see, eg, M Hunt, 'Sovereignty's Blight: Why Contemporary Public Law Needs the Concept of "Due Deference"' in N Bamforth and P Leyland (eds), *Public Law in a Multi-layered Constitution* (Oxford, Hart Publishing, 2003); TRS Allan, 'Human Rights and Judicial Review: A Critique of "Due Deference"' (2006) 65 *Cambridge Law Journal* 671; JA King, 'Institutional Approaches to Judicial Restraint' (2008) 28 *Oxford Journal of Legal Studies* 409. See also ch 4, section III.B.

[78] See ch 1, text accompanying nn 59ff.

[79] *McCloy v New South Wales* (2015) 257 CLR 178, 220 [90]–[91] (French CJ, Kiefel, Bell and Keane JJ). See also *Unions NSW v New South Wales* (2013) 252 CLR 530, 553 [34], 556 [45]

As this passage demonstrates, the Court's rejection of deference is closely tied to its conception of its own role. The effect is that there is little room for considering how to evaluate the factual determinations made by other branches of government. Yet this approach has led to unsatisfactory results and a lack of clarity in the Court's reasoning. While the Court has long insisted that its duty is to determine the relevant facts,[80] as Susan Kenny has observed, in practice it often attributes 'virtually conclusive force' to factual decisions made by other branches of government.[81]

## II. RECOGNISING FACTS: IMPLICATIONS FOR PROCEDURE

Given these limitations surrounding the Court's current approaches to fact-finding, it is instructive to ask whether differentiating between the facts that arise at the various stages of proportionality reasoning can inform the processes by which courts find facts. Returning to Davis' foundational distinction between legislative and adjudicative facts, which was analysed in Chapter 2, it is apparent that Davis himself recognised that there were procedural implications flowing from his proposed taxonomy of facts. Indeed, one of the motivating factors behind his categorisation was the discrepancy he observed between the current practices of the US Supreme Court and the rules of evidence. Since at least the beginning of the twentieth century,[82] the Supreme Court had been accepting 'briefs' of non-legal, extrinsic materials under what appears to have been an expanded concept of judicial notice.[83] Davis argued that the traditional rules of evidence, which were designed with adjudicative facts in mind, were ill-suited and inappropriate when it came to legislative facts. These facts could not always be supported by evidence, much less by evidence supplied by the parties themselves.[84] This idea – that classification might inform process – has also permeated other attempts at taxonomy.[85]

(French CJ, Hayne, Crennan, Kiefel and Bell JJ); *Unions (No 2)* (n 27) 617 [51] (Kiefel CJ, Bell and Keane JJ); *Clubb v Edwards; Preston v Avery* (2019) 267 CLR 171, 262 [263] (Nettle J).

[80] *Australian Communist Party v Commonwealth* (1951) 83 CLR 1, 193 (Dixon J), 205 (McTiernan J), 222 (Williams J), 264 (Fullagar J), 272–73 (Kitto J).

[81] Kenny (n 23) 164.

[82] Davis attributes this practice to the brief prepared by Mr Louis Brandeis in *Muller v Oregon* 208 US 412 (1908), but it has been suggested that the practice in fact dates from *Munn v Illinois* 94 US 113 (1876); see ch 3, n 43.

[83] See *Muller* (n 82) 421, where Brewer J referred to taking 'judicial cognizance of all matters of general knowledge'. See also E Margolis, 'Beyond Brandeis: Exploring the Uses of Non-legal Materials in Appellate Briefs' (2000) 34 *University of San Francisco Law Review* 197, 203–04; and more generally, see DL Faigman, *Constitutional Fictions: A Unified Theory of Constitutional Facts* (New York, Oxford University Press, 2008) ch 5.

[84] See, eg, KC Davis, *Administrative Law Treatise*, 2nd edn (San Diego, KC Davis Publishing Co, 1979) vol 2, 413.

[85] See the other classifications of fact that are discussed in ch 3, section II.

As I have argued in this book, the nature and significance of facts depends on the context in which they are being used. As will be recalled, the facts that are relevant at each stage of proportionality reasoning will often exhibit different characteristics. It is useful, then, to consider the procedural implications that arise at the different stages of proportionality reasoning.

## A. The Suitability Stage

At the suitability stage, a court must examine the connection between a particular measure and the legitimate aim which it is said to advance. As the comparative experience reveals, it is relatively uncommon for laws to fail the proportionality inquiry at this stage.[86] Although the suitability test is likely to be construed as a question of law, a court's conclusion will be underpinned, at least implicitly, by various facts about the purpose to be pursued by the law, the background context in which the law operates, and the practicalities of how the law works in practice. Knowledge about these circumstances will enable the court to answer the (legal) question of whether the law is *capable of* advancing the legitimate objective. These facts, as explained in previous chapters, raise different considerations than ordinary, adjudicative facts.

### *i. The Burden and Standard of Proof*

At the suitability stage, the relevant legal threshold is relatively low as the court only needs to be satisfied that the law is *capable* of advancing the legitimate objective. As previous chapters have established, a court will often be able to answer the question of suitability on the basis of reason or logic; that is, evidence will not always be necessary for a court to assess the relevant connection between a law and its purpose. This suggests that the burden of proof will in many cases have no application at this stage of the inquiry. In some cases, however, a court's assessment of suitability will be assisted by extrinsic materials. In *McCloy*,[87] for instance, the Court referred to various reports to demonstrate that a problem of corruption existed in New South Wales and, second, that the legislation was designed to reduce the risk of corruption or undue influence.[88] While the majority in *McCloy* accepted that the burden of justification rested with the State (ie, the persuasive burden), the extent to which evidence was necessary to discharge this burden was not explicitly addressed.[89]

[86] See ch 4, n 20 and the text accompanying n 93.
[87] *McCloy* (n 79).
[88] ibid 208–09 [48]–[53] (French CJ, Kiefel, Bell and Keane JJ). See also the discussion in ch 6, sections II.B and II.D.
[89] *McCloy* (n 79) 201 [24] (French CJ, Kiefel, Bell and Keane JJ).

Another issue that remains unaddressed is the relevant standard of proof at the suitability stage. Although the balance of probabilities will apply, the nature of the facts that the Court is seeking to establish needs to be borne in mind. In *McCloy*, the Court did not need to make a definitive finding that corruption had *actually* occurred, nor did it need to ascertain the extent of the corruption. Instead, the reports were used to establish that there was *some evidence* of a problem of corruption and, correspondingly, that Parliament had a reasonable basis for acting. To establish these facts requires less evidence (and therefore a lower or more flexible standard of proof) than if the Court was required to make positive findings about the extent of corruption. This reflects, consistently with *Briginshaw* and the cases that have followed it, that the degree of certainty or satisfaction will vary depending on 'the nature and consequences of the fact or facts to be proved'.[90] In other words, the nature of the facts that are relevant to the suitability inquiry suggests that less evidence (or, in some cases, even no evidence) may be sufficient to satisfy this standard.

### *ii. Judicial Notice*

When a court refers to extrinsic materials to demonstrate suitability, as it did in *McCloy*, there is a question about whether this falls within the scope of judicial notice. A strict application of the doctrine of judicial notice, as was suggested by the majority in *Aytugrul*,[91] would mean that any facts to be judicially noticed must comply with the restrictive requirements of section 144 of the *Evidence Act 1995*.[92] As well as being 'not reasonably open to question',[93] the knowledge must be 'capable of verification by reference to a document the authority of which cannot be reasonably questioned'.[94] This approach to judicial notice might, potentially, be able to encompass the use of the Independent Commission Against Corruption (ICAC) and other reports that were referred to in *McCloy*. These reports were included in the special case materials by agreement of the parties.[95] This is not to say that there was agreement as to the content and accuracy of the reports[96] but, as explained above, the Court was only concerned with establishing that a genuine problem existed.

So, while this use of judicial notice might be able to explain *some* of the Court's use of extrinsic materials, particularly where a matter has proceeded by way of special case,[97] it is far from clear that it will always be sufficient.

[90] *Briginshaw* (n 40) 362 (Dixon J). See also the cases referred to at n 43 above.
[91] *Aytugrul* (n 66) 183 [21] (French CJ, Hayne, Crennan and Bell JJ).
[92] This would appear to be the case in uniform *Evidence Act* jurisdictions: see n 67, above.
[93] *Evidence Act 1995* (Cth), s 144(1).
[94] ibid s 144(1)(b).
[95] 'Special Case Book', *McCloy v New South Wales*, S211/2014, 28 January 2015.
[96] Transcript of Proceedings, *McCloy v New South Wales* [2015] HCATrans 141 (10 June 2015) 835–40.
[97] As indicated above, under the special case procedure, the parties must identify the facts and documents which are necessary for the Court to answer the stated questions of law.

For example, if there *is* disagreement about the relevant facts a strict application of section 144 would curtail the Court's ability to take judicial notice of published materials. In addition, at the suitability stage, it will not always be appropriate for the Court to require the parties to produce evidence. To demand evidence in all cases might, as Sujit Choudhry has suggested in the Canadian context, serve to hamper government activity.[98] Similarly, as the High Court has recognised, Parliament must be able to deal 'prophylactically' with 'inferred legislative imperatives'.[99] There may not always be evidence available in advance that can establish that there is a particular problem to be addressed. To require proof in these circumstances could serve to impede the work of both the courts[100] and the legislature.[101]

This suggests that it would be helpful if, at least at the suitability stage, there is some relaxation of the requirements of section 144. The types of facts that are relevant to proportionality reasoning will often be open to question and may fail to meet the demands of the provision. To demand evidence and formal proof in every case would be unworkable, particularly given the need for parliaments to be able to respond to future threats or problems. The critical question is *when* the Court should be able to rely on its own general knowledge of the world, including referring to extrinsic materials, and when it should require formal proof.

It is here that the Canadian approach might be instructive. As discussed in Chapter 4, in the case of *R v Spence*, the Supreme Court sought to define the limits of judicial notice when it comes to legislative facts.[102] Although acknowledging that the boundaries will be 'inevitably somewhat elastic',[103] the Court defined the dividing line in terms of the degree to which the legislative fact approaches the 'dispositive issue' in the case.[104] In other words, how central is the fact to the ultimate question to be decided? As Binnie J explained in *Spence*:

> [M]ore stringent proof may be called for of facts that are close to the center of the controversy between the parties (whether social, legislative or adjudicative) as distinguished from background facts at or near the periphery.[105]

Under this approach, where the fact is critical to the outcome, a strict approach should be taken and judicial notice should be confined.[106]

[98] S Choudhry, 'So What is the Real Legacy of *Oakes*? Two Decades of Proportionality Analysis under the Canadian *Charter*'s Section 1' (2006) 34 *Supreme Court Law Review* 501, 524–25.

[99] *Spence v Queensland* (2019) 93 ALJR 643, 671 [96] (Kiefel CJ, Bell, Gageler and Keane JJ), quoting Nettle J in *McCloy* (n 79) 262 [233]. See also *Brown* (n 17) 421–22 [288], where Nettle J made the same point.

[100] See Odgers (n 66) 1281 [EA 144.90].

[101] See ch 4, text accompanying n 118.

[102] *R v Spence* [2005] 3 SCR 458 (hereinafter '*Spence*').

[103] ibid 490–91 [63] (Binnie J, writing for the Court).

[104] ibid 490 [61].

[105] ibid 490 [60].

[106] ibid 491 [64]. See the discussion in ch 4, text accompanying nn 156ff.

The suitability stage of the proportionality inquiry, as I have explained, represents a low hurdle and is seldom determinative of the outcome of a case. All that needs to be established at this stage is that the law is *capable* of advancing the legitimate objective. In these circumstances, a more relaxed approach to judicial notice appears appropriate.[107] Rather than insisting on strict compliance with section 144,[108] the Court should be able to find that a rational connection exists based on reason or logic, combined with its own knowledge about the world (even if no empirical material is offered in support). Of course, if there is uncertainty or dispute about the suitability stage, this would indicate that a stricter approach should be taken and evidence may be needed. This is discussed further below in the context of the necessity and balancing stages.

### *iii. Deference or Restraint*

Despite the High Court's general disdain for the concept of deference, this does not mean that deference has no work to do. Under the Court's current approach, the question of what weight is afforded to the decisions of other branches of government is largely unexpressed. In other words, such considerations are built into the Court's reasoning, but without being clearly articulated.[109] As others have recognised, it would be preferable for structured proportionality to be accompanied by a more explicit approach to deference or restraint.[110] Proportionality is, as previously explained, an inherently flexible standard, and articulating potential grounds for deference or restraint (however this is labelled) may increase the transparency and therefore the legitimacy of judicial decision-making.

In terms of the suitability inquiry, at this stage a court needs to determine a law's purpose and whether the law has the requisite connection with that purpose. The critical question is whether there might be any grounds – either in terms of legitimacy or expertise – to defer to the views of the legislature. Of course, to defer entirely to the assessment made by the legislature would dilute this inquiry of any real force. The nature of the inquiry at the suitability stage is similar to those inquiries that routinely arise in the course of statutory interpretation. Answering these questions, then, falls squarely within the Court's conception of its own role and its accepted approach to judicial power, meaning there are no particular legitimacy concerns that arise at this stage. In other words, it is part of the Court's duty to answer these questions.

[107] Subject to giving the parties an opportunity to respond.

[108] Which, as noted above, in practice the Court tends not to do in any event.

[109] M Wesson, 'Crafting a Concept of Deference for the Implied Freedom of Political Communication' (2016) 27 *Public Law Review* 101, 105.

[110] ibid 108; S Chordia, *Proportionality in Australian Constitutional Law* (Sydney, Federation Press, 2020) 201.

In terms of the facts that arise at this stage of the analysis, courts may at times lack the relevant empirical knowledge to make an assessment of suitability. For example, the nature of the problem may concern a future risk or there may be little or even no evidence available. In such circumstances, it may sometimes be appropriate to accord some weight to the views of other branches of government, who are better placed to assess this risk. To demand evidence may, as indicated above, stifle the government's ability to act in relation to future risk. In practice, the nature of the suitability inquiry (which requires only that there be a rational connection) means that questions of deference are unlikely to assume much prominence at this stage.[111]

## B. The Necessity and Balancing Stages

The necessity and balancing stages of proportionality reasoning tend to be more pivotal in terms of a court's overall conclusion about proportionality. It is at the necessity stage that questions of fact are particularly prominent as the inquiry is one of 'empirical prognosis'.[112] Under this sub-test, the court must ask whether the legitimate objective could be achieved by other measures that are less restrictive of the particular right. This involves considering the effect not only of the impugned law itself, but also any hypothetical alternatives. Facts are also relevant to the final stage of balancing. Although at this stage judges are ultimately required to choose between two competing interests, meaning that normative considerations will often dominate, this decision takes place against the backdrop of the previous two inquiries. In other words, courts do not balance in isolation; rather, the process of weighing up competing interests relies upon empirical assessments about both the degree of infringement and the extent of any benefits to be achieved.[113]

### *i. The Burden and Standard of Proof*

The allocation of the burden of proof has arisen most sharply in relation to the question of necessity. In *Brown v Tasmania*, Nettle J was the only member of the Court to address this question directly, and he rejected the plaintiffs' submission that Tasmania had a burden to persuade the Court that there were no less restrictive alternatives available.[114] Such an approach, according to Nettle J, would be 'illogical', as there was 'nothing in principle or authority' to suggest

[111] Chordia (n 110) 82.
[112] J Rivers, 'The Presumption of Proportionality' (2014) 77 *Modern Law Review* 409, 415.
[113] Whether these factual questions are considered at this stage or earlier in the analysis will depend partly on how a court structures its proportionality inquiry.
[114] *Brown* (n 17) 421 [288].

that 'a plaintiff should be relieved of the burden of persuasion as to an essential element of his or her cause of action'.[115] Nettle J cautioned that to require a defendant to rebut any possible alternative measure would require evidence and an assessment of competing legislative models. He was keen to avoid this type of factual inquiry, as it would require the court to adjudicate 'contestable issues of policy'.[116]

To support his position, Nettle J relied on the 'presumption of constitutionality', which refers to a general presumption in favour of the validity of Commonwealth and State legislation.[117] This was used to bolster his conclusion that the plaintiffs must bear the burden of establishing the relevant facts. Similarly, in the academic literature, there has been some suggestion that the presumption of constitutionality might assist with resolving factual disputes in constitutional claims.[118] Yet, as Nettle J himself acknowledged, the presumption remains under-developed in the Australian context.[119] While it might potentially have a role in the allocation of the burden of proof, it is not apparent that it should apply in the same way to all types of facts. Legislative and constitutional facts, as I have explained, are different in nature from conventional adjudicative facts. It may not, as the Court itself has recognised on other occasions, be appropriate to apply the burden of proof in the ordinary way.[120] The comparative experience suggests, for example, that the burden of adducing evidence of justification often shifts to the party seeking to defend the legislation.[121] In addition, there may be institutional reasons why plaintiffs may be ill-equipped to provide the relevant evidence.[122]

In *Unions (No 2)*, the Court explicitly addressed the question of which party bears the burden of justification in the context of the implied freedom. Both the plurality (who applied structured proportionality) and Gageler J and Gordon J (who did not) agreed that the burden rested with the party seeking to uphold the legislation.[123] According to the plurality, while 'Parliament does not generally

[115] ibid.

[116] ibid.

[117] ibid.

[118] See, eg, Burmester, who suggests that the presumption might be developed to place a burden of proof on those wishing to challenge legislation: H Burmester, 'The Presumption of Constitutionality' (1982) 13 *Federal Law Review* 277. Similarly, Dixon suggests that if a plaintiff cannot persuade the Court that the relevant facts exist that would make the legislation invalid, then the legislation should be upheld: Dixon (n 5) 471–72.

[119] *Brown* (n 17) 421 [288].

[120] *Tanner* (n 51) 179 (Brennan J); *Gerhardy* (n 28) 141–42 (Brennan J).

[121] See the discussion in section I.B.i above.

[122] For instance, as Chan suggests, an individual litigant may have inferior resources, means of access to information or expertise in policy-making: C Chan, 'The Burden of Proof under the *Human Rights Act*' (2014) 19 *Judicial Review* 46, 50.

[123] Note also that Nettle J seemed to adopt a more flexible approach to the burden of proof than he had in *Brown*, noting that 'what is required to justify an effective burden on the implied freedom depends on the circumstances of the case': *Unions (No 2)* (n 27) 640 [117].

need to provide evidence to prove the basis for legislation which it enacts', the position is different in relation to laws that burden the implied freedom, as 'any effective burden [must] be justified'.[124] Justice Gageler and Gordon J noted that differing views had been expressed on this question in the past, but, like the plurality, held that the onus of establishing justification rested on the State.[125] Justice Gordon noted that this may include 'where necessary … ensuring sufficient evidence is put on to support its case'.[126] This approach to the allocation of the burden of proof brings the Australian approach broadly in line with the approach adopted in Canada and South Africa, and also makes sense in terms of the institutional resources of the parties. It also recognises that the facts that underpin proportionality reasoning are, by their very nature, quite different from ordinary adjudicative facts.

When it comes to the standard of proof, the inquiries at both the necessity and balancing stages are designed to be more searching; that is, they entail a greater degree of judicial scrutiny. While at the suitability stage the relatively low degree of judicial scrutiny tends to correspond with a relatively low standard of proof, as a matter of principle there are arguments in favour of imposing a slightly higher standard of proof at the later two stages. For a start, experience shows us that the facts relevant to these inquiries are more likely to be critical to the Court's overall assessment. To attenuate the standard of proof too much would, as McLachlin J warned in the Canadian context, risk relieving the State of the burden of justification;[127] that is, it would risk decisions that are not properly supported by empirical material and that might not reflect the realities of how the world works. This suggests that although the standard of proof will remain the balance of probabilities, it might be reasonable for a court to require more evidence to find this standard satisfied.

However, at the same time, the very facts relevant to the necessity and balancing stages are likely to be more difficult to establish. They are, as was discussed in Chapter 3, more likely to be predictive or even hypothetical in nature, and to require assessments of likelihood. In this way, they are less likely to resemble conventional, backward-looking facts that describe the existing empirical world. In addition, there may be less evidence available or the evidence may be more contested. In this way, the significance of facts at the necessity and balancing stages seems to coincide with potential limits of the Court's capacity in terms of both expertise and institutional competence. Yet, rather than relaxing the standard of proof to a degree that it becomes meaningless, recognising these limits can potentially offer guidance in terms of both the scope of judicial notice and the weight to be accorded to the factual assessments of other branches of government.

[124] *Unions (No 2)* (n 27) 616 [45] (Kiefel CJ, Bell and Keane JJ).
[125] ibid 631 [93] (Gageler J), 650 [151] (Gordon).
[126] ibid 650 [151].
[127] *RJR-MacDonald* (n 46) 333 [138].

### *ii. Judicial Notice*

When considering the limits of judicial notice, the critical question is *when* it is appropriate for the Court to invoke judicial notice and rely on its own knowledge about facts, and when it should require evidence. Under the Canadian approach, as explained above, the Supreme Court has defined the relevant dividing line in terms of the degree to which the legislative fact approaches the 'dispositive issue' in the case.[128] If this is applied to proportionality reasoning, it is apparent that it is at the necessity and balancing stages that the Court's conclusions are more likely to be determinative in terms of the outcome of the case. Correspondingly, the facts that underpin these inquiries are more likely to play an important role in the Court's conclusion. Although the High Court has limited its consideration to alternatives that are 'obvious and compelling'[129] – thereby trying to avoid extensive factual engagement – the empirical dimensions of the necessity inquiry cannot be avoided altogether. In addition, the facts that arise at the necessity stage are more likely to contain elements of evaluation or expertise which extend beyond the Court's own knowledge.

This suggests that, when dealing with the question of necessity, a somewhat stricter approach to judicial notice may at times be called far. As these facts are likely to be closer to the dispositive issue, and contestable, it becomes less appropriate for the Court to rely on its own knowledge via judicial notice. The alternative, of course, is that these facts would have to be established by normal processes, which for the High Court may include referring the matter to a single justice of the Court or remitting the matter to a lower court.[130] In the *Palmer v Western Australia* case, which involved a challenge to Western Australia's border closer on the basis of section 92 of the *Australian Constitution*, the Court adopted the latter approach, and extensive factual findings were made by a judge of the Federal Court.[131] Such an approach enables relevant evidence to be tendered by the parties and, if necessary, experts to be called and cross-examined, which ensures a proper factual foundation upon which the High Court can assess the substantive claim.

### *iii. Deference or Restraint*

When it comes to considering whether there are grounds for allocating weight to the factual assessments made by other branches of government, again it is apparent that these questions are likely to be more acute at the necessity and balancing stages. The necessity inquiry, for instance, may give rise to considerable empirical

[128] *Spence* (n 102) 490 [61] (Binnie J, writing for the Court).

[129] See, eg, *McCloy* (n 79) 211 [58] (French CJ, Kiefel, Bell and Keane JJ). See also *Clubb* (n 79) 265–66 [267]–[269] (Nettle J), 337 [479] (Edelman J).

[130] *Judiciary Act 1903* (Cth), ss 42, 44.

[131] See *Palmer v Western Australia* (2021) 95 ALJR 229; *Palmer v Western Australia* [2020] FCA 1221 (Rangiah J).

uncertainty[132] and it may be that the other branches of government are better equipped to gather or monitor relevant empirical information, to consult with the public or to consider the feasibility of alternatives.[133] In such circumstances, empirical deference – that is, deference on the grounds of the decision-maker's superior expertise – might sometimes be appropriate at the necessity stage. In contrast, at the balancing stage, the evaluative nature of the inquiry, and the need to consider competing policy considerations, might sometimes suggest that there are normative reasons for deference.[134] In other words, the legislature may be better suited to perform the complex balancing of competing interests.

However, as explained above, complete deference at either the necessity or balancing stages would be antithetical to the Court's constitutional duty and would dilute the force of the proportionality inquiry. If the relevant legal test to be applied involves the three stages of proportionality, the Court itself must independently assess each of these stages. As former High Court justice Kenneth Hayne commented extra-judicially: 'Once a task is validly committed to the courts they must perform that task.'[135] Yet even if we reject a blanket or absolute notion of deference, there may on occasion be good reasons for giving some weight to the factual assessments made by other branches of government. The Court should not, for example, simply accept at face value statements from the legislature as to a law's purpose or effects, nor should it unhesitatingly accept that the legislature will *always* have superior competence. Instead, it will be relevant for the Court to assess the degree to which the legislature might have specific competence or expertise to determine factual questions in a particular case and the degree to which the legislature itself undertook the relevant deliberations.[136] This might involve asking whether the legislature had before it specific evidence of the problem, what the nature of this evidence was, and whether it had commissioned reports or engaged in a consultative process.[137] These types of reasons might be understood as 'second-order' reasons, as they relate to the government's competence and processes (rather than the merits of the particular case).[138] It may be that it can be demonstrated that in relation to a specific issue, the legislature *is* in fact better placed to make the required empirical assessment and in this scenario some weight should be given to the government's findings.

[132] Chordia (n 110) 78–79.
[133] Henckels (n 72) 39.
[134] Chordia (n 110) 78–79.
[135] KM Hayne, 'Deference: An Australian Perspective' [2011] *Public Law* 75, 82.
[136] G Appleby and A Carter, 'Parliament, Proportionality and Facts' (2021) *Sydney Law Review* (forthcoming).
[137] In the US context, it has been argued that the superior competence of legislatures to make factual findings should not be assumed; see, eg, CE Borgmann, 'Rethinking Judicial Deference to Legislative Fact-Finding' (2009) 84 *Indiana Law Journal* 1.
[138] C Chan, 'Proportionality and Invariable Baseline Intensity of Review' (2013) 33 *Legal Studies* 1, 11–14, 18–21.

## III. CHANGING FACTS AND THE PROBLEM OF PRECEDENT

A more open recognition of the facts underpinning proportionality reasoning raises the problem of changing facts. As was foreshadowed in Chapter 6, in *Murphy v Electoral Commissioner*,[139] which concerned provisions of the *Commonwealth Electoral Act 1918* (Cth) that prevented amending or updating the Electoral Roll for a period before an election, the plaintiffs argued that 'an inevitable consequence' of applying proportionality reasoning was that changes in the relevant facts might affect constitutional validity.[140] They submitted that changes in the constitutional facts meant that there was no longer a 'substantial reason' to justify restrictions on the franchise.[141] Only Keane J specifically addressed this argument and he was quick to reject what he described as '[c]reeping unconstitutionality'.[142] In his Honour's view, constitutional validity could not be dependent on changes in the factual circumstances in which an Act operates.[143] While Keane J acknowledged the relevance of facts – and the possibility that these facts may change – in relation to the defence power and section 92 of the *Australian Constitution*, he rejected this possibility in the context of Parliament's power to make laws regulating elections.[144] However, as suggested in the previous chapter, this argument is difficult to maintain given that across a range of areas, the Court now employs reasoning that contains common elements of proportionality.[145]

The problem of changing facts was again considered by Edelman J in *Clubb v Edwards; Preston v Avery*.[146] His Honour confirmed that a court can consider the facts and circumstances at the time Parliament enacted the legislation, but queried whether this would extend to 'taking into account unforeseeable subsequent, potentially radical, changes in facts and circumstances'.[147] He acknowledged the difficulties this might cause in terms of validity: legislation that was once suitable, necessary or adequate in its balance may cease to be so. While he acknowledged the 'strong opposition' some members of the Court had expressed towards such 'waxing and waning' of validity,[148] he considered that this question did not need to be resolved in the present case. Even though some of the material provided to the Court was subsequent to the enactment of the

[139] *Murphy v Electoral Commissioner* (2016) 261 CLR 28.
[140] Anthony John Murphy, 'Plaintiff's Annotated Submissions', Submission in *Murphy v Electoral Commissioner*, M247/2015, 11 April 2016, [8].
[141] ibid.
[142] *Murphy* (n 139) 90 [191].
[143] ibid 92 [196].
[144] ibid 92–93 [199]–[200].
[145] See ch 6, text accompanying nn 36ff.
[146] *Clubb* (n 79).
[147] ibid 334 [470].
[148] ibid 334 [471], referring to *XYZ v The Commonwealth* (2006) 227 CLR 532, 608 [218] and *Murphy* (n 139) 55 [42], 92–93 [196]–[199].

legislation, there was 'no suggestion' that this material 'reflected any changes in underlying facts and circumstances'.[149]

A related question concerns the extent to which the doctrine of precedent attaches to findings of legislative or constitutional fact. While ordinary facts, whether established via the normal processes of proof or via judicial notice, do not attract the application of stare decisis,[150] legislative facts stand in a different category. To the extent that they form part of the ratio decidendi of a case, it would appear that they do attract the operation of stare decisis.[151] The effect, of course, is that a subsequent (lower) court would technically be bound to follow the precedent even if the findings were considered 'incorrect, inadequate or out of date'.[152] The situation is different when it comes to the High Court; the Court is not formally bound by its own decisions, which means that changes in the facts may be reviewed in subsequent cases.

The obvious disadvantage of recognising changing factual circumstances is that it will lead to instability and uncertainty. Indeed, in Australia this has traditionally been one of the reasons used to explain the High Court's reluctance to develop fact-dependent standards.[153] In the US, Stuart Minor Benjamin has commented:

> Rapidly changing facts weaken the force of stare decisis by undermining the stability of precedents. Appellate opinions are only as robust as the facts on which they are based. When those facts evaporate, the opinion on which they rest is weakened as well.[154]

Yet the alternative, which Benjamin also acknowledges, is even more problematic. To simply ignore changing factual circumstances, where these are relevant to the application of the constitutional test, might result in decisions that no longer reflect the real world. This would have the effect of undermining the authority on which precedent is based.[155] While current precedents would not automatically cease to be binding or lose their authoritative force, it does suggest that in a future case, a significant change to the factual circumstances

[149] *Clubb* (n 79) 334–35 [471].

[150] See Heydon (n 14) 228 [3125]; Carter (n 54) 94.

[151] Carter (n 54) 94. Yet, as Heydon observes, not all legislative facts will form part of the precedent: JD Heydon, 'Developing the Common Law' in JT Gleeson and RCA Higgins (eds), *Constituting Law: Legal Arguments and Social Values* (Sydney, Federation Press, 2011) 117.

[152] Serpell (n 66) 139.

[153] Stellios (n 20). In the US context, see Faigman (n 83) 16, 178–80.

[154] SM Benjamin, 'Stepping into the Same River Twice: Rapidly Changing Facts and the Appellate Process' (1999) 78 *Texas Law Review* 269, 272.

[155] As Duxbury has observed: 'Perhaps it is because case-law is often treated and presented as if it were itself a body of legal rules that it is sometimes assumed that precedents have binding force rather as statutory rules have binding force. But the reality is that precedents, unlike statutes, do not bind judges in an all-or-nothing fashion, that the binding force of a precedent is best explained not in terms of its validity (this being a non-scalar concept) but in terms of its authority (of which there can be degrees)': N Duxbury, *The Nature and Authority of Precedent* (Cambridge, Cambridge University Press, 2008) 23.

may provide a reason for a court coming to a different conclusion when applying proportionality. Given the importance of stability, however, a court would not make this decision lightly and would require persuasive evidence to substantiate the relevant changes in factual circumstances.

Again, this is an issue that has been addressed in other jurisdictions where proportionality reasoning is more firmly established. In Canada, for example, the Supreme Court has recently clarified that the threshold for revisiting a matter will be high. Chief Justice McLachlin, writing for the Court in *Canada (Attorney-General) v Bedford*, indicated that this threshold may be met 'if there is a change in the circumstances or evidence that fundamentally shifts the parameters of the debate'.[156] According to McLachlin CJ, this approach 'balances the need for finality and stability with the recognition that when an appropriate case arises for revisiting precedent, a lower court must be able to perform its full role'.[157] In Germany, likewise, the Federal Constitutional Court has indicated it is prepared to revisit factual questions where the underlying factual circumstances have significantly changed.[158] Given that the Australian High Court already acknowledges, at least in some circumstances, the relevance of facts, a similar approach may be warranted if significant changes to the underlying facts can be demonstrated. To fail to do so risks decisions that no longer reflect the real world.

## IV. CONCLUSION

As demonstrated in this chapter, a greater recognition of the facts underpinning proportionality reasoning has implications in terms of procedure. In particular, a more precise articulation of the facts relevant to each stage of proportionality reasoning has the potential to inform three important but unresolved issues: the burden and standard of proof; the scope of judicial notice; and the role of deference or restraint. This chapter has suggested that a more nuanced understanding of the facts that arise at each stage of proportionality reasoning might assist in identifying the limits of courts' expertise and capacity, and the point at which the courts will require evidence to support their factual findings. This will help to ensure that the facts are appropriately justified and that the proportionality test remains an effective method of review.

[156] *Canada (Attorney-General) v Bedford* [2013] 3 SCR 1101, 1127–28 [42].

[157] ibid 1128 [44]. See also *Carter v Canada (Attorney-General)* [2015] 1 SCR 331, 361 [44] (McLachlin CJ, LeBel, Abella, Rothstein, Cromwell, Moldaver, Karakatsanis, Wagner and Gascon JJ). For some discussion, see M Bloodworth, 'A Fact is a Fact is a Fact: *Stare Decisis* and the Distinction between Adjudicative and Social Facts in *Bedford* and *Carter*' (2014) 32 *National Journal of Constitutional Law* 193; J Hughes, V MacDonnell and K Pearlston, 'Equality & Incrementalism: The Role of Common Law Reasoning in Constitutional Rights Cases' (2013) 44 *Ottawa Law Review* 467.

[158] An illustration of this is the *Parental Custody Decisions* of 2003 and 2010; see ch 4, nn 188 and 189.

# 8

# *Conclusion: Why Facts Matter*

THIS BOOK HAS sought to understand the relationship between facts and proportionality in constitutional adjudication. Despite the prevalence of proportionality reasoning in recent decades and the burgeoning literature on the subject, there has been little sustained attention given to the role of facts. In Australia, the use of proportionality reasoning remains contested as the High Court is divided over whether it constitutes an appropriate or useful method of constitutional review. In light of this uncertainty, this book has sought to clarify how facts are relevant to proportionality reasoning both conceptually and as a matter of practice.

I have argued in this book that facts are relevant to all three stages of proportionality reasoning. Although a court's overall conclusion in relation to proportionality is likely to be characterised as a question of law, this conclusion rests upon various propositions of fact. At each of the suitability, necessity and balancing stages, courts must rely (even if implicitly) on certain views about the world. It is at the necessity stage that facts are likely to be most prominent, as courts at this stage are required to assess the efficacy of the impugned measure and any hypothetical alternatives. However, the Australian and comparative jurisprudence illustrates that the extent to which questions of fact have been recognised in practice varies. The factual underpinnings of proportionality are not always explicitly acknowledged, and there is judicial disagreement about whether evidence is necessary or appropriate and how such evidence should be adduced.

What, then, is the nature of the facts that underpin proportionality reasoning? I have proposed that in order to understand the significance of facts, there is a need to distinguish more clearly between the types of empirical claims that arise at the different stages of proportionality analysis; in other words, there is a need to develop a context-specific approach to facts. The facts that arise at the suitability, necessity and balancing stages will often display different characteristics and will require the court to make different types of judgments. Although, as Chapter 3 suggested, it is useful to distinguish between adjudicative and non-adjudicative facts (which may be variously labelled), proportionality contains its own distinctive set of questions and it is instructive to consider each stage separately.

Against this conceptual framework, the book has examined how the courts themselves have applied proportionality reasoning and the degree to which facts have been recognised as relevant. The comparative analysis of Germany, Canada and South Africa, all of which have extensive experience with applying tests of proportionality, showed that in all three jurisdictions, courts have acknowledged that facts may be relevant to proportionality. This recognition has been most explicit in Canada, where the Supreme Court has adopted a fact-sensitive approach to section 1 of the *Charter*. The comparative jurisprudence revealed that there are some signs of a different approach to facts emerging at the various stages of the proportionality inquiry. The comparative analysis also helped to identify some of the difficulties surrounding the recognition and proof of facts, and how these have been resolved, which can usefully inform the Australian approach.

In the second half of the book, the focus shifted to Australia. The High Court has, as Chapters 5 and 6 demonstrated, adopted a number of differently worded tests which can be seen to incorporate aspects of the tripartite model of proportionality. Since 2015, a majority of the Court has adopted a structured test of proportionality in the context of the implied freedom of political communication and, more recently, in relation to section 92, but the Court remains divided over the role and nature of this test. The book has clarified the extent to which the various tests adopted by the Court incorporate the elements of suitability, necessity and balancing. Moreover, it has examined the extent to which the Court has recognised the relevance of facts within each of these different tests. As part of this analysis, the book has considered whether the development of a more structured test of proportionality has resulted in a more fact-sensitive approach to adjudication. I have argued, based on the jurisprudence to date, that there is no simple correlation between the framing of constitutional tests and facts. In other words, the turn towards a more structured test of proportionality in Australia has not necessarily increased the role of facts.

Finally, the book has begun the task of addressing the procedural implications that flow from a greater recognition of facts. In particular, I have suggested that distinguishing more clearly between the types of factual claims that arise at each of the three stages of proportionality might offer insights in terms of the burden and standard of proof, the scope of judicial notice and the role of judicial deference or restraint.

Having established that facts *are* relevant to judicial assessments of proportionality, it is worth pausing to consider why facts matter. In other words, why do we care about facts, and what role do they play in judicial decisions? At the outset, it must be acknowledged that facts may not always matter in terms of the result of a case; that is, they will not necessarily be determinative of a court's conclusion about whether a measure satisfies the requirements of proportionality. This is because while facts are relevant, on their own they do not direct a particular result. Judges must also rely on other factors to inform their assessments of proportionality, such as the importance of the different interests at stake and the extent of the interference with the constitutional guarantee. It is these evaluative judgments that will, in many cases, be most significant in determining the result. That facts, or evidence in support of the facts, will not always be decisive can be seen in the Australian case of *McCloy v New South Wales*.[1] As discussed in Chapter 6, while there was extrinsic material before the High Court regarding the problem of corruption, it appears this material was mainly used to bolster the Court's findings about the purpose of the legislation. It did not appear to have been determinative in the application of the necessity and balancing stages.[2] At other times, however, a lack of evidence may be important or even decisive to the question of validity. For instance, in *Unions NSW v New South Wales (No 2)*, there was a significant evidentiary gap which meant that the impugned provisions could not be justified.[3] Similarly, in the comparative jurisdictions, there are examples where the courts have directed the filing of further evidence[4] or have invalidated legislation partly on the basis of insufficient evidence of justification.[5]

Even though facts will not always be decisive, it remains important to understand how facts underpin and inform the proportionality inquiry. First, identifying where facts are relevant has the potential to increase the transparency of judicial decisions. One of the main criticisms of proportionality, as discussed in Chapter 1, is that it can serve to conceal what a court is doing. This potential for opaqueness may be even more pronounced when judges do not articulate clearly which stage of proportionality is being relied upon. While much will of course depend on how judicial reasons are expressed, a more careful identification of the facts and assumptions on which a court relies can serve to clarify judicial decision-making. Unlike David Beatty,[6] whose argument was considered in Chapter 2, I do not suggest that a greater recognition of facts will transform proportionality into a purely neutral or objective standard. Isolating the factual elements, however, can help to reveal where value judgments come into play and might therefore illuminate where and how the 'work' of proportionality is being performed.

Second, a greater recognition of facts might have a bearing upon the intensity of review. Proportionality is a flexible method of review that can be applied with varying degrees of intensity. The degree of scrutiny with which proportionality is applied might be affected by a court's approach to questions of fact. For example, if a court adopts a deferential approach, simply accepting assertions

[1] *McCloy v New South Wales* (2015) 257 CLR 178.
[2] See ch 6, nn 151ff and accompanying text.
[3] *Unions NSW v New South Wales (No 2)* (2019) 264 CLR 595.
[4] See ch 4, nn 48ff and accompanying text.
[5] See ch 4, nn 65ff and accompanying text.
[6] DM Beatty, *The Ultimate Rule of Law* (Oxford, Oxford University Press, 2004) ch 5.

of justification put forward by government parties, the standard of review would be considerably weakened. At the same time, it is clear that demanding empirical support for questions of fact is not always practicable; as recognised by courts both in Australia and abroad, there is risk that governments might be prevented from taking action in relation to future threats or harms.

Third, and perhaps most crucially, facts matter in terms of ensuring that judicial decisions accurately reflect the empirical world. As explained in Chapter 3, the idea of justification is central to judicial fact-finding.[7] Justification involves considering whether the facts are, or can be, supported by empirical evidence. Justification provides some basis for assessing the degree to which facts can be said to have been established. To completely ignore facts, of course, risks judicial decisions that are divorced from the realities of how the world works. Although the relevant facts may not be able to be verified to the same degree of certainty as conventional, adjudicative facts, this does not mean that justification has no role. Instead, as this book has argued, recognising differences between facts directs attention to what it is reasonable to expect in terms of justification.

In reflecting on the findings of this book, it is helpful to consider what this research might reveal more broadly in terms of both proportionality and facts. There are a couple of caveats to this discussion. First, the book primarily concerns Australian constitutional adjudication and decisions of the High Court. The relatively recent adoption of structured proportionality testing in Australia means that the Court's jurisprudence in this area is not yet fully developed, and aspects of the Court's approach remain to be clarified. Second, the cases discussed are illustrative, not exhaustive.[8] These two factors mean that any conclusions about patterns emerging from the Court's jurisprudence must necessarily be somewhat tentative at this stage. The book's findings may also not be readily translatable to courts in other jurisdictions, in part due to the level of generality at which the decisions and techniques of other courts are often treated. There are also aspects of the Australian approach, such as the reticence about proportionality and the general reluctance to adopt fact-dependent standards, that will be less applicable in other jurisdictions. In addition, lower courts in the Australian court hierarchy largely follow the ordinary adversarial trial processes and so different procedural considerations will apply.

Notwithstanding these limitations, this book contributes to the existing literature by offering insights into the nature of both proportionality reasoning and facts. As explained in Chapter 1, the book brings together the scholarship on proportionality and fact-finding.[9] While considerable work has been

[7] See ch 3, section I.
[8] See the discussion in ch 1, sections II and III regarding the scope of the book and selection of cases.
[9] See ch 1, nn 18ff and 35ff and accompanying text.

done in each area (most prominently, of course, in terms of charting the global popularity of proportionality), there has been little attempt to connect the two bodies of literature. The factual dimensions of the proportionality inquiry tend to have been overshadowed by other aspects, such as the role of judicial balancing. In terms of facts, there has been some discussion that courts are not very good at deciding complex questions of policy or evaluating conflicting social science data. However, this claim – that courts often get these sorts of facts wrong – only matters if the role and significance of facts is first understood. It is to this end that this book was principally directed.

Primarily, this book has helped to clarify the types of judgments that courts must make when applying tests of proportionality. By isolating those inquiries that are factual in nature, the book helps to illuminate what exactly courts are doing when they apply proportionality reasoning. This enables a court's factual claims to be evaluated and also helps to reveal where normative judgments come into play. In addition, the book has begun the task of examining the correlation between facts and proportionality. While it is often assumed that proportionality reasoning will propel courts into fact-finding exercises for which they are inherently ill-suited, the actual connection between proportionality and facts has not been examined with any precision. As I have demonstrated, in Australia at least, the adoption of a structured test of proportionality has not necessarily resulted in a greater focus on facts.

In addition, when it comes to facts, this book has argued that it would be helpful to develop a more nuanced categorisation of facts. While the existing classifications can provide a useful starting point, they were not developed specifically with proportionality reasoning in mind. There is considerable variety within the category of legislative and constitutional facts, and it is instructive to consider the differences that arise at each of the stages of suitability, necessity and balancing. These differences might be relevant when considering a court's capacity to answer the relevant questions, the need for evidence and the appropriate procedural mechanisms.

The findings of this book have a number of implications, both substantively and procedurally. For a start, developing a more sophisticated understanding of the relevance of facts to proportionality can offer insights in terms of doctrinal design. This is particularly significant in the Australian context, where the role and nature of proportionality in constitutional adjudication remains in a state of flux. As Chapter 5 has explained, the High Court remains divided over whether structured proportionality is a useful method of review both in the context of the implied freedom of political communication and the guarantee of free trade, commerce and intercourse in section 92. The use of proportionality beyond these contexts also remains unclear. A more careful identification of the relevance of facts has implications in terms of the framing of constitutional tests of validity. There are already signs of this in the Australian context, as for much of its history the Court has tended to avoid fact-dependent standards. More recently, too, the Court's confining of alternatives within the proportionality inquiry to those that are 'obvious and compelling' can minimise the need to undertake detailed factual inquiries.[10]

This book also has implications in terms of the processes by which the relevant facts can and should be ascertained. The High Court has, on the whole, failed to develop appropriate procedures for the ascertainment of non-adjudicative facts. While these issues defy easy solutions, distinguishing more carefully between different types of facts is instructive. As Chapter 7 explored, a recognition of the differences emerging at the various stages of proportionality reasoning might yield insights in terms of how the relevant facts are established. While further work in this area is needed, it was suggested that this understanding of facts might offer some guidance in terms of the degree of satisfaction required, the appropriate scope of judicial notice and the limits of the court's institutional capacity. While the book has not sought to recommend specific reforms, it raises questions about *how* the Court ought to be informed of empirical matters. These questions invite further consideration of specific mechanisms, such as the role of amicus briefs, interventions and expert evidence, along with the associated repercussions in terms of the length and cost of constitutional litigation.

Finally, this book has implications not only for the work of the courts but also for parliamentary processes. A greater recognition of facts by the courts is likely to prompt a greater demand for empirical evidence. This will, in turn, place pressure on governments to justify their decisions and to produce empirical support.[11] The creation of too high an evidentiary hurdle would have the effect of stifling government action. As Justice Nettle has emphasised in the Australian context, Parliament must be able to act in response to 'inferred' legislative imperatives;[12] that is, there need not always be empirical evidence to support a legislative objective. At the same time, to ignore the factual basis of proportionality risks judicial decisions that do not accurately reflect the empirical world. The critical question, therefore, is how much empirical support it is reasonable to expect from law-makers. By clarifying the nature of the facts that are relevant to the proportionality inquiry, the analysis in this book goes some way towards answering this question.

Overall, this book has established that facts *matter* to judicial assessments of proportionality. I have argued that it is helpful to distinguish more clearly between the types of factual claims that arise at the different stages of proportionality analysis. The implications of this approach to facts remain to be worked out, particularly in Australia as the jurisprudence on proportionality unfolds. Further research, both comparatively and in Australia, will enable a

[10] *McCloy* (n 1) 211 [58] (French CJ, Kiefel, Bell and Keane JJ).

[11] For some discussion in the UK context, see M Hunt, 'Enhancing Parliaments' Role in the Protection and Realisation of Human Rights' in M Hunt, HJ Hooper and P Yowell (eds), *Parliaments and Human Rights: Redressing the Democratic Deficit* (Oxford, Hart Publishing, 2015) 472–74.

[12] *McCloy* (n 1) 262 [233]; *Brown v Tasmania* (2017) 261 CLR 328, 422 [288].

more detailed picture of the correlation between proportionality and facts to be established. Such work might helpfully examine the prevalence of judicial recognition of facts, the differences that arise within and between jurisdictions, the criteria for evaluating facts, and the practical implications of this revised framework. Whichever way the jurisprudence in Australia evolves, the Court must confront the relevance of facts to ensure that its assessments of proportionality are appropriately justified.

# *Bibliography*


Adams, EM, 'Canada's "Newer Constitutional Law" and the Idea of Constitutional Rights' (2006) 51 *McGill Law Journal* 435

Agarwal, R, and Lalani, F, 'Noting the Obvious: A Reflection on the Supreme Court of Canada's Application of Judicial Notice under Sections 7 and 15 of the *Charter*' (2016) 35 *National Journal of Constitutional Law* 131

Alarie, BRD, and Green, AJ, 'Interventions at the Supreme Court of Canada: Accuracy, Affiliation, and Acceptance' (2010) 48 *Osgoode Hall Law Journal* 381

Aleinikoff, TA, 'Constitutional Law in the Age of Balancing' (1987) 96 *Yale Law Journal* 943

Alexy, R, *A Theory of Constitutional Rights*, reprinted edn (J Rivers trans, Oxford, Oxford University Press, 2010)

Alexy, R, and Dreier, R, 'Statutory Interpretation in the Federal Republic of Germany' in N MacCormick and RS Summers (eds), *Interpreting Statutes: A Comparative Study* (Aldershot, Dartmouth, 1991) 73–121

Allan, TRS, 'Human Rights and Judicial Review: A Critique of "Due Deference"' (2006) 65 *Cambridge Law Journal* 671

Allars, M, 'Proportionality, Tradition and Constitutional Framework: Borrowing Foreign Legal Notions in Australian Public Law' in G Doeker-Mach and KA Ziegert (eds), *Law and Legal Culture in Comparative Perspective* (Stuttgart, Franz Steiner Verlag, 2004) 286–312

Anderson, T, Schum, DA, and Twining, WL, *Analysis of Evidence*, 2nd edn (Cambridge, Cambridge University Press, 2005)

Appleby, G, 'Proportionality and Federalism: Can Australia Learn from the European Community, the US and Canada?' (2007) 26 *University of Tasmania Law Review* 1

——. 'Functionalism in Constitutional Interpretation: Factual and Participatory Challenges: Comment on Dixon' (2015) 43 *Federal Law Review* 493

Appleby, G, and Carter, A, 'Parliaments, Proportionality and Facts' (2021) *Sydney Law Review* (forthcoming)

Aronson, M, Groves, M, and Weeks, G, *Judicial Review of Administrative Action and Government Liability*, 6th edn (Sydney, Thomson Reuters, 2017)

Baade, HW, 'Social Science Evidence and the Federal Constitutional Court of West Germany' (1961) 23 *Journal of Politics* 421

Bar-Siman-Tov, I, 'Semiprocedural Judicial Review' (2012) 6 *Legisprudence* 271

Barak, A, *Proportionality: Constitutional Rights and Their Limitations* (Cambridge, Cambridge University Press, 2012)

Beatty, DM, *The Ultimate Rule of Law* (Oxford, Oxford University Press, 2004)

Bell, AS, 'Section 92, Factual Discrimination and the High Court' (1991) 20 *Federal Law Review* 240

Benda, E, 'The Position and Function of the *Bundesverfassungsgericht* (Federal Constitutional Court) in a Reunited Germany' in E McWhinney, J Zaslove and W Wolf (eds), *Federalism-in-the-Making: Contemporary Canadian and German Constitutionalism, National and Transnational* (Dordrecht, Kluwer Academic Publishers, 1992) 29–39

Benjamin, SM, 'Stepping into the Same River Twice: Rapidly Changing Facts and the Appellate Process' (1999) 78 *Texas Law Review* 269

Bilchitz, D, 'Necessity and Proportionality: Towards a Balanced Approach?' in L Lazarus, C McCrudden and N Bowles (eds), *Reasoning Rights: Comparative Judicial Engagement* (Oxford, Hart Publishing, 2014) 41–62

Birks, P, 'Equity in the Modern Law: An Exercise in Taxonomy' (1996) 26 *University of Western Australia Law Review* 1
Bjørge, E, *Domestic Application of the ECHR: Courts as Faithful Trustees* (Oxford, Oxford University Press, 2015)
Black, M, 'The *Tasmanian Dam Case*: An Advocate's Memoir' (2015) 24 *Griffith Law Review* 22
Blackshield, T, 'Realism' in T Blackshield, M Coper and G Williams (eds), *The Oxford Companion to the High Court of Australia* (Melbourne, Oxford University Press, 2001) 582–85
Bloodworth, M, 'A Fact is a Fact is a Fact: *Stare Decisis* and the Distinction Between Adjudicative and Social Facts in *Bedford* and *Carter*' (2014) 32 *National Journal of Constitutional Law* 193
Bomhoff, J, 'Genealogies of Balancing as Discourse' (2010) 4 *Law & Ethics of Human Rights* 107
Borgmann, CE, 'Rethinking Judicial Deference to Legislative Fact-Finding' (2009) 84 *Indiana Law Journal* 1
——. 'Appellate Review of Social Facts in Constitutional Rights Cases' (2013) 101 *California Law Review* 1185
Borowski, M, 'The Beginnings of Germany's Federal Constitutional Court' (2003) 16 *Ratio Juris* 155
Botha, H, 'Democracy and Rights: Constitutional Interpretation in a Postrealist World' (2000) 63 *Journal of Contemporary Roman-Dutch Law* 561
——. 'Metaphoric Reasoning and Transformative Constitutionalism (part 1)' [2002] *Tydskrif vir die Suid-Afrikaanse Reg* 612
Boughey, J, 'The Reasonableness of Proportionality in the Australian Administrative Law Context' (2015) 43 *Federal Law Review* 59
——. 'Brett Cattle: New Limits on Delegated Law-Making Powers' (2020) 31 *Public Law Review* 347
Brady, ADP, *Proportionality and Deference under the UK Human Rights Act: An Institutionally Sensitive Approach* (Cambridge, Cambridge University Press, 2012)
Brazil, P, 'The Ascertainment of Facts in Australian Constitutional Cases' (1970) 4 *Federal Law Review* 65
Bredt, CD, 'The Right to Equality and *Oakes*: Time for Change' (2009) 27 *National Journal of Constitutional Law* 59
Bredt, CD, and Dodek, AM, 'The Increasing Irrelevance of Section 1 of the *Charter*' (2001) 14 *Supreme Court Law Review* 175
Bredt, CD, and Pessione, HK, 'The Death of *Oakes*: Time for a Rights-Specific Approach' (2013) 62 *Supreme Court Law Review* 486
Brodie, I, *Friends of the Court: The Privileging of Interest Group Litigants in Canada* (Albany, State University of New York Press, 2002)
Bröhmer, J, 'Legislative and Executive Branch versus the Federal Constitutional Court and the Judiciary – Conflict or Cooperation' in J Bröhmer (ed), *The German Constitution Turns 60: Basic Law and Common Constitution German and Australian Perspectives* (Peter Lang, 2011) 145–65
Bröhmer, J, Hill, C, and Spitzkatz, M (eds), *60 Years German Basic Law: The German Constitution and its Court*, 2nd edn (Kuala Lumpur, Malaysian Current Law Journal Sdn Bhd, 2012)
Broun, KS (ed), *McCormick on Evidence*, 6th edn (St Paul, Thomson West, 2006) vol 2
Brown, J, 'The Doctrine of Proportionality: A Comparative Analysis of the Proportionality Principle Applied to Free Speech Cases in Canada, South Africa and the European Convention on Human Right and Freedoms' (Master of Laws thesis, Central European University, 2012)
Budlender, G, 'Amicus Curiae' in S Woolman, T Roux and M Bishop (eds), *Constitutional Law of South Africa*, 2nd edn (Cape Town, Juta) vol 1, 1–17
Burmester, H, 'The Presumption of Constitutionality' (1982) 13 *Federal Law Review* 277
Burns, K, 'It's Just Not Cricket: The High Court, Sport and Legislative Facts' (2002) 10 *Torts Law Journal* 234
——. 'The Way the World is: Social Facts in High Court Negligence Cases' (2004) 12 *Torts Law Journal* 216
——. 'The High Court and Social Facts: A Negligence Case Study' in M Bryan (ed), *Private Law in Theory and Practice* (London, Routledge-Cavendish, 2007) 85–115

——. 'Judicial Use and Construction of Social Facts in Negligence Cases in the Australian High Court' (PhD thesis, Griffith University, 2011)

——. 'The Australian High Court and Social Facts: A Content Analysis Study' (2012) 40 *Federal Law Review* 317

——. 'It's Not Just Policy: The Role of Social Facts in Judicial Reasoning in Negligence Cases' (2013) 21 *Torts Law Journal* 73

Caleo, C, 'Section 90 and Excise Duties: A Crisis of Interpretation' (1987) 16 *Melbourne University Law Review* 296

Callaghan, GD, 'Intervenors at the Supreme Court of Canada' (2020) 44 *Dalhousie Law Journal* 33

Campbell, E, 'Fact Finding in Constitutional Cases' in Constitutional Commission, *Final Report of the Constitutional Commission* (Canberra, Australian Government Publishing Service, 1988) vol 2, 1099–114

Cane, P, *Controlling Administrative Power: An Historical Comparison* (Cambridge, Cambridge University Press, 2016)

Cappalli, RB, 'Bringing Internet Information to Court: Of Legislative Facts' (2002) 75 *Temple Law Review* 99

Cappelletti, M, and Cohen, W, *Comparative Constitutional Law: Cases and Materials* (Indianapolis, Bobbs-Merrill, 1979)

Carter, A, 'The Definition and Discovery of Facts in Native Title: The Historian's Contribution' (2008) 36 *Federal Law Review* 301

——. 'Political Donations, Political Communication and the Place of Proportionality Analysis: Case Note on *McCloy v New South Wales*' (2015) 26 *Public Law Review* 245

——. 'Proportionality in Australian Constitutional Law: Towards Transnationalism' (2016) 76 *Heidelberg Journal of International Law* 951

——. 'Moving Beyond the Common Law Objection to Structured Proportionality' (2021) 49 *Federal Law Review* 73

Carter, PB, 'Judicial Notice: Related and Unrelated Matters' in E Campbell and L Waller (eds), *Well and Truly Tried: Essays on Evidence in Honour of Sir Richard Eggleston* (Sydney, Law Book Co, 1982) 88–99

Cass, DZ, 'Through the Looking Glass: The High Court and the Right to Speech' (1993) 4 *Public Law Review* 229

Challenor, B, 'The Balancing Act: A Case for Structured Proportionality under the Second Limb of the *Lange* Test' (2015) 40 *University of Western Australia Law Review* 267

Chan, C, 'Deference, Expertise and Information-Gathering Powers' (2013) 33 *Legal Studies* 598

——. 'Proportionality and Invariable Baseline Intensity of Review' (2013) 33 *Legal Studies* 1

——. 'The Burden of Proof under the *Human Rights Act*' (2014) 19 *Judicial Review* 46

Charney, RE, 'Evidence in *Charter* Cases: Expert Evidence and Proving Purpose' (2004) 16 *National Journal of Constitutional Law* 1

Charney, RE, and Green, SZ, 'Prophets of Doom, Seers of Fortune: 20 Years of Expert Evidence under the *Oakes* Test' (2006) 34 *Supreme Court Law Review* 479

Chesterman, M, 'Criminal Trial Juries in Australia: From Penal Colonies to a Federal Democracy' (1999) 62 *Law and Contemporary Problems* 69

Chordia, S, *Proportionality in Australian Constitutional Law* (Sydney, Federation Press, 2020)

Choudhry, S, 'So What is the Real Legacy of *Oakes*? Two Decades of Proportionality Analysis under the Canadian *Charter*'s Section 1' (2006) 34 *Supreme Court Law Review* 501

Cockrell, A, 'Rainbow Jurisprudence' (1996) 12 *South African Journal on Human Rights* 1

Cohen-Eliya, M, and Porat, I, 'American Balancing and German Proportionality: The Historical Origins' (2010) 8 *International Journal of Constitutional Law* 263

——. *Proportionality and Constitutional Culture* (Cambridge, Cambridge University Press, 2013)

Cohn, M, 'Legal Transplant Chronicles: The Evolution of Unreasonableness and Proportionality Review of the Administration in the United Kingdom' (2010) 58 *American Journal of Comparative Law* 583

Coper, M, *Freedom of Interstate Trade under the Australian Constitution* (Sydney, Butterworths, 1983)

——. 'Section 92 of the Australian *Constitution* since *Cole v Whitfield*' in HP Lee and G Winterton (eds), *Australian Constitutional Perspectives* (Sydney, Law Book Co, 1992) 129–47

Corder, H, *Judges at Work: The Role and Attitudes of the South African Appellate Judiciary, 1910–50* (Cape Town, Juta, 1984)

Coyle, I, and Halon, R, 'Humpty Dumpty and Risk Assessment: A Reply to Slobogin' in Patrick Keyzer (ed), *Preventive Detention: Asking the Fundamental Questions* (Cambridge, Intersentia, 2013) 193–222

Craig, P, 'Proportionality, Rationality and Review' [2010] *New Zealand Law Review* 265

——. 'The Nature of Reasonableness Review' (2013) 66 *Current Legal Problems* 131

——. 'Proportionality and Judicial Review: A UK Historical Perspective' in S Vogenauer and S Weatherill (eds), *General Principles of Law: European and Comparative Perspectives* (Oxford, Hart Publishing, 2017) 145–66

Currie, I, 'Judicious Avoidance' (1999) 15 *South African Journal on Human Rights* 138

Currie, I, and de Waal, J, *The Bill of Rights Handbook*, 6th edn (Cape Town, Juta, 2013)

Da Silva, M, 'Trial Level References: In Defence of a New Presumption' (2012) 2(2) *Western Journal of Legal Studies* 1

Damaška, MR, *Evidence Law Adrift* (New Haven, Yale University Press, 1997)

Danneman, G, 'Comparative Law: Study of Similarities or Differences?' in M Reimann and R Zimmermann (eds), *The Oxford Handbook of Comparative Law*, 2nd edn (Oxford, Oxford University Press, 2019) 390–422

Davies, ACL, and Williams, JR, 'Proportionality in English Law' in S Ranchordás and B de Waard (eds), *The Judge and the Proportionate Use of Discretion: A Comparative Study* (Abingdon, Routledge, 2016) 73–108

Davis, KC, 'An Approach to Problems of Evidence in the Administrative Process' (1942) 55 *Harvard Law Review* 364

——. 'Official Notice' (1949) 62 *Harvard Law Review* 537

——. 'Judicial Notice' (1955) 55 *Columbia Law Review* 945

——. *Administrative Law Treatise* (St Paul, West Publishing Co, 1958) vol 2

——. 'Judicial Notice' [1969] *Law and the Social Order* 513

——. *Administrative Law Treatise*, 2nd edn (San Diego, KC Davis Publishing Co, 1979) vol 2

——. 'Facts in Lawmaking' (1980) 80 *Columbia Law Review* 931

Dawson, D, and Nicholls, M, 'Sir Owen Dixon and Judicial Method' (1986) 15 *Melbourne University Law Review* 543

De Vos, P, and Freedman, W, (eds), *South African Constitutional Law in Context* (Cape Town, Oxford University Press, 2014)

De Waal, J, 'Constitutional Law' in GC van der Merwe and JE du Plessis (eds), *Introduction to the Law of South Africa* (Kluwer Law International, 2004) 55–106

Dedek, H, and Schermaier, MJ, 'German Law' in JM Smits (ed), *Elgar Encyclopedia of Comparative Law*, 2nd edn (Cheltenham, Edward Elgar, 2012) 349–370

Dennis, IH, *The Law of Evidence*, 5th edn (London, Sweet & Maxwell, 2013)

Deturbide, M, and Hughes, EJ, 'Canada' in JM Smits (ed), *Elgar Encyclopedia of Comparative Law*, 2nd edn (Cheltenham, Edward Elgar, 2012) 132–36

Dharmanda, J, 'Using Parliamentary Material in Interpretation: Insights from Parliamentary Process' (2018) 41 *University of New South Wales Law Journal* 4

Dixon, O, 'Address upon Taking the Oath of Office in Sydney as Chief Justice of the High Court of Australia on 21st April, 1952' in S Crennan and W Gummow (eds) *Jesting Pilate: And Other Papers and Addresses* (Sydney, Federation Press, 2019) 287–91

Dixon, R, 'The Functional Constitution: Re-reading the 2014 High Court Constitutional Term' (2015) 43 *Federal Law Review* 455

——. 'Proportionality & Comparative Constitutional Law versus Studies' (2018) 12 *Law & Ethics of Human Rights* 203

Douglas, H, 'Social Framework Evidence: Its Interpretation and Application in Victoria and Beyond' in K Fitz-Gibbon and A Freiberg (eds), *Homicide Law Reform in Victoria: Retrospect and Prospects* (Sydney, Federation Press, 2015) 94–109

Doyle, JJ, 'Judicial Law Making – Is Honesty the Best Policy?' (1995) 17 *Adelaide Law Review* 161

Du Plessis, L, 'Religious Freedom and Equality as Celebration of Difference: A Significant Development in Recent South African Constitutional Case-Law' (2009) 12 *Potchefstroom Electronic Law Journal* 10

Du Plessis, L, and Corder, H, *Understanding South Africa's Transitional Bill of Rights* (Cape Town, Juta, 1994)

Dugard, J, *Human Rights and the South African Legal Order* (Princeton, Princeton University Press, 1978)

——. 'Judging the Judges: Towards an Appropriate Role for the Judiciary in South Africa's Transformation' (2007) 20 *Leiden Journal of International Law* 965

Duxbury, N, *The Nature and Authority of Precedent* (Cambridge, Cambridge University Press, 2008)

Dwyer, DM, *The Judicial Assessment of Expert Evidence* (Cambridge, Cambridge University Press, 2008)

Edgar, A, 'Judicial Review of Delegated Legislation: Why Favour Substantive Review over Procedural Review?' in J Bell, M Elliott, JNE Varuhas and P Murray (eds), *Public Law Adjudication in Common Law Systems: Process and Substance* (Oxford, Hart Publishing, 2016) 189–211

Elliott, M, 'Proportionality and Deference: The Importance of a Structured Approach' in C Forsyth et al (eds), *Effective Judicial Review: A Cornerstone of Good Governance* (Oxford, Oxford University Press, 2010) 264–86

Emiliou, N, *The Principle of Proportionality in European Law: A Comparative Study* (London, Kluwer Law International, 1996)

Endicott, T, 'Questions of Law' (1998) 114 *Law Quarterly Review* 292

——. 'Proportionality and Incommensurability' in G Huscroft, BW Miller and G Webber (eds), *Proportionality and the Rule of Law: Rights, Justification, Reasoning* (Cambridge, Cambridge University Press, 2014) 311–42

Faigman, DL, *Constitutional Fictions: A Unified Theory of Constitutional Facts* (New York, Oxford University Press, 2008)

Feldman, D, 'Comparison, Realism and Theory in Public Law' in J Bell, M Elliott, JNE Varuhas and P Murray (eds), *Public Law Adjudication in Common Law Systems: Process and Substance* (Oxford, Hart Publishing, 2016) 367–79

Fitzgerald, BF, 'Proportionality and Australian Constitutionalism' (1993) 12 *University of Tasmania Law Review* 263

Freckelton, IR, *Expert Evidence: Law, Practice, Procedure and Advocacy*, 6th edn (Sydney, Thomson Reuters, 2019)

Free, S, 'Commentary on Chapter 6' in J Griffiths and J Stellios (eds), *Current Issues in Australian Constitutional Law: Tributes to Professor Leslie Zines* (Sydney, Federation Press, 2020) 202–08

Gageler, S, 'Foundations of Australian Federalism and the Role of Judicial Review' (1987) 17 *Federal Law Review* 162

——. 'Fact and Law' (2009) 11 *Newcastle Law Review* 1

——. 'Deference' (2015) 22 *Australian Journal of Administrative Law* 151

——. 'Whitmore and the Americans: Some American Influences on the Development of Australian Administrative Law' (2015) 38 *University of New South Wales Law Journal* 1316

——. 'Alternative Facts in the Courts' (2019) 93 *Australian Law Journal* 585

Galligan, B, and Morton, FL, 'Australian Exceptionalism: Rights Protection without a Bill of Rights' in T Campbell, J Goldsworthy and A Stone (eds), *Protecting Rights without a Bill of Rights: Institutional Performance and Reform in Australia* (Aldershot, Ashgate, 2006) 17–39

Gardbaum, S, 'Positive and Horizontal Rights: Proportionality's Next Frontier or a Bridge Too Far?' in VC Jackson and M Tushnet (eds), *Proportionality: New Frontiers, New Challenges* (Cambridge, Cambridge University Press, 2017) 221–47

Goldsworthy, J, 'Australia: Devotion to Legalism' in J Goldsworthy (ed), *Interpreting Constitutions: A Comparative Study* (Oxford, Oxford University Press, 2007) 106–60

Götz, V, 'Legislative and Executive Power under the Constitutional Requirements Entailed in the Principle of the Rule of Law' in C Starck (ed), *New Challenges to the German Basic Law: the German Contributions to the Third World Congress of the International Association of Constitutional Law* (Baden-Baden, Nomos Verlagsgesellschaft, 1991) 141–66

Grando, MT, *Evidence, Proof, and Fact-Finding in WTO Dispute Settlement* (Oxford, Oxford University Press, 2009)

Grechenig, KR, and Gelter, M, 'The Transatlantic Divergence in Legal Thought: American Law and Economics vs German Doctrinalism' (2008) 31 *Hastings International and Comparative Law Review* 295

Greer, S, '"Balancing" and the European Court of Human Rights: A Contribution to the Habermas-Alexy Debate' (2004) 63 *Cambridge Law Journal* 412

Grimm, D, 'Proportionality in Canadian and German Constitutional Jurisprudence' (2007) 57 *University of Toronto Law Journal* 383

——. 'Values in German Constitutional Law' in D Davis, A Richter and C Saunders (eds), *An Inquiry into the Existence of Global Values: Through the Lens of Comparative Constitutional Law* (Oxford, Hart Publishing, 2015) 199–214

Groves, M, Boughey, J, and Meagher, D, 'Rights, Rhetoric and Reality: An Overview of Rights Protection in Australia' in M Groves, J Boughey and D Meagher (eds), *The Legal Protection of Rights in Australia* (Oxford, Hart Publishing, 2019) 1–16

Haack, S, *Evidence and Inquiry: A Pragmatist Reconstruction of Epistemology*, 2nd expanded edn (New York, Prometheus Books, 2009)

——. *Evidence Matters: Science, Proof, and Truth in the Law* (Cambridge, Cambridge University Press, 2014)

Habermas, J, *Between Facts and Norms: Contributions to a Discourse Theory of Law and Democracy* (W Rehg trans, Cambridge, Polity Press, 1996)

Hailbronner, M, 'Rethinking the Rise of the German Constitutional Court: From Anti-Nazism to Value Formalism' (2014) 12 *International Journal of Constitutional Law* 626

Hamer, D, 'The Civil Standard of Proof Uncertainty: Probability, Belief and Justice' (1994) 16 *Sydney Law Review* 506

Hanks, P, Gordon, F, and Hill, G, *Constitutional Law in Australia*, 3rd edn (Sydney, LexisNexis Butterworths, 2012)

——. *Constitutional Law in Australia*, 4th edn (Sydney, LexisNexis Butterworths, 2017)

Hayne, KM, 'Deference: An Australian Perspective' [2011] *Public Law* 75

Henckels, C, *Proportionality and Deference in Investor-State Arbitration: Balancing Investment Protection and Regulatory Autonomy* (Cambridge, Cambridge University Press, 2015)

Heydon, JD, 'Developing the Common Law' in JT Gleeson and RCA Higgins (eds), *Constituting Law: Legal Arguments and Social Values* (Sydney, Federation Press, 2011) 93–136

——. *Cross on Evidence*, 12th Australian edn (Sydney, LexisNexis Butterworths, 2020)

Hickman, T, 'Proportionality: Comparative Law Lessons' (2007) 12 *Judicial Review* 31

Ho, HL, *A Philosophy of Evidence Law* (Oxford, Oxford University Press, 2008)

Hogg, PW, 'Section 1 Revisited' (1991) 1 *National Journal of Constitutional Law* 1

——. 'Canada: From Privy Council to Supreme Court' in J Goldsworthy (ed), *Interpreting Constitutions: A Comparative Study* (Oxford, Oxford University Press, 2007) 55–105

——. *Constitutional Law of Canada*, 5th edn (Toronto, Thomson Carswell, 2007) vol 2

——. *Constitutional Law of Canada*, 2014 student edn (Toronto, Carswell, 2014)

Holmes, JD, 'Evidence in Constitutional Cases' (1949) 23 *Australian Law Journal* 235

Horowitz, DL, *The Courts and Social Policy* (Washington DC, Brookings Institution, 1977)

Hughes, J, and MacDonnell, V, 'Social Science Evidence in Constitutional Rights Cases in Germany and Canada: Some Comparative Observations' (2013) 32 *National Journal of Constitutional Law* 23

Hughes, J, MacDonnell, V, and Pearlston, K, 'Equality & Incrementalism: The Role of Common Law Reasoning in Constitutional Rights Cases' (2013) 44 *Ottawa Law Review* 467

Hunt, M, 'Sovereignty's Blight: Why Contemporary Public Law Needs the Concept of "Due Deference"' in N Bamforth and P Leyland (eds), *Public Law in a Multi-layered Constitution* (Oxford, Hart Publishing, 2003) 337–70

——. 'Enhancing Parliaments' Role in the Protection and Realisation of Human Rights' in M Hunt, HJ Hooper and P Yowell (eds), *Parliaments and Human Rights: Redressing the Democratic Deficit* (Oxford, Hart Publishing, 2015) 469–83

Huscroft, G, Miller, BW, and Webber, G, 'Introduction' in G Huscroft, BW Miller and G Webber (eds), *Proportionality and the Rule of Law: Rights, Justification, Reasoning* (Cambridge University Press, 2014) 1–17

Jackson, BS, *Law, Fact and Narrative Coherence* (Liverpool, Deborah Charles, 1988)

Jackson, JD, and Summers, SJ, *The Internationalisation of Criminal Evidence: Beyond the Common Law and Civil Law Traditions* (Cambridge, Cambridge University Press, 2012)

Jackson, VC, 'Being Proportional about Proportionality: The Ultimate Rule of Law' (2004) 21 *Constitutional Commentary* 843

——. 'Methodological Challenges in Comparative Constitutional Law' (2009) 28 *Penn State International Law Review* 319

——. 'Comparative Constitutional Law: Methodologies' in M Rosenfeld and A Sajó (eds), *The Oxford Handbook of Comparative Constitutional Law* (Oxford, Oxford University Press, 2012) 54–74

——. 'Constitutional Law in an Age of Proportionality' (2015) 124 *Yale Law Journal* 3094

Jamal, M, 'Legislative Facts in *Charter* Litigation: Where are We Now?' (2005) 17 *National Journal of Constitutional Law* 1

James, GF, 'Relevancy, Probability and the Law' (1941) 29 *California Law Review* 689

Jasiak, A, *Constitutional Constraints on Ad Hoc Legislation: A Comparative Study of the United States, Germany and the Netherlands* (Cambridge, Intersentia, 2011)

Jolowicz, JA, 'Fact-Based Classification' in JA Jolowicz (ed), *The Division and Classification of the Law* (London, Butterworths, 1970) 1–9

——. 'Adversarial and Inquisitorial Models of Civil Procedure' (2003) 52 *International and Comparative Law Quarterly* 281

Jones, FWD, 'High Court Procedure under the *Judiciary Act*' (1994) 68 *Australian Law Journal* 442

Josev, T, *The Campaign Against the Courts: A History of the Judicial Activism Debate* (Sydney, Federation Press, 2017)

Kavanagh, A, *Constitutional Review under the UK Human Rights Act* (Cambridge, Cambridge University Press, 2009)

——. 'Proportionality and Parliamentary Debates: Exploring Some Forbidden Territory' (2014) 34 *Oxford Journal of Legal Studies* 443

Keeton, RE, 'Legislative Facts and Similar Things: Deciding Disputed Premise Facts' (1988) 73 *Minnesota Law Review* 1

Kelsen, H, 'Who Ought to Be the Guardian of the Constitution? Kelsen's Reply to Schmitt' (1931) in L Vinx (ed), *The Guardian of the Constitution: Hans Kelsen and Carl Schmitt on the Limits of Constitutional Law* (Cambridge, Cambridge University Press, 2015) 174–221

Kenny, D, 'Proportionality, the Burden of Proof, and Some Signs of Reconsideration' (2014) 52 *Irish Jurist* 141

——. 'Proportionality and the Inevitability of the Local: A Comparative Localist Analysis of Canada and Ireland' (2018) 66 *American Journal of Comparative Law* 537

Kenny, S, 'Constitutional Fact Ascertainment' (1990) 1 *Public Law Review* 134

——. 'Interveners and Amici Curiae in the High Court' (1998) 20 *Adelaide Law Review* 159

Keyzer, P, 'Attorneys-General, Solicitors-General and "the Public Interest" in Australian Constitutional Cases: A Case for Citizen Input into the Development of Constitutional Policy' in G Appleby, P Keyzer and J Williams (eds), *Public Sentinels: A Comparative Study of Australian Solicitors-General* (Abingdon, Routledge, 2016) 105–16

Kiefel, S, 'English, European and Australian Law: Convergence or Divergence?' (2005) 79 *Australian Law Journal* 220

——. 'Section 92: Markets, Protectionism and Proportionality – Australian and European Perspectives' (2010) 36 *Monash University Law Review* 1

——. 'Proportionality: A Rule of Reason' (2012) 23 *Public Law Review* 85

——. 'Standards of Review in Constitutional Review of Legislation' in C Saunders and A Stone (eds), *The Oxford Handbook of the Australian Constitution* (Oxford, Oxford University Press, 2018) 488–509

King, JA, 'Institutional Approaches to Judicial Restraint' (2008) 28 *Oxford Journal of Legal Studies* 409

Kirby, M, 'Judicial Activism? A Riposte to the Counter-Reformation' (2004) 24 *Australian Bar Journal* 219

Kirk, J, 'Constitutional Guarantees, Characterisation and the Concept of Proportionality' (1997) 21 *Melbourne University Law Review* 1

——. 'Section 92 in its Second Century' in J Griffiths and J Stellios (eds), *Current Issues in Australian Constitutional Law: Tributes to Professor Leslie Zines* (Sydney, Federation Press, 2020) 253–82

Klare, KE, 'Legal Culture and Transformative Constitutionalism' (1998) 14 *South African Journal on Human Rights* 146

Klatt, M, and Schmidt, J, 'Epistemic Discretion in Constitutional Law' (2012) 10 *International Journal of Constitutional Law* 69

Klein, E, 'The Importance and Challenges of Values-Based Legal Orders' (2015) 10 *Intercultural Human Rights Law Review* 1

Klug, H, 'South Africa: From Constitutional Promise to Social Transformation' in J Goldsworthy (ed), *Interpreting Constitutions: A Comparative Study* (Oxford, Oxford University Press, 2007) 266–320

Koch, C, 'The Sky is Falling if Judges Decide Religious Controversies! – Or is it? The German Experience of Religious Freedom under a Bill of Rights' in P Babie and N Rochow (eds), *Freedom of Religion under Bills of Rights* (Adelaide, University of Adelaide Press, 2013) 190–215

Kokott, J, *The Burden of Proof in Comparative and International Human Rights Law: Civil and Common Law Approaches with Special Reference to the American and German Legal Systems* (The Hague, Kluwer Law International, 1998)

Kommers, DP, and Miller, RA, *The Constitutional Jurisprudence of the Federal Republic of Germany*, 3rd edn (Durham, NC, Duke University Press, 2012)

Kumm, M, 'Political Liberalism and the Structure of Rights: On the Place and Limits of the Proportionality Requirement' in G Pavlakos (ed), *Law, Rights and Discourse: The Legal Philosophy of Robert Alexy* (Oxford, Hart Publishing, 2007) 131–66

——. 'On the Past and Future of European Constitutional Scholarship' (2009) 7 *International Journal of Constitutional Law* 401

Lane, PH, 'Facts in Constitutional Law' (1963) 37 *Australian Law Journal* 108

——. *The Australian Federal System*, 2nd edn (Sydney, Law Book Co, 1979)

Larsen, AO, 'Confronting Supreme Court Fact Finding' (2012) 98 *Virginia Law Review* 1255

——. 'Constitutional Law in an Age of Alternative Facts' (2018) 93 *New York University Law Review* 175

Law Reform Commission, *Evidence*, Interim Report No 26 (1985) vol 1

——. *Evidence*, Report No 38 (1987)

Leckey, R, *Bills of Rights in the Common Law* (Cambridge, Cambridge University Press, 2015)

Ledford, KF, 'Formalizing the Rule of Law in Prussia: The Supreme Administrative Law Court, 1876–1914' (2004) 37 *Central European History* 203

Lee, HP, 'Proportionality in Australian Constitutional Adjudication' in G Lindell (ed), *Future Directions in Australian Constitutional Law* (Sydney, Federation Press, 1994) 126–49

Leeming, M, 'Fact Finding' in T Blackshield, M Coper and G Williams (eds), *The Oxford Companion to the High Court of Australia* (Melbourne, Oxford University Press, 2001) 268–69

——. 'The Federal and State Courts on Constitutional Law: The 2013 Term' [2014] *New South Wales Judicial Scholarship* 5
Legg, A, *The Margin of Appreciation in International Human Rights Law: Deference and Proportionality* (Oxford, Oxford University Press, 2012)
Lennan, J, 'How to Find Facts in Constitutional Cases' (2011) 30 *Civil Justice Quarterly* 304
Lepsius, O, 'Constitutional Review of Tax Laws and the Unconstitutionality of the German Inheritance Tax' (2015) 16 *German Law Journal* 1191
Letsas, G, *A Theory of Interpretation of the European Convention on Human Rights* (Oxford, Oxford University Press, 2007)
Ligertwood, A, and Edmond, G, *Australian Evidence: A Principled Approach to the Common Law and Uniform Acts*, 6th edn (Sydney, LexisNexis Butterworths, 2017)
Lovric, D, *Deference to the Legislature in WTO Challenges to Legislation* (Alphen aan den Rijn, Kluwer Law International, 2010)
Lübbe-Wolff, G, 'The Principle of Proportionality in the Case-Law of the German Federal Constitutional Court' (2014) 34 *Human Rights Law Journal* 12
Main, TO, 'The Procedural Foundation of Substantive Law' (2010) 87 *Washington University Law Review* 801
Malbon, J, 'Judicial Values' in I Freckelton and H Selby (eds), *Appealing to the Future: Michael Kirby and His Legacy* (Sydney, Lawbook Co, 2009) 579–606
Margolis, E, 'Beyond Brandeis: Exploring the Uses of Non-legal Materials in Appellate Briefs' (2000) 34 *University of San Francisco Law Review* 197
Marsch, N, and Tünsmeyer, V, 'The Principle of Proportionality in German Administrative Law' in S Ranchordás and B de Waard (eds), *The Judge and the Proportionate Use of Discretion: A Comparative Study* (Abingdon, Routledge, 2016) 13–42
Martin, M, and Horne, A, 'Proportionality: Principles and Pitfalls – Some Lessons from Germany' [2008] *Judicial Review* 169
Mason, A, 'Interveners and Amici Curiae in the High Court: A Comment' (1998) 20 *Adelaide Law Review* 173
——. 'The Use of Proportionality in Australian Constitutional Law' (2016) 27 *Public Law Review* 109
Mason, K, 'Ethics and the Environment' (2011) 10 *The Judicial Review* 187
Mathen, C, 'Rational Connections: *Oakes*, Section 1 and the *Charter*'s Legal Rights' (2012) 43 *Ottawa Law Review* 491
McClellan, P, and Doyle, A, 'Legislative Facts and Section 144 – A Contemporary Problem?' (2016) 12 *The Judicial Review* 421
McCrudden, C, 'Judicial Comparativism and Human Rights' in E Örücü and D Nelken (eds), *Comparative Law: A Handbook* (Oxford, Hart Publishing, 2007) 371–97
McDonald, S, 'Involuntary Detention and the Separation of Judicial Power' (2007) 35 *Federal Law Review* 1
Meagher, D, 'The Brennan Conception of the Implied Freedom: Theory, Proportionality and Deference' (2011) 30 *University of Queensland Law Journal* 119
Mendes, EP, 'Section 1 of the *Charter* after 30 Years: The Soul or the Dagger at its Heart?' in E Mendes and S Beaulac (eds), *The Canadian Charter of Rights and Freedoms*, 5th edn (Markham, LexisNexis, 2013) 293–336
Meßerschmidt, K, 'The Race to Rationality Review and the Score of the German Federal Constitutional Court' (2012) 6 *Legisprudence* 347
——. 'The Good Shepherd of Karlsruhe: The "*Hartz IV*" Decision on Unemployment Benefits and Social Allowances – A Good Example of Regulatory Review by the German Federal Constitutional Court?' in P Popelier, A Mazmanyan and W Vandenbruwaene (eds), *The Role of Constitutional Courts in Multilevel Governance* (Cambridge, Intersentia, 2013) 235–47

Michaels, R, 'The Functional Method of Comparative Law' in M Reimann and R Zimmermann (eds), *The Oxford Handbook of Comparative Law*, 2nd edn (Oxford, Oxford University Press, 2019) 345–89

Miller, RA, 'Germany's German Constitution' (2017) 57 *Virginia Journal of International Law* 95

Miller, RA, and Kommers, DP, '*Das Bundesverfassungsgericht*: Procedure, Practice and Policy of the German Federal Constitutional Court' (2009) 3 *Journal of Comparative Law* 194

Mitchell, AD, *Legal Principles in WTO Disputes* (Cambridge, Cambridge University Press, 2008)

Möller, K, 'Balancing and the Structure of Constitutional Rights' (2007) 5 *International Journal of Constitutional Law* 453

——. *The Global Model of Constitutional Rights* (Oxford University Press, 2012)

——. 'Proportionality: Challenging the Critics' (2012) 10 *International Journal of Constitutional Law* 709

——. 'Dworkin's Theory of Rights in the Age of Proportionality' (2018) 12 *Law & Ethics of Human Rights* 281

Möllers, C, 'Scope and Legitimacy of Judicial Review in German Constitutional Law – the Court versus the Political Process' in H Pünder and C Waldhoff (eds), *Debates in German Public Law* (Oxford, Hart Publishing, 2014) 3–25

Möllers, C, and Birkenkotter, H, 'Towards a New Conceptualism in Comparative Constitutional Law, or Reviving the German Tradition of the *Lehrbuch*' (2014) 12 *International Journal of Constitutional Law* 603

Monahan, J, and Walker, L, 'Social Authority: Obtaining, Evaluating, and Establishing Social Science in Law' (1986) 134 *University of Pennsylvania Law Review* 477

——. *An Introduction to Social Science in Law* (New York, Foundation Press, 2006)

——. 'Twenty-Five Years of Social Science in Law' (2011) 35 *Law and Human Behavior* 72

Monahan, J, Walker, L, and Mitchell, G, 'Contextual Evidence of Gender Discrimination: The Ascendance of "Social Frameworks"' (2008) 94 *Virginia Law Review* 1715

Morgan, EM, 'Judicial Notice' (1944) 57 *Harvard Law Review* 269

Morton, FL, and Brodie, I, 'The Use of Extrinsic Evidence in *Charter* Litigation Before the Supreme Court of Canada' (1993) 3 *National Journal of Constitutional Law* 1

Moulds, S, *Committees of Influence: Parliamentary Rights Scrutiny and Counter-Terrorism Lawmaking in Australia* (Singapore, Springer, 2020)

Mounsey, R, 'Social Science Evidence as Proof of Legislative Fact in Constitutional Litigation: A Proposed Framework for a Reliability Analysis' (2014) 32 *National Journal of Constitutional Law* 127

Mullane, GR, 'Evidence of Social Science Research: Law, Practice, and Options in the Family Court of Australia' 72 *Australian Law Journal* 434

Murray, PL, and Stürner, R, *German Civil Justice* (Durham, Carolina Academic Press, 2004)

Newton, MA, and May, L, *Proportionality in International Law* (New York, Oxford University Press, 2014)

Nicolson, D, 'Truth, Reason and Justice: Epistemology and Politics in Evidence Disclosure' (1994) 57 *Modern Law Review* 726

Nolte, G, 'General Principles of German and European Administrative Law – A Comparison in Historical Perspective' (1994) 57 *Modern Law Review* 191

Odgers, S, *Uniform Evidence Law*, 15th edn (Sydney, Thomson Reuters, 2020)

Oreb, N, 'Betting across Borders – *Betfair Pty Limited v Western Australia*' (2009) 31 *Sydney Law Review* 607

Palmer, VV, 'Mixed Jurisdictions' in JM Smits (ed), *Elgar Encyclopedia of Comparative Law*, 2nd edn (Cheltenham, Edward Elgar, 2012) 590–99

Pardo, MS, 'The Field of Evidence and the Field of Knowledge' (2005) 24 *Law and Philosophy* 321

——. 'The Gettier Problem and Legal Proof' (2010) 16 *Legal Theory* 37

Pearce, D, *Statutory Interpretation in Australia*, 9th edn (Sydney, LexisNexis Butterworths, 2019)

Pearce, D, and Argument, S, *Delegated Legislation in Australia*, 5th edn (Sydney, LexisNexis Butterworths, 2017)

Pepall, JT, 'What's the Evidence? The Use the Supreme Court of Canada Makes of Evidence in *Charter* Cases' in AA Peacock (ed), *Rethinking the Constitution: Perspectives on Canadian Constitutional Reform, Interpretation, and Theory* (Toronto, Oxford University Press, 1996) 161–76

Perry, SR, 'Second-Order Reasons, Uncertainty and Legal Theory' (1988) 62 *Southern California Law Review* 913

Perryman, B, 'Adducing Social Science Evidence in Constitutional Cases' (2018) 44 *Queens's Law Journal* 121

Petersen, N, 'Avoiding the Common-Wisdom Fallacy: The Role of Social Sciences in Constitutional Adjudication' (2013) 11 *International Journal of Constitutional Law* 294

——. 'How to Compare the Length of Lines to the Weight of Stones: Balancing and the Resolution of Value Conflicts in Constitutional Law' (2013) 14 *German Law Journal* 1387

——. 'Proportionality and the Incommensurability Challenge in the Jurisprudence of the South African Constitutional Court' (2014) 30 *South African Journal on Human Rights* 405

——. 'Balancing and Judicial Self-Empowerment: A Case Study on the Rise of Balancing in the Jurisprudence of the Federal Constitutional Court' (2015) 4 *Global Constitutionalism* 49

——. *Proportionality and Judicial Activism: Fundamental Rights Adjudication in Canada, Germany and South Africa* (Cambridge, Cambridge University Press, 2017)

——. 'Alexy and the "German" Model of Proportionality: Why the Theory of Constitutional Rights Does Not Provide a Representative Reconstruction of the Proportionality Test' (2020) 21 *German Law Journal* 163

Pirker, B, *Proportionality Analysis and Models of Judicial Review: A Theoretical and Comparative Study* (Groningen, Europa Law Publishing, 2013)

Poole, T, 'The Reformation of English Administrative Law' (2009) 68 *Cambridge Law Journal* 142

——. 'Proportionality in Perspective' [2010] *New Zealand Law Review* 369

Popelier, P, 'Preliminary Comments on the Role of Courts as Regulatory Watchdogs' (2012) 6 *Legisprudence* 257

——. 'The Court as Regulatory Watchdog: The Procedural Approach in the Case Law of the European Court of Human Rights' in P Popelier, A Mazmanyan and W Vandenbruwaene (eds), *The Role of Constitutional Courts in Multilevel Governance* (Cambridge, Intersentia, 2013) 249–67

Raz, J, *Practical Reason and Norms* (first published by Hutchinson 1975, Oxford, Oxford University Press, 1999 edn)

Réaume, D, *Limitations on Constitutional Rights: The Logic of Proportionality*, University of Oxford Legal Research Paper Series, Paper No 26/2009 (2009)

Reimann, M, 'Nineteenth Century German Legal Science' (1989) 31 *Boston College Law Review* 837

Rivers, J, 'Proportionality and Variable Intensity of Review' (2006) 65 *Cambridge Law Journal* 174

——. 'Proportionality, Discretion and the Second Law of Balancing' in G Pavlakos (ed), *Law, Rights and Discourse: The Legal Philosophy of Robert Alexy* (Oxford, Hart Publishing, 2007) 167–88

——. 'The Presumption of Proportionality' (2014) 77 *Modern Law Review* 409

Roberts, A, 'Probative Value, Reliability, and Rationality' in A Roberts and J Gans (eds), *Critical Perspectives on the Uniform Evidence Law* (Sydney, Federation Press, 2017) 63–79

Roberts, H, 'A Mirror to the Man – Reflecting on Justice William Deane: A Private Man in Public Office' (2011) 32 *Adelaide Law Review* 17

Rose, D, '*Cole v Whitfield*: "Absolutely Free" Trade?' in HP Lee and G Winterton (eds), *Australian Constitutional Landmarks* (Cambridge, Cambridge University Press, 2003) 335–54

Rosenberg, GN, and Williams, JM, 'Do Not Go Gently Into That Good Right: The First Amendment in the High Court of Australia' (1997) *Supreme Court Law Review* 439

Roux, T, 'Transformative Constitutionalism and the Best Interpretation of the South African Constitution: Distinction without a Difference' (2009) 20 *Stellenbosch Law Review* 258

——. *The Politics of Principle: The First South African Constitutional Court, 1995–2005* (Cambridge, Cambridge University Press, 2013)

Saks, MJ, 'Judicial Attention to the Way the World Works' (1990) 75 *Iowa Law Review* 1011

Saunders, C, 'Interpreting the *Constitution*' (2004) 15 *Public Law Review* 289

——. 'The Use and Misuse of Comparative Constitutional Law' (2006) 13 *Indiana Journal of Global Legal Studies* 37

——. 'Australia: Interpretation and Review' in AR Brewer-Carías (ed), *Constitutional Courts as Positive Legislators: A Comparative Law Study* (Cambridge, Cambridge University Press, 2011) 213–50

——. *The Constitution of Australia: A Contextual Analysis* (Oxford, Hart Publishing, 2011)

Saunders, C, and Donaldson, M, 'Values in Australian Constitutionalism' in D Davis, A Richter and C Saunders (eds), *An Inquiry into the Existence of Global Values: Through the Lens of Comparative Constitutional Law* (Oxford, Hart Publishing, 2015) 15–66

Sawer, G, *Australian Federalism in the Courts* (Melbourne, Melbourne University Press, 1967)

Schauer, F, 'Balancing, Subsumption, and the Constraining Role of Legal Text' (2010) 4 *Law & Ethics of Human Rights* 35

Schwikkard, PJ, and van der Merwe, SE, *Principles of Evidence*, 4th edn (Cape Town, Juta, 2016)

Selway, B, 'The Rise and Rise of the Reasonable Proportionality Test in Public Law' (1996) 7 *Public Law Review* 212

——. 'The Use of History and Other Facts in the Reasoning of the High Court of Australia' (2001) 20 *University of Tasmania Law Review* 129

Serpell, AJ, *The Reception and Use of Social Policy Information in the High Court of Australia* (Sydney, Lawbook Co, 2006)

Sharpe, RJ, and Roach, K, *The Charter of Rights and Freedoms*, 5th edn (Toronto, Irwin Law, 2013)

Simpson, A, 'Grounding the High Court's Modern Section 92 Jurisprudence: The Case for Improper Purpose as the Touchstone' (2005) 33 *Federal Law Review* 445

——. 'Section 92 as a Transplant Recipient?' in J Griffiths and J Stellios (eds), *Current Issues in Australian Constitutional Law: Tributes to Professor Leslie Zines* (Sydney, Federation Press, 2020) 283–94

Slovenko, R, 'The Superfluous Rule of Evidence on Judicial Notice' (1998) 2 *International Journal of Evidence and Proof* 51

Somek, A, 'The Indelible Science of Law' (2009) 7 *International Journal of Constitutional Law* 424

Stellios, J, *Zines's The High Court and the Constitution*, 6th edn (Sydney, Federation Press, 2015)

——. 'The Masking of Judicial Power Values: Historical Analogies and Double Function Provisions' (2017) 28 *Public Law Review* 138

Stoljar, J, 'Invisible Cargo: The Introduction of English Law into Australia' in JT Gleeson, JA Watson and RCA Higgins (eds), *Historical Foundations of Australian Law* (Sydney, Federation Press, 2013) vol 1, 194–211

Stone, A, 'The Limits of Constitutional Text and Structure: Standards of Review and the Freedom of Political Communication' (1999) 23 *Melbourne University Law Review* 668

——. 'Australia's Constitutional Rights and the Problem of Interpretive Disagreement' (2005) 27 *Sydney Law Review* 29

——. 'The Limits of Constitutional Text and Structure Revisited' (2006) 29 *University of New South Wales Law Journal* 842

——. 'Constitutional Orthodoxy in the United Kingdom and Australia: The Deepening Divide' (2014) 38 *Melbourne University Law Review* 836

——. 'Judicial Reasoning' in C Saunders and A Stone (eds), *The Oxford Handbook of the Australian Constitution* (Oxford, Oxford University Press, 2018) 472–87

——. 'Proportionality and its Alternatives' (2020) 48 *Federal Law Review* 123

Stone, J, 'A Government of Laws and Yet of Men' (1948) 1 *University of Western Australia Law Review* 461

Stone, J, and Wells, WAN, *Evidence: Its History and Policies* (Sydney, Butterworths, 1991)

Stone Sweet, A, and Mathews, J, 'Proportionality Balancing and Global Constitutionalism' (2008) 47 *Columbia Journal of Transnational Law* 72

——. *Proportionality Balancing & Constitutional Governance: A Comparative & Global Approach* (Oxford, Oxford University Press, 2019)

Stubbs, MT, 'From Foreign Circumstances to First Instance Considerations: Extrinsic Material and the Law of Statutory Interpretation' (2006) 34 *Federal Law Review* 103

——. 'A Brief History of the Judicial Review of Legislation under the *Australian Constitution*' (2012) 40 *Federal Law Review* 227

Sullivan, ET, and Frase, RS, *Proportionality Principles in American Law: Controlling Excessive Government Actions* (Oxford, Oxford University Press, 2009)

Taylor, G, 'Teachers' Religious Headscarves in German Constitutional Law' (2017) 6 *Oxford Journal of Law and Religion* 93

Towfigh, EV, 'Empirical Arguments in Public Law Doctrine: Should Empirical Legal Studies Make a "Doctrinal Turn"?' (2014) 12 *International Journal of Constitutional Law* 670

Trakman, LE, Cole-Hamilton, W, and Gatien, S, '*R v Oakes* 1986–1997: Back to the Drawing Board' (1998) 36 *Osgoode Hall Law Journal* 83

Tran, C, 'Facts and Evidence in Litigation under the *Charter of Human Rights and Responsibilities Act 2006* (Vic) and the *Human Rights Act 2004* (ACT)' (2012) 36 *Melbourne University Law Review* 287

Tsakyrakis, S, 'Proportionality: An Assault on Human Rights?' (2009) 7 *International Journal of Constitutional Law* 468

Tushnet, M, 'The Possibilities of Comparative Constitutional Law' (1999) 108 *Yale Law Journal* 1225

Twining, W, 'Some Scepticism about Some Scepticism' (1984) 11 *Journal of Law and Society* 137

——. 'The Rationalist Tradition of Evidence Scholarship', first published in E Campbell and L Waller (eds), *Well and Truly Tried: Essays on Evidence in Honour of Sir Richard Eggleston* (Sydney, Law Book Co, 1982), republished with some additions in W Twining, *Rethinking Evidence: Exploratory Essays*, 2nd edn (Cambridge, Cambridge University Press, 2006) 35–98

——. 'Taking Facts Seriously – Again' in P Roberts and M Redmayne (eds), *Innovations in Evidence and Proof: Integrating Theory, Research and Teaching* (Oxford, Hart Publishing, 2007) 65–86

Twining, W, and Miers, D, *How to Do Things with Rules* (Cambridge, Cambridge University Press, 2010)

Twining, W, O'Donovan, K, and Paliwala, A, 'Ernie and the Centipede: Some Theoretical Aspects of Classification for the Purposes of Law Reform' in JA Jolowicz (ed), *The Division and Classification of the Law* (London, Butterworths, 1970) 10–29

Urbina, FJ, 'Is it Really That Easy? A Critique of Proportionality and "Balancing as Reasoning"' (2014) 27 *Canadian Journal of Law and Jurisprudence* 167

Van der Schyff, G, *Judicial Review of Legislation: A Comparative Study of the United Kingdom, the Netherlands and South Africa* (Dordrecht, Springer, 2010)

Van Wees, N, 'Judicial Review of Legislators' Motives' (2017) 45 *Federal Law Review* 681

Vanberg, G, *The Politics of Constitutional Review in Germany* (Cambridge, Cambridge University Press, 2005)

Varuhas, JNE, 'Taxonomy and Public Law' in M Elliott, JNE Varuhas and SW Stark (eds), *The Unity of Public Law? Doctrinal, Theoretical and Comparative Perspectives* (Oxford, Hart Publishing, 2018) 39–78

Villalta Puig, G, *The High Court of Australia and Section 92 of the Australian Constitution* (Sydney, Lawbook Co, 2008)

Von Bernstorff, J, 'Proportionality without Balancing: Why Judicial Ad Hoc Balancing is Unnecessary and Potentially Detrimental to the Realisation of Individual and Collective Self-Determination' in L Lazarus, C McCrudden and N Bowles (eds), *Reasoning Rights: Comparative Judicial Engagement* (Oxford, Hart Publishing, 2014) 63–86

Von Bogdandy, A, 'The Past and Promise of Doctrinal Constructivism: A Strategy for Responding to the Challenges Facing Constitutional Scholarship in Europe' (2009) 7 *International Journal of Constitutional Law* 364

Von Brünneck, A, 'Constitutional Review and Legislation in Western Democracies' in C Landfried (ed), *Constitutional Review and Legislation: An International Comparison* (Baden-Baden, Nomos Verlagsgesellschaft, 1988) 219–60

Waldron, J, 'The Core of the Case against Judicial Review' (2006) 115 *Yale Law Journal* 1346
Walker, L, and Monahan, J, 'Social Frameworks: A New Use of Social Science in Law' (1987) 73 *Virginia Law Review* 559
Webber, G, *The Negotiable Constitution: On the Limitation of Rights* (Cambridge, Cambridge University Press, 2009)
——. 'Judicial Power and Judicial Responsibility' (2017) 36 *University of Queensland Law Journal* 205
——. 'Proportionality, Balancing, and the Cult of Constitutional Rights Scholarship' (2010) 23 *Canadian Journal of Law and Jurisprudence* 179
Weinrib, LE, 'Canada's *Charter of Rights*: Paradigm Lost'? (2001) 6 *Review of Constitutional Studies* 119
——. 'The Postwar Paradigm and American Exceptionalism' in S Choudhry (ed), *The Migration of Constitutional Ideas* (Cambridge, Cambridge University Press, 2007) 84–111
Weinrib, S, 'The Emergence of the Third Step of the *Oakes* Test in *Alberta v Hutterian Brethren of Wilson Colony*' (2010) 68 *University of Toronto Faculty of Law Review* 77
Weis, LK, 'On Just Terms, Revisited' (2017) 45 *Federal Law Review* 223
Wells, WAN, *Natural Logic, Judicial Proof and Objective Facts* (Sydney, Federation Press, 1994)
Welsh, R, 'A Path to Purposive Formalism: Interpreting Chapter III for Judicial Independence and Impartiality' (2012) 39 *Monash University Law Review* 66
Wesson, M, 'Crafting a Concept of Deference for the Implied Freedom of Political Communication' (2016) 27 *Public Law Review* 101
Wesson, M, and du Plessis, M, 'Fifteen Years On: Central Issues Relating to the Transformation of the South African Judiciary' (2008) 24 *South African Journal on Human Rights* 187
Wheatle, S, *Principled Reasoning in Human Rights Adjudication* (Oxford, Hart Publishing, 2017)
Wigmore, JH, *The Science of Judicial Proof, as given by Logic, Psychology, and General Experience, and Illustrated in Judicial Trials*, 3rd edn (Boston, Little, Brown, 1937)
Willheim, E, 'Amici Curiae and Access to Constitutional Justice in the High Court of Australia' (2010) 22 *Bond Law Review* 126
Williams, G, Brennan, S, and Lynch, A, *Blackshield and Williams Australian Constitutional Law and Theory: Commentary and Materials*, 7th edn (Sydney, Federation Press, 2018)
Williams, LA, 'The Role of Courts in the Quantitative-Implementation of Social and Economic Rights: A Comparative Study' [2010] *Constitutional Court Review* 141
Wiseman, D, 'Managing the Burden of Doubt: Social Science Evidence, the Institutional Competence of Courts and the Prospects for Anti-poverty *Charter* Claims' (2014) 33 *National Journal of Constitutional Law* 1
Woolhandler, A, 'Rethinking the Judicial Reception of Legislative Facts' (1988) 41 *Vanderbilt Law Review* 111
Woolman, S, and Botha, H, 'Limitations: Shared Constitutional Interpretation, An Appropriate Normative Framework and Hard Choices' in S Woolman and M Bishop (eds), *Constitutional Conversations* (Pretoria, Pretoria University Law Press, 2008) 149–86
Yowell, P, 'Empirical Research in Rights-Based Judicial Review of Legislation' in KS Ziegler and P Huber (eds), *Current Problems in the Protection of Human Rights: Perspectives from Germany and the UK* (Oxford, Hart Publishing, 2013) 155–86
——. 'Proportionality in United States Constitutional Law' in L Lazarus, C McCrudden and N Bowles (eds), *Reasoning Rights: Comparative Judicial Engagement* (Oxford, Hart Publishing, 2014) 87–114
Zines, L, *The High Court and the Constitution*, 5th edn (Sydney, Federation Press, 2008)

# *Index*

www.ingramcontent.com/pod-product-compliance
Ingram Content Group UK Ltd.
Pitfield, Milton Keynes, MK11 3LW, UK
UKHW021907150926
475560UK00003B/232

9 781509 936984